# Windows Server 2008 Portable Command Guide: MCTS 70-640, 70-642, 70-643, and MCITP 70-646, 70-647

Darril Gibson

Pearson Education
800 East 96th Street
Indianapolis, Indiana
46240
USA

# Windows Server 2008 Portable Command Guide: MCTS 70-640, 70-642, 70-643, and MCITP 70-646, 70-647

## Copyright © 2011 by Pearson Education, Inc.

ISBN-13: 978-0-7897-4737-2

ISBN-10: 0-7897-4737-5

*Library of Congress Cataloging-in-Publication data is on file.*

Printed in the United States of America

First Printing: May 2011

Trademarks

All terms mentioned in this book that are known to be trademarks or service marks have been appropriately capitalized. Pearson IT Certification cannot attest to the accuracy of this information. Use of a term in this book should not be regarded as affecting the validity of any trademark or service mark.

Warning and Disclaimer

Every effort has been made to make this book as complete and as accurate as possible, but no warranty or fitness is implied. The information provided is on an "as is" basis. The author and the publisher shall have neither liability nor responsibility to any person or entity with respect to any loss or damages arising from the information contained in this book.

Bulk Sales

Pearson IT Certification offers excellent discounts on this book when ordered in quantity for bulk purchases or special sales. For more information, please contact

**U.S. Corporate and Government Sales**

**1-800-382-3419**

**corpsales@pearsontechgroup.com**

For sales outside the United States, please contact

**International Sales**

**international@pearson.com**

**Associate Publisher**
Dave Dusthimer

**Acquisitions Editor**
Betsy Brown

**Development Editor**
Jeff Riley

**Series Editor**
Scott Empson

**Managing Editor**
Sandra Schroeder

**Senior Project Editor**
Tonya Simpson

**Copy Editor**
Deadline Driven Publishing

**Proofreader**
Leslie Joseph

**Technical Editor**
David Camardella

**Publishing Coordinator**
Vanessa Evans

**Book Designer**
Gary Adair

**Composition**
Bronkella Publishing

# Contents at a Glance

# Table of Contents

## Part IX: Working with Some Server Roles from the Command Line

## Part X: Using Visual Basic Scripts (VB Script)

## Part XI: Using PowerShell

## About the Author

**Darril Gibson** is the CEO of Security Consulting and Training, LLC. He regularly teaches, writes, and consults on a wide variety of security and technical topics. He has been a Microsoft Certified Trainer since 1999 and holds several certifications, including MCSE (NT 4.0, 2000, 2003), MCDBA (SQL Server), MCITP (Windows 7, Server 2008, and SQL Server), ITIL v3, Security+, and CISSP. He has authored, coauthored, or contributed to more than a dozen books. You can view a listing of most of his current books on Amazon at http://amzn.to/bL0Obo.

## About the Series Editor

**Scott Empson** is the associate chair of the Bachelor of Applied Information Systems Technology degree program at the Northern Alberta Institute of Technology in Edmonton, Alberta, Canada, where he teaches Cisco routing, switching, and network design courses. Scott is also the program coordinator of the Cisco Networking Academy Program at NAIT, a Regional Academy covering Central and Northern Alberta. He has earned three undergraduate degrees: a Bachelor of Arts, with a major in English; a Bachelor of Education, again with a major in English/Language Arts; and a Bachelor of Applied Information Systems Technology, with a major in Network Management. Scott also has a Masters of Education degree from the University of Portland. He holds several industry certifications, including CCNP, CCAI, Network+, and C|EH.

Scott is the series creator and one of the authors of the Portable Command Guide Series. Portable Command Guides are filled with valuable, easy-to-access information to quickly refresh your memory. Each guide is portable enough for use whether you're in the server room or the equipment closet.

## About the Technical Editor

**David Camardella** has more than 10 years of experience in networking, including providing technical support and services such as designing and maintaining Cisco Internetworks, Active Directory, messaging infrastructures, and desktop deployment systems. Over the years, David has performed technical editing on several Cisco and Microsoft books. He holds a Bachelor of Science in Business Management as well as several levels of IT certifications, including the MCITP Enterprise Admin/Server Admin Certifications.

## Dedication

*To my wife, who continues to provide me with love and encouragement. I'm thankful we are sharing our lives together.*

## Acknowledgments

I'm grateful for all the hard work done behind the scenes by the people at Pearson. I'm thankful to Scott Empson, who had the original vision for these books, and I'm grateful that David Dusthimer had faith in me to head up many of the books in the Microsoft series. I especially appreciated the efforts of the editors: Jeff Riley, David Camardella, Ginny Bess, and Tonya Simpson. This book is much better due to their efforts.

## We Want to Hear from You!

As the reader of this book, *you* are our most important critic and commentator. We value your opinion and want to know what we're doing right, what we could do better, what areas you'd like to see us publish in, and any other words of wisdom you're willing to pass our way.

As an associate publisher for Pearson IT Certification, I welcome your comments. You can email or write me directly to let me know what you did or didn't like about this book—as well as what we can do to make our books better.

*Please note that I cannot help you with technical problems related to the topic of this book. We do have a User Services group, however, where I will forward specific technical questions related to the book.*

When you write, please be sure to include this book's title and author as well as your name, email address, and phone number. I will carefully review your comments and share them with the author and editors who worked on the book.

Email:      feedback@pearsonitcertification.com

Mail:       David Dusthimer
            Associate Publisher
            Pearson IT Certification
            800 East 96th Street
            Indianapolis, IN 46240 USA

## Reader Services

Visit our website and register this book at pearsonitcertification.com for convenient access to any updates, downloads, or errata that might be available for this book.

# Introduction

Thanks for buying the *Windows Server 2008 Portable Command Guide: MCTS 70-640, 70-642, 70-643, and MCITP 70-646, 70-647*. I'd love to say that this book was my idea, but the real credit goes to Scott Empson who originally developed the vision of this book with Cisco certifications. I've worked with Scott and Pearson Education to help bring the same type of books he created for Cisco products to professionals working on Microsoft products. Scott's vision started with the idea that many IT professionals who have already learned the theory still sometimes need help remembering how to implement it.

The book doesn't go into depth teaching these concepts. The idea is that you already understand them. Instead, the goal is to provide enough information to help you remember what you can do and how to do it. The book is purposely written to be a small, portable, and useful journal, not an encyclopedic-sized volume. However, even if a concept is new to you, there's enough information for you to start typing at the command prompt to gain a better understanding.

As an example, you probably know that you can force the registration of SRV records in DNS by stopping and restarting a specific service. However, you might not remember the specific commands are **net stop netlogon** and **net start netlogon**. You might remember that you have to join a Server Core computer to a domain using the **netdom** command, but you might not remember the full syntax off the top of your head. In other words, you know the theory behind why you'd stop and restart the netlogon service and why you have to join a Server Core computer to a domain from the command prompt, but you might not always remember the syntax. This book is a ready reference of useful commands and procedures with clear-cut examples. It shows the exact syntax of many of the commands needed for administrative tasks performed regularly by Windows Server 2008 (and Windows Server 2008 R2) administrators.

I started the outline of this book by ensuring that command prompt commands covered by the Microsoft Certified Information Technology Professional (MCITP) certifications on Windows Server 2008 were included. This includes the 70-640, 70-642, 70-643, 70-646, and 70-647 exams for the MCITP Server Administrator and MCITP: Enterprise Administrator certifications. I then added the commands I've found valuable in my day-to-day work on networks and from classroom teaching.

Many IT professionals use an engineering journal to help them remember key information needed on the job. It might include specific commands that they sometimes forget, IP addressing schemes used on their networks, steps for important maintenance tasks that are performed infrequently, or anything else they want to easily recall by looking at the journal. If you already have an engineering journal of your own, you can add this as a Windows Server 2008 addendum. If you don't have one, you can start with this book. It includes the same "Create Your Own Journal Here" appendix that Scott uses in the Cisco series. There are blank pages you can use to add your own notes and make this your journal, not mine.

## Command Syntax Conventions

The conventions used to present command syntax in this book are as follows:

- **Boldface** indicates syntax that is entered literally as shown.
- *Italic* indicates syntax for which you supply actual values.
- Vertical bars | separate alternative, mutually exclusive choices.
- Square brackets [ ] indicate an optional element.
- Braces { } indicate a required choice.

# CHAPTER 1

# Launching and Using the Command Prompt

This chapter provides information and commands concerning the following topics:

- Launching the command prompt
- Launching with elevated privileges
- Using the built-in doskey program
- Creating mini macros with **doskey**
- Cutting and pasting to and from the command prompt
- Changing the options and display

## Launching the Command Prompt

The command prompt is pinned to the **Start** menu by default in Windows Server 2008. You can access it by clicking **Start** and selecting **Command Prompt**. If it has been removed from the **Start** menu, you can also launch it using one of these methods:

- Click **Start**, type **CMD** in the **Start Search** box, and then press **Enter**.
- Click **Start**, **All Programs**, **Accessories**, and then select **Command Prompt**.

The command prompt opens and looks similar to Figure 1-1.

**Figure 1-1** The command prompt window

If you regularly use the command prompt, you can add some shortcuts to pin it to the **Quick Launch** menu or to the **Start** menu using one of the following methods:

- Click **Start**, type **CMD** in the **Start Search** box, right-click **CMD**, and select either **Add to Quick Launch** or **Pin to Start Menu**.
- Click **Start**, **All Programs**, **Accessories**, right-click **Command Prompt**, and select either **Add to Quick Launch** or **Pin to Start Menu**.

**NOTE**   Quick Launch is available only in Windows Server 2008. It is not available in Windows Server 2008 R2.

## Launching with Elevated Privileges

Many of the commands entered from the command prompt require elevated privileges, or administrative permissions. For example, if you wanted to stop and restart the net-logon service to re-create SRV records on a DNS server, you can use the following two commands:

```
sc stop netlogon
sc start netlogon
```

However, the first command fails with an Access Is Denied error similar to the follow-ing if the command isn't executed from an elevated prompt:

```
c:\ >sc stop netlogon
[SC] OpenService FAILED 5:
Access is denied.
```

The solution is to launch the command prompt with administrator permissions by right-clicking the menu item or shortcut and selecting **Run As Administrator**.

**NOTE**   The command prompt starts in the windows\system32 folder by default when started with administrator permissions and includes Administrator in the title.

Figure 1-2 shows how to launch the command prompt with administrator permissions from the **Start** menu.

Figure 1-3 shows the command prompt launched with administrator permissions. Notice that the title screen is changed from simply **Command Prompt** to **Administrator: Command Prompt** to let you know you have administrative permissions. Additionally, it starts in the windows\system32 folder instead of the user's profile folder.

**TIP**   If you log on to the server with the administrator account, the command prompt is automatically started with administrator permissions.

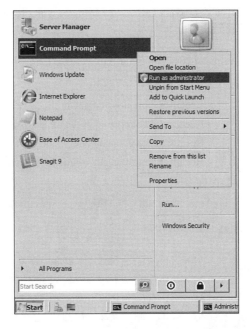

**Figure 1-2**   Launching the command prompt with Run As Administrator

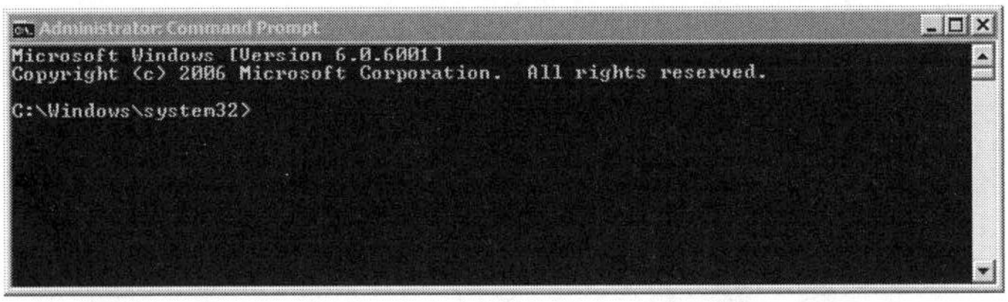

**Figure 1-3**   The command prompt window launched as an administrator

## Using the Built-in doskey Program

doskey is built in to the command prompt and keeps a history of all the commands you enter in the current command prompt session. You can easily retrieve previous commands so that you don't have to type them again. For example, suppose you're trying to export a DNS zone with the **dnscmd /zoneexport pearson.pub pearson.txt** command. However, instead, you enter the following command with only one "e" in **zoneexport** instead of two:

```
dnscmd /zonexport pearson.pub pearson.txt
```

**dnscmd** gives an error and then displays help. You don't have to retype the entire command. Instead, you can just press the up arrow to retrieve the command, press the left arrow until the cursor is positioned after zone, add the second e, and then press **Enter**. The same command executes again without retyping it from scratch.

**TIP**   After making an edit, you don't have to reposition the cursor at the end of the line. Simply press **Enter** to continue.

The following table shows the keys you can use to retrieve commands.

| Keyboard Key | Description |
| --- | --- |
| Up arrow | Recalls the previous command. |
| Down arrow | Recalls the next command in the doskey buffer. |
| Page up | Recalls the oldest command in the current session. |
| Page down | Recalls the most recent command in the current session. |

You can use the following keys when editing a retrieved doskey command.

| Keyboard Key or Key Combination | Description |
| --- | --- |
| Left arrow | Moves the cursor back one character at a time. |
| Right arrow | Moves the cursor forward one character at a time. |
| CTRL + left arrow | Moves the cursor back one word. |
| CTRL + right arrow | Moves the cursor forward one word. |
| Home | Moves the cursor to the beginning of the line. |
| End | Moves the cursor to the end of the line. |
| Esc | Clears the command from the display. |

**NOTE**   The doskey buffer holds the last 50 commands by default; however, you can change that with the **/listsize** switch. For example, to extend the history buffer to 75, use the following command:

```
doskey /listsize = 75
```

**TIP**   You can also change the buffer size by right-clicking the title bar, selecting **Properties**, and changing the buffer size. The buffer size value is the same as the **listsize** value.

The following are some of the useful commands you can use with doskey.

| doskey Command | Description |
| --- | --- |
| `c:\> doskey /history` | Lists all commands in the history buffer. |
| F7 | Displays the command history in a selectable popup dialog box. |
| `c:\> doskey /reinstall` | Installs a new copy of doskey.exe and clears the command history buffer. |
| `doskey /listsize = number`<br>`c:\> doskey /listsize = 999` | Changes the size of the **doskey** buffer to the provided number. The example sets the buffer size to 999. |

## Creating Mini Macros with doskey

You can create mini macros to make them available to you in a command prompt session. For example, imagine that you expect to enter **sc stop netlogon** and **sc start netlogon** many times. You can create two macros with the following commands:

```
doskey stpnl = sc stop netlogon
doskey sttnl = sc start netlogon
```

Now, you can simply enter **stpnl** at the command prompt to stop the netlogon service, and enter **sttnl** to start it.

> **NOTE**  Macros are available only in the current session. If you close the command prompt and reopen it, the macro is lost.

| doskey Command | Description |
|---|---|
| `doskey macroKey = command`<br>`c:\>doskey stpnl = sc stop netlogon`<br>`c:\>doskey sttnl = sc start netlogon` | Creates a macro that executes the command when the macro key is entered. The examples create two macros named stop and start that can be used to stop and start the netlogon service. |
| `c:\>stpnl`<br>`c:\>sttnl` | Executing the macro is the same as executing the command. These examples show how to execute the macros. |
| `c:\>doskey /macros` | Displays all **doskey** macros in the session. |

## Cutting and Pasting to and from the Command Prompt

You can cut text from, and paste text to, the command prompt. The process is a little different depending on how the **Quick Edit Mode** option is configured. Figure 1-4 shows the **Options** tab of the Properties dialog box. You can access this by right-clicking the title bar of the command prompt window and selecting **Properties**.

The **QuickEdit Mode** option changes the way you can cut and paste from the command line. The **Insert Mode** option works just like the Insert key of the keyboard. It enables you to insert characters in the line when enabled or overwrite characters in the line when disabled.

> **TIP**  If you want your changes to apply anytime the command prompt window is open instead of only the current session, right-click the title bar, select **Defaults**, and then select the options.

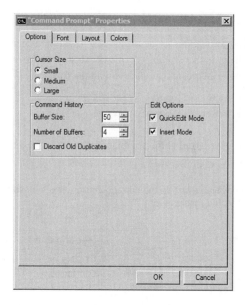

**Figure 1-4** Options tab of Command Prompt Properties window

## Copying from the Command Prompt Window

You can copy data from the command line to the Clipboard.

| Quick Edit Mode Option | Result |
| --- | --- |
| If Quick Edit Mode is enabled (checked) | Use the mouse to highlight text and press the **Enter** key to copy highlighted text. |
| If Quick Edit Mode is not enabled (unchecked) | Right-click in the command prompt window and select **Mark**. Use the mouse to highlight text and press the **Enter** key to copy highlighted text. |

**NOTE** Both of these methods copy the data to the Clipboard. You can then paste it into any other application (such as Notepad).

## Pasting Data to the Command Prompt Window

You can paste any data that is in the Clipboard to the command line.

| Quick Edit Mode Option | Result |
| --- | --- |
| If Quick Edit Mode is enabled (checked) | Right-click in the command prompt window and the data is pasted. |
| If Quick Edit Mode is not enabled (unchecked) | Right-click in the command prompt window and select **Paste**. |

NOTE   If you copy a carriage return with the command, the carriage return is pasted into the command prompt window. In other words, when you paste it, it executes.

## Changing the Options and Display

Figure 1-4 (shown earlier) showed the **Options** tab and the **Edit Options** selections on this tab. This tab includes additional options, as shown in the following table.

| Options Tab Selections | Comments |
|---|---|
| Cursor Size | You can change this to Small, Medium, or Large. |
| Command History - Buffer Size | The buffer size can be changed to as high as 999 and directly relates to the **/listsize** switch of **doskey**. |
| Command History - Number of Buffers | This identifies how much memory can be used to hold and display the buffer. |
| Command History - Discard Old Duplicates | Duplicate commands are not kept in the history when this is checked. |

Figure 1-5 shows the **Font** tab of the Properties dialog box. This enables you to change the size of the font and pick other fonts, though you don't have many choices available.

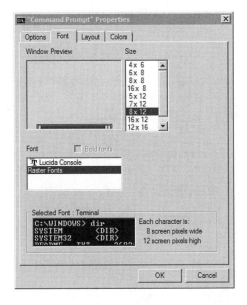

**Figure 1-5**   Font tab of Command Prompt Properties window

Figure 1-6 shows the **Layout** tab of the Properties dialog box. The most valuable setting here is the **Height** of the **Screen Buffer Size**. If you change this to 9999, the screen buffer captures as many as 9,999 lines. This can be useful when your command has more than 300 lines of output data. For example, the **gpresult /z** command (used to show current group policy settings using super verbose mode) can easily exceed the default buffer.

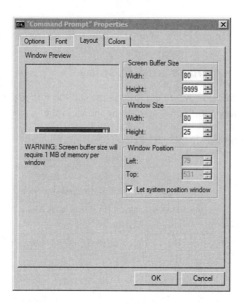

**Figure 1-6**   Layout tab of Command Prompt Properties window

Figure 1-7 shows the **Colors** tab of the Properties dialog box. You can change the background color and the text color here. This can be especially useful if you're displaying the text for multiple people to see.

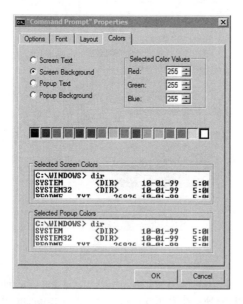

**Figure 1-7**   Colors tab of Command Prompt Properties window

**TIP**   When using an overhead or data projector, text in the command prompt shows up best as black text on a white background.

# CHAPTER 2

# Basic Rules When Using the Command Prompt

This chapter provides information and commands concerning the following topics:

- Using uppercase or lowercase
- Using quotes
- Understanding variables
- Understanding switches
- Understanding wildcards
- Getting help
- Understanding paths
- Using basic commands
- Redirecting output to files

## Using Uppercase or Lowercase

In almost all instances, you can enter command prompt commands as uppercase, lowercase, or a combination of the two. In other words, the following commands are all interpreted the same:

| Mixed Case | Lowercase | Uppercase |
|---|---|---|
| RepAdmin /SyncAll | Repadmin /syncall | REPADMIN /SYNCALL |
| ADPrep /ForestPrep | adprep /forestprep | ADPREP /FORESTPREP |
| DCPromo | Dcpromo | DCPROMO |

Documentation and help files commonly show the first letter as uppercase and when the command has two words in it, both words are uppercase, such as **RepAdmin**. This is sometimes called Pascal-casing (from the Pascal language) or camel casing (because the uppercase letters resemble the humps of a camel). It's done for readability and doesn't affect how the command is interpreted at the command line.

> **NOTE**   In this book, all commands are shown as all lowercase unless you must enter the command using specific upper- or lowercase letters.

There are some exceptions where case does matter, but they are rare. For example, when adding roles to a Windows Server 2008 Server Core installation, the case of the role is important. The proper case when adding the DHCP Server role with the **ocsetup** command is **DHCPServerCore**. The following table shows how to use the **ocsetup** command with the incorrect case and the proper case.

| start ocsetup Command | Description |
|---|---|
| `start ocsetup serverrole` | The **start ocsetup** command is used to add roles to a Server Core installation; however, the role must be entered in a specific case. |
| `c:\>start ocsetup`<br>`dhcpservercore` | The **start ocsetup** command must be entered using the exact case. The example command will fail (as shown in Figure 2-1) because **DHCPServerCore** isn't entered with the proper case. |
| `c:\>start ocsetup`<br>`DHCPServerCore` | This command will succeed because **DHCPServerCore** is entered with the proper case. |

**Figure 2-1**   Error from **ocsetup** command

## Using Quotes

The command-line interpreter understands a space as the next part of the command. For example, consider how **ping** is used in the following table.

| ping Command | Description |
|---|---|
| `C:\>ping dc1` | The space after **ping** indicates that ping is the command, and what follows (**dc1**) is a parameter for the **ping** command. This sends four echo requests to **dc1** and gets four echo replies back if the server is operational. |

Some parameters can have spaces. When a parameter has a space, the parameter must be enclosed in quotes. For example, you can use the **netsh** command to change the configuration of a network interface card (NIC). The default name of the first NIC is **Local Area Connection** but because **Local Area Connection** has spaces, it must be enclosed in quotes as "Local Area Connection" so that the **netsh** command can interpret it correctly.

> **TIP** The **netsh** command is the only way to configure the NIC for a Server Core installation. Server Core is covered in Chapters 20, 21, and 22.

| netsh Command | Description |
|---|---|
| `netsh interface ipv4 set address name` = *Name of NIC* static *ip address subnet mask* | The **netsh** command changes the configuration of a NIC. It needs the name of the NIC, an IP address, and a subnet mask. <br><br> **NOTE** Chapter 11, "Working with Active Directory Accounts," covers **netsh** in more depth. |
| `C:\>netsh interface ipv4 set address name = "local area connection" static 192.168.1.15 255.255.255.0` | This command works, setting the IP address and subnet mask of the NIC. <br><br> The default name of the first NIC is Local Area Connection and because it includes a space, it must be enclosed in quotes. |
| `C:\>netsh interface ipv4 set address name = local area connection static 192.168.1.15 255.255.255.0` `Invalid source parameter (area).` | This command fails. <br><br> If **local area connection** is not enclosed in quotes, **netsh** interprets *local* as the name of the NIC but doesn't understand *area*. |

## Understanding Variables

A variable is simply a placeholder for an actual value. You don't have to know the actual value as long as you know the placeholder. For example, the location of the Windows Server 2008 operating system folder is usually c:\Windows, but it can be on another drive and even have a different name. However, the **%systemroot%** variable always points to the actual location of the operating system folder.

For example, if you want to see the path to the sysvol folder, you can use this command:

```
echo %systemroot%\sysvol
```

> **TIP** Variables always start and end with a percent symbol (%). You can easily see the value of any variable by using the **echo** command followed by the variable.

Some of the commonly referenced variables are shown in the following table.

| Variable | Description |
|---|---|
| `%systemroot%` `%windir%` | Shows the path to the Windows folder (typically C:\Windows). |
| `%programfiles%` | Shows the path to the Program Files folder (typically C:\Program Files). |
| `%systemdrive%` | Returns the drive of the root directory (typically C:\). |
| `%appdata%` | Returns the location where applications store data by default. |
| `%userdomain%` | Gives the name of the domain that contains the currently logged-on user's account. |
| `%logonserver%` | Lists the name of the domain controller that validated the current logon session (when the system is joined to a domain). |
| `%processor_architecture%` | Returns the architecture of the processor (such as x856 for 32-bit or AMD64 for 64-bit processors). |
| `%userprofile%` | Lists the location of the profile for the current user. |
| `%allusersprofile%` | Lists the location of the All Users Profile. |
| `%cd%` | Lists the current directory string. |
| `%date%` | Returns the current date. |
| `%time%` | Returns the current time. |
| `%errorlevel%` | Gives the error number of the last executed command. Anything other than 0 indicates an error occurred. |

**TIP**  You can use variables in commands at the command prompt. For example, if you want to open the Windows update log (windowsupdate.log), you can use the following command:

```
notepad %systemroot%\windowsupdate.log
```

**TIP**  You can view a listing of all variables with the **set** command.

It's also possible to create your own variables. This can sometimes be useful in scripts.

| Variable | Description |
|---|---|
| `set variable-name = value` `C:\>set myvariable = test` | Creates the variable and assigns a value. |
| `C:\>echo %myvariable%` `Test` | Shows the value of the variable. |

## Understanding Switches

You can modify most commands by using one or more switches. A switch is preceded by a space and a forward slash (/) or a space and a dash (-). For example, if you want to flush the DNS cache, you use the **ipconfig** command and modify it with the **/flushdns** switch like this:

```
ipconfig /flushdns
```

Some commands can use either a forward slash or a dash, whereas others work only with one or the other.

| Command | Description |
|---|---|
| C:\>ipconfig -flushdns<br>C:\>ipconfig /flushdns | Both of these commands work the same. |
| C:\>ipconfig/flushdns | This works. Even though the space is omitted before the slash, the **ipconfig** command recognizes it. |
| C:\>ipconfig-flushdns<br>ipconfig-flushdns is not recognized as an internal or external command, operable program, or batch file. | This fails. The **ipconfig** command doesn't recognize the dash (-) as a switch without a space. |

**TIP**    It's best to always use a space before the switch because this consistently works. Some commands do not work if you use the forward slash (/) or dash (-) without a space preceding it.

## Understanding Wildcards

Wildcards are used to represent one or more characters. Two wildcard characters are available at the command prompt: the asterisk and the question mark.

| Wildcard | Description |
|---|---|
| * | Takes the place for zero or more characters. |
| C:\>dir *.txt | Shows all files that end with .txt. |
| C:\>dir a* | Shows all files that start with A. |
| C:\>dir a*.txt | Shows all files that start with A and end with .txt. |
| ? | Takes the place for one character. |
| C:\>dir week?.txt | Shows all .txt files that start with week and end with one character and .txt (such as week1.txt, week2.txt, and so on). |

**NOTE**    The **dir** command provides a listing of files in the current directory.

## Getting Help

The goal of this book is not to cover every possible switch of every possible command. Instead, the goal is to give you the common commands covered by the Server 2008 MCITP exams and most on-the-job tasks. If you work with Server 2008 long enough, there will come a time when you'll need a little more information.

Thankfully, the command prompt includes a lot of built-in help if you know how to use it. For example, if you enter just **Help**, you'll get a list of commands that you can enter at the command line. The following table shows some of these commands.

| Command | Description |
|---------|-------------|
| assoc | Displays or modifies file extension associations. |
| attrib | Sets and displays attributes for files. |
| bcdedit | Sets properties in the boot configuration data store to control the boot process. |
| call | Calls one batch program from another. |
| cd or chdir | Displays the name of a directory when entered alone, or changes the current directory when a path is given. |
| chkdsk | Checks a disk and displays a status report, and can also repair disk errors. |
| compact | Displays or alters the compression of files on NTFS partitions. |
| convert | Converts FAT volumes to NTFS. You cannot convert the current drive without rebooting. Also, you cannot convert from NTFS to FAT without reformatting. |
| copy | Copies one or more files to another location. |
| date | Displays or sets the date. |
| del or erase | Deletes one or more files. |
| dir | Displays a list of files and subdirectories in a directory. |
| diskpart | Displays or configures disk partition properties. |
| doskey | Edits command lines, recalls Windows commands, and creates macros. |
| driverquery | Displays the current device driver status and properties. |
| echo | Displays messages or turns command echoing on or off. |
| exit | Quits the CMD.EXE program (command interpreter). |
| for | Runs a specified command for each file in a set of files. |
| format | Formats a disk for use with Windows. |
| fsutil | Displays or configures the file system properties. |
| ftype | Displays or modifies file types used in file extension associations. |
| goto | Directs the Windows command interpreter to a labeled line in a batch program. |
| gpresult | Displays Group Policy information that is applied to the local system. |
| help | Provides Help information for Windows commands. |

| Command | Description |
|---|---|
| **icacls** | Displays, modifys, backs up, or restores access control lists (ACL) for files and directories. |
| **if** | Performs conditional processing in batch programs. |
| **label** | Creates, changes, or deletes the volume label of a disk. |
| **md or mkdir** | Creates a directory. |
| **more** | Displays output one screen at a time. |
| **path** | Displays or sets a search path for executable files. |
| **rd or rmdir** | Removes a directory. |
| **rem** | Records comments (remarks) in batch files or CONFIG.SYS. |
| **ren or rename** | Renames a file or files. |
| **robocopy** | Advanced robust copy utility used to copy files and directory trees. |
| **set** | Displays, sets, or removes Windows environment variables. |
| **sc** | Displays or configures services (background processes). |
| **schtasks** | Schedules commands and programs to run on a computer. |
| **shutdown** | Allows proper local or remote shutdown of a machine. |
| **systeminfo** | Displays machine-specific properties and configuration. |
| **tasklist** | Displays all currently running tasks including services. |
| **taskkill** | Kills or stops a running process or application. |
| **time** | Displays or sets the system time. |
| **tree** | Graphically displays the directory structure of a drive or path. |
| **xcopy** | Copies files and directory trees. |
| **wmic** | Displays Windows Management Instrumentation (WMI) information inside an interactive command shell. |

**NOTE**   The help doesn't show all commands that are available at the command prompt. For example, the **dsacls** command doesn't appear but can be used to display or modify ACLs for Active Directory Domain Services objects. Chapter 8, "Using Advanced ds Commands," covers the **dsacls** command.

There are two ways you can get help for individual commands. You can use the **/?** switch or enter **help** followed by the command; however, only the **/?** switch method works consistently.

| Command | Description |
|---|---|
| /?<br>`C:\>sc /?` | Using the **/?** switch provides help for any command. |
| **help** command<br>`C:\>help sc` | Some commands provide help by entering the word **help** followed by the command |
| `C:\>help dsacls`<br>`This command is not sup-`<br>`ported by the help util-`<br>`ity. Try "dsacls /?".` | This fails and generates the error. |

When you ask for help on any commands, you'll see a lot of help is available; however, you need to know how to read it. The following table outlines the conventions used in the help output.

| Help Notation | Description | Example |
|---|---|---|
| Text without brackets or braces | Items you must type as shown | **ipconfig [/allcompartments] [/all] [/renew[adapter]] [/release[adapter]] [/renew6[adapter]] [/release6[adapter]] [/flushdns] [/displaydns] [/registerdns] [/showclassidadapter] [/setclassidadapter [classid]]**<br><br>**ipconfig** is without brackets, so it must be entered as **ipconfig**. |
| [Text inside square brackets] | Optional items | **echo [message]**<br><br>The message is in brackets [], indicating it is optional. In other words, you can enter **echo** to see whether echo is turned on or off for the system, or you can enter **echo** with a message to echo to the screen. |
| <Text inside angle brackets> | Placeholder for which you must supply a value | **echo [message]**<br><br>You provide the message. For example, you can enter **echo %programfiles%** to view the value of the variable. |
| {Text inside braces} | Set of required items; choose one | **gpupdate [/target:{computer \| user}] [/force] [/wait:<value>] [/logoff] [/boot] [/sync]**<br><br>If **/target** is used, the user must enter either computer or user. In this case, **/target** is optional and if it is omitted, it executes against both the computer and the user. |
| Vertical bar (\|) | Separator for mutually exclusive items; choose one | **gpresult [/s system [/u username [/p [password]]]] [/scope scope] [/user targetusername] [/r \| /v \| /z] [(/x \| /h) <filename> [/f]]**<br><br>Several items in this command cannot be used with others, so they are grouped together in the brackets and separated with the vertical bar. If you want to use **/r**, **/v**, or **/z**, you must choose only one. Similarly, if you want to use **/x** or **/h**, you must choose only one. |
| Ellipsis (...) | Items that can be repeated | **winrm operation resource_uri [-switch:value [-switch:value] ...] [@{key=value[;key=value]...}]**<br><br>The ellipsis indicates that multiple switch values and multiple key values can be entered in the same line. |

## Understanding Paths

The command prompt shows the current path at the prompt. For example, if you open a prompt with administrator privileges, you'll see the following prompt:

```
c:\Windows\system32>
```

When executing a command, the system always looks in the current location for the file or executable command. For example, if you have a file named 70-642.txt in the current path, you can use the following command to open it with Notepad:

```
C:\studynotes>notepad 70-642.txt
```

You can also specify a path with the command. For example, if your file is in a folder named studynotes on the c: drive, you can use the following command:

```
C:\>notepad c:\studynotes\70-642.txt
```

In the second example that includes the path, it doesn't matter what your current path is because you specified it in the command.

You might notice that the command is **notepad**, but the path to **notepad** is not needed when it is executed. Notepad is located in the c:\windows folder and Windows Server 2008 is already aware of this path. Windows Server 2008 is aware of the following paths by default:

- c:\windows
- c:\windows\system32
- c:\windows\wystem32\wbem

**TIP** Windows Server 2008 R2 is also aware of the path to PowerShell by default (c:\windows\system32\windowspowershell\v1.0\). Windows Server 2008 (not R2) adds this path when PowerShell is installed.

You can view the path with the commands shown in the following table.

| Command | Comments |
|---------|----------|
| `c:\>echo %path%` | The output is<br><br>c:\Windows\system32;c:\Windows;c:\Windows\System32\Wbem;c:\Windows\System32\WindowsPowerShell\v1.0\ |
| `c:\>path` | The output is<br><br>PATH=C:\Windows\system32;C:\Windows;C:\Windows\System32\Wbem;C:\Windows\System32\WindowsPowerShell\v1.0\ |

You can also modify the path with the commands in the following table.

| Command | Comments |
|---|---|
| `c:\>path = c:\mypath` | Sets the path for the current command prompt session to only c:\mypath. When you close the session and open another session, the path reverts to the value in the **%path%** variable. |
| `c:\>path = %path%;c:\mypath` | Appends the current path with the value you include (in the example, c:\mypath). When you close the session and open another session, the path reverts to the value in the **%path%** variable. |

# Using Basic Commands

The following table shows many of the basic commands used at the command prompt.

> **NOTE**   The term *directories* was used in the original DOS commands, and Windows uses the term folders. However, *directories* and *folders* refer to the same thing. In other words, directories and folders are synonymous.

| Command | Comments |
|---|---|
| `dir`<br>`c:\>dir`<br>`c:\>dir *.txt`<br>`c:\>dir appcmd*.* /s` | Retrieves a listing of the current folder.<br><br>Wildcards can be used. The example displays all files with a .txt extension.<br><br>The **/s** switch looks in subdirectories also. The example lists all instances of the **appcmd** file on the c: drive. |
| `cd`<br>`c:\>cd data\study`<br>`c:\data\study>cd ..`<br>`c:\data\>cd \`<br>`c:\>` | Changes directory.<br><br>The **cd ..** command moves up one folder.<br><br>The **cd \** command moves to the root of the current drive. |
| `md`<br>`c:\>md tmpdata` | Makes a directory. |
| `rd`<br>`c:\>rd tmpdata`<br>`c:\>rd tmpdata /s`<br>`c:\>rd tmpdata /s /q` | Removes a directory if it is empty.<br><br>The first example removes the folder named tmpdata, but only if it is empty.<br><br>The next example (with **/s** for subfolders) removes the folder and any subfolders even if there is data in any of the folders.<br><br>The last example (with **/q** for quite mode) suppresses the confirmation prompt. |
| `exit`<br>`c:\>exit` | Ends the current command prompt session and closes the command prompt window. |

## Redirecting Output to Files

Many times you'll want the output of a command sent to a file. You can do this with the redirector symbol (>), as shown in the following table.

| Redirector | Description |
|---|---|
| `>`<br>`Command > `*`filename`*<br>`c:\> gpresult /z > grouppolicies.txt` | Sends output to a file. The file is created if it doesn't exist and over-written if it exists. |
| `>>`<br>`Command >> `*`filename`*<br>`c:\> gpresult /z >> grouppolicies.txt` | Appends output to a file. Existing data is not overwritten. |

# CHAPTER 3

# Manipulating Files, Folders, and Shares

This chapter provides information and commands concerning the following topics:

- Copying files with **copy**, **xcopy**, and **robocopy**
- Compressing files with **compact**
- Encrypting files with **cipher**
- Manipulating shadow copies with **vssadmin**
- Manipulating shares with **net share**
- Mapping drives with **net use**
- Manipulating users and groups with the **net** command
- Modifying NTFS permissions with **icacls**

## Copying Files with copy, xcopy, and robocopy

There are three primary commands that are useful for copying files.

| Command | Description |
|---------|-------------|
| Copy | Basic file copy command. You can use this when you want to merge multiple files into one. |
| xcopy | Extended copy command. You can use this when you want to include subdirectories. |
| robocopy | Robust file copy command. You can use this to copy folder structures and include existing permissions. |

### copy

You can use the **copy** command for basic file copying. The format is

```
copy source [destination]
```

It can also combine multiple files into a single file. The format when copying multiple files is

```
copy sourceFile1 + sourceFile2 [+ sourceFileN] destinationFile
```

**NOTE** You can include as many source files as desired.

The following table shows some examples using the **copy** command.

| copy command | Comments |
|---|---|
| `c:\>copy test.txt`<br>`test2.txt` | Creates a new file named test2.txt from an existing source file named test.txt. |
| `c:\>copy test1.txt`<br>`+ test2.txt`<br>`combined.txt` | Combines test1.text and test2.txt into a single file named combined.txt. The entire contents of test1.txt are at the beginning of the file and the entire contents of test2.txt are at the end. |
| `c:\>copy *.txt`<br>`combined.txt` | Copies all the .txt files in the current directory into a single file named combined.txt. |
| `c:\data>copy *.*`<br>`c:\archive` | Copies all files from the current folder (c:\data in the example) to the target folder (c:\archive in the example). The *.* wildcards indicate that all files should be copied. |

## xcopy

**xcopy** extends the basic **copy** command and provides additional capabilities. The most notable capability with **xcopy** is the capability to copy subdirectories. The basic format of the command is

`xcopy source destination`

| xcopy Command | Comments |
|---|---|
| `/s`<br>`c:\>xcopy c:\data d:\data /s`<br>`c:\>xcopy c:\data d:\data\ /s` | The **/s** switch copies all the files, directories, and subdirectories from the source to the destination. The example copies all the files on the c: drive to the d: drive.<br><br>Use the trailing backslash (\) on the destination if the destination folder doesn't exist. If the trailing backslash on the destination is omitted (*d:\data* instead of *d:\data\*) and the destination folder doesn't exist, you are prompted to send the data to a file or a directory. If you select a file, all the data is combined into a single file. If you choose directory, the entire folder structure is re-created. |
| `/e`<br>`c:\>xcopy c:\data d:\data\ /s /e` | The **/e** switch includes empty folders. This copies the entire contents of the c:\data folder, including all empty subfolders, to the d: drive. |
| `/t`<br>`c:\>xcopy c:\data d:\data\ /s /e /t` | The **/t** switch is used to copy the directory structure only. Files are not copied. |

| xcopy Command | Comments |
|---|---|
| /y<br><br>`c:\>xcopy c:\data d:\data\ /s /e /y` | The **/y** switch suppresses prompting to overwrite files. This is useful in scripts when you want the process automated without prompting you to take action.<br><br>If the destination folder exists and the **/y** switch is omitted, **xcopy** prompts the user to overwrite the folder. |

## robocopy

**robocopy** is a robust file copy command. It can do everything that **xcopy** can do and more, including copy permissions. The basic syntax is

`robocopy sourceDirectory destinationDirectory`

One of the most valuable features of **robocopy** is the capability to copy metadata associated with a file. You identify the metadata you want to copy by using specific flags, as shown in the following table. Any of the flags can be used with the **/copy** switch to specify what metadata to copy.

| robocopy Metadata Flag | Description |
|---|---|
| d<br>`c:\>robocopy c:\data`<br>`d:\data\ /copy:d` | Data flag. The **d** flag identifies the file itself. |
| a<br>`c:\>robocopy c:\data`<br>`d:\data\ /copy:da` | Attributes flag. This includes attributes such as hidden or read-only. |
| t<br>`c:\>robocopy c:\data`<br>`d:\data\ /copy:dat`<br>`c:\>robocopy c:\data`<br>`d:\data\` | Timestamps flag. Timestamps include when the file was created and when it was modified. The **d**, **a**, and **t** flags are used by default. In other words, the two example commands are the same. |
| s<br>`c:\>robocopy c:\data`<br>`d:\data\ /copy:dats` | Security flag. This includes all of the NTFS access control lists (ACL). In other words, it includes all of the assigned permissions. |
| o<br>`c:\>robocopy c:\data`<br>`d:\data\ /copy:datso` | Owner flag. This flag enables you to retain the original owner of the file. If this isn't used, the owner of the copied file is the user who executes the command. |
| u<br>`c:\>robocopy c:\data`<br>`d:\data\ /copy:datsou` | Auditing information flag. This includes all of the security access control lists (SACL) that identify auditing information for files and folders. |

The following table shows some common uses of the **robocopy** command.

| Common robocopy Commands | Description |
|---|---|
| `c:\>robocopy c:\data d:\data\`<br>`c:\>robocopy c:\data d:\data\ /copy:dat` | Copies all the files in the c:\data folder to the d: drive. It does not include subfolders. Note that this includes the data, the attributes, and the timestamps and is the same as using the **/copy:dat** switch. |
| `/s`<br>`c:\>robocopy c:\data d:\data\ /s` | The **/s** switch includes nonempty subfolders. It copies the entire contents of the c:\data folder to the d: drive. It includes all nonempty subfolders. |
| `/e`<br>`c:\>robocopy c:\data d:\data\ /e` | If you want to include empty folders, use the **/e** switch. It copies the entire contents of the c:\data folder (including nonempty subfolders) to the d: drive. Note that **/s** is implied but does not need to be included. |
| `/purge`<br>`c:\>robocopy c:\data d:\data\ /e /purge` | The **/purge** switch deletes files at the destination that no longer exist at the destination. |
| `/mir`<br>`c:\>robocopy c:\data d:\data\ /mir` | Using the **/mir** switch mirrors the source contents at the destination. This is the same as using the **/e** and **/purge** switches. |
| `/mov`<br>`c:\>robocopy c:\data d:\data\ /mov` | The **/mov** switch specifies that the files should be copied to the destination and then deleted from the source. This is similar to a cut and paste operation. It does not include subdirectories. |
| `/move`<br>`c:\>robocopy c:\data d:\data\ /move` | You can add an e to the **/mov** switch (**/move**) to include all subdirectories, including empty subdirectories. This works like **/mov** but includes all subfolders. |
| `/copy:copyflag(s)`<br>`c:\>robocopy c:\data d:\data\ /copy:datsou`<br>`c:\>robocopy c:\data d:\data\ /copy:all` | The **/copy** flag enables you to include additional metadata in the copy operation. The **/copy:datsou** command copies all the metadata and works the same as **/copy:all.** |
| `c:\>robocopy c:\data d:\data\ /copy:dats`<br>`c:\>robocopy c:\data d:\data\ /sec` | If you want to copy the permissions without the owner and auditing information, you can use the **/copy:dats** switch. This works the same as the **/sec** switch. |

The output of the **robocopy** command provides useful information. It shows how many files and folders were copied, whether any files were skipped, whether any failures occurred, the speed of the copy, and more, as shown in the following partial output:

```
C:\>robocopy c:\scripts e:\scripts\ /copy:datsou
```

```
-------------------------------------------------------------------

   ROBOCOPY     ::     Robust File Copy for Windows

-------------------------------------------------------------------


  Started : Sun Nov 07 18:36:22 2010

   Source : c:\scripts\
     Dest : e:\scripts\


    Files : *.*

  Options : *.* /COPYALL /R:1000000 /W:30


-------------------------------------------------------------------


            New Dir          8    c:\scripts\
100%        New File              201         logon.vbs
100%        New File               47         ipconfig.ps1
100%        New File              482         shutdown.ps1
100%        New File              321         createou.wsh
100%        New File              182         createuser.wsh
100%        New File            11298         processes.txt


-------------------------------------------------------------------


            Total   Copied   Skipped  Mismatch    FAILED    Extras
   Dirs :       1        1         0         0         0         0
  Files :       8        8         0         0         0         0
  Bytes :   12.2 k   12.2 k        0         0         0         0
  Times : 0:00:00  0:00:00                      0:00:00   0:00:00


  Speed :              156637 Bytes/sec.
  Speed :              8.962 MegaBytes/min.

  Ended : Sun Nov 07 18:36:23 2010
```

As a reminder, you can capture the output of any command using the > symbol to redirect the output to a text file like this:

```
c:\>robocopy c:\scripts e:\scripts\ /copy:datsou > robooutput.txt
```

## Compressing Files with compact

The **compact** command compresses and uncompress files and folders on NTFS drives. The two primary switches you'll use are **/c** to compress files and **/u** to uncompress them. When files are compressed, Windows Explorer displays them with blue text. The following table shows some examples using the **compact** command.

| compact Command | Description |
|---|---|
| c:\data>**compact**<br>Listing c:\Data\<br> New files added to this directory will<br>not be compressed.<br>  3617 : 3617 = 1.0 to 1    70-640.rtf<br>  1641 : 1641 = 1.0 to 1    70-642.rtf<br>  2629 : 2629 = 1.0 to 1    70-647.rtf<br>Of 3 files within 1 directories<br>0 are compressed and 4 are not com-<br>pressed.<br>7887 total bytes of data are stored in<br>7887 bytes.<br>The compression ratio is 1.0 to 1. | If you enter the command without switches, it shows you the size and current state of compression for files in the current folder.<br><br>The output shows the actual size of the files in bytes and the compression ratio. A compression ratio of 1.0 to 1 indicates the file is not compressed.<br><br>This also shows the uncompressed size and the actual amount of space taken by the files. Compressed files usually take less space on the disk than uncompressed files. |
| c:\data>**compact /c test.txt** | You compress an individual file by using the **/c** switch and then including the name of the file. |
| c:\data>**compact /c** | If you want to compress all files in the current folder, you can use the **/c** switch by itself. This also changes the folder attribute to compressed, causing new files added to the folder to be compressed. |
| c:\data>**compact /c /s** | You can add the **/s** switch to include subfolders. New files added to any of the folders are compressed. |
| c:\data>**compact /u /s** | The **/u** switch uncompresses files. This example uncompresses all files in the folder and subfolders. New files added to any of the folders are not compressed. |

| compact Command | Description |
|---|---|
| c:\data>compact /c /f test.txt | You can use the /f switch to force compression on the file. This is useful if the original attempt to compress the file is interrupted, leaving the file in a partially compressed state. |

# Encrypting Files with cipher

You can encrypt files on NTFS using the **cipher** command. These files are encrypted using the Encrypting File System (EFS) feature of NTFS. The two primary switches you use are /e to encrypt files and /d to decrypt them. When files are encrypted, Windows Explorer displays them with green text.

> **NOTE** Files can be compressed or encrypted, however, they cannot be compressed and encrypted.

| cipher Commands | Comments |
|---|---|
| c:\data>**cipher**<br>Listing c:\data\study\Server2008\<br>New files added to this directory<br>will not be encrypted.<br>E 70-640.rtf<br>U 70-642.rtf<br>U 70-647.rtf | If you enter **cipher** without any switches, it shows the current state of the encryption attribute.<br><br>Encrypted files are shown with E.<br><br>The U attribute indicates the files are not encrypted.<br><br>**cipher** /c provides the same output. |
| /e<br>c:\data>**cipher /e** | The /e switch used by itself encrypts all the files in the current folder and changes the folder attribute to Encrypted. New files added to the folder are encrypted. |
| /e file<br>c:\data>**cipher /e 70-642.rtf** | You can add a file name with the /e switch to encrypt only the named file. This doesn't affect other files or the folder attribute. |
| /d<br>c:\data>**cipher /d** | The /d switch decrypts encrypted files and folders. This example decrypts all the files in the current folder as long as the user has appropriate privileges.<br><br>The user must have encrypted the file, been added as an authorized user for the file, or be a data recovery agent. |
| /d file<br>c:\data>**cipher /d 70-642.rtf** | You can unencrypt a single file by specifying the file with the /u switch. |

| cipher Commands | Comments |
|---|---|
| /u /n<br>`c:\>cipher /u`<br>`c:\data>cipher /u /n >`<br>`encryptedfileslist.txt` | The **/u** switch can be used to locate all encrypted files on all local drives of a system and update them with the data recovery agent's certificate if it has changed.<br><br>This switch is useful if the keys have changed, such as when a new data recovery agent is designated.<br><br>When used with the **/n** switch, it lists the files but does not update them. This is useful for creating a list of encrypted files on a system |
| `c:\data>cipher /k` | Creates a new file encryption key for the user. |
| /w<br>`c:\data>cipher /w:e:`<br>To remove as much data as possible, please close all other applications while<br>running CIPHER /W.<br>Writing 0x00<br>. . . . . . . . . . . . . . . . . . . . . . . . . . . . . .<br>. . . . . . . . . . . . . . . . . . . . . . . . . . . . . .<br>. . . . . . . . . . . . .<br>Writing 0xFF<br>. . . . . . . . . . . . . . . . . . . . . . . . . . . . . .<br>. . . . . . . . . . . . . . . . . . . . . . . . . . . . . .<br>. . . . . . . . . . . . .<br>Writing Random Numbers<br>. . . . . . . . . . . . . . . . . . . . . . . . . . . . . .<br>. . . . . . . . . . . . . . . . . . . . . . . . . . . . . .<br>. . . . . . . . . . . . . | Removes data from available unused disk space on a drive.<br><br>When files are first encrypted, it's possible that remnants of these files are left on the drive. You can remove all remnants of these files with the **/w** switch. The example sanitizes the unused disk space on drive E:. Note that it first writes all 0s (0x00) to the unused disk space, writes all 1s (0xFF), and then writes random numbers to the drive.<br><br>This can also be done on any NTFS drive, even if there aren't any encrypted files on the drive. |

## Manipulating Shadow Copies with vssadmin

**vssadmin** is the volume shadow copy service administrative command-line tool. You can use it to view and manipulate shadow copies.

> **TIP**   You should be familiar with the **vssadmin** tool when taking the 70-642 exam.

Volume shadow copies are used to create previous versions of files (as shown in Figure 3-1) and when doing backups by allowing open files to be copied.

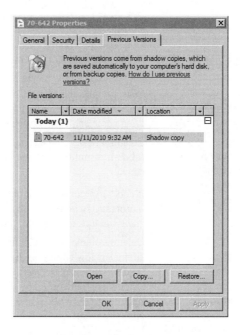

**Figure 3-1**    Restoring a previous version of a file

The following table shows some common uses of the **vssadmin** tool.

| vssadmin Command | Comments |
|---|---|
| `query reverts`<br>`vssadmin query reverts`<br>`/for=x: | /all`<br>`c:\>vssadmin query reverts`<br>`/all`<br>`c:\>vssadmin query reverts`<br>`/for=e:` | Queries the progress of the in-progress previous version restore operations. You can query the status of a restore operation for a specific drive or for all drives.<br><br>**TIP**   This is useful if a large file is being restored using previous versions and you want to check the status. |
| `revert shadow`<br>`vssadmin revert shadow`<br>`/shadow={`*guid*`}`<br>`[/forcedismount]`<br>`c:\>vssadmin revert shadow`<br>`/shadow={54e0d057-fcf7-4aa2-`<br>`95ef-72390436d420}`<br>`c:\>vssadmin revert shadow`<br>`/shadow={54e0d057-fcf7-4aa2-`<br>`95ef-72390436d420}`<br>`/forcedismount` | Reverts a volume to a shadow copy. The shadow copy is identified by the GUID (which is obtained from the **vssadmin list shadows** command). Spaces are not allowed before or after the equal sign (=) in the **/shadow** switch.<br><br>**TIP**   This is the same as accessing the Shadow Copies properties from Computer Management, selecting a shadow copy, and clicking the **Revert** button (as shown in Figure 3-2).<br><br>**WARNING**   Any changes made to files since the shadow copy was created will be lost. |

| vssadmin Command | Comments |
|---|---|
| `list shadows`<br>`c:\>vssadmin list shadows` | Lists existing volume shadow copies. This output includes the time each shadow copy is created and the globally unique identifier (GUID). |
| `list volumes`<br>`c:\>vssadmin list volumes` | Lists volumes that can be, or are, configured for shadow copies. Volumes are identified by the drive name and by the drive GUID. |
| `create shadow`<br>`vssadmin create shadow`<br>`/for=x: [/autoretry=mins]`<br>`c:\>vssadmin create shadow`<br>`/for=e: /autoretry = 10` | Creates a new volume shadow copy. This is useful if you want to create an unscheduled shadow copy.<br><br>If another process is creating a shadow copy, the **/autoretry** switch can be used to specify how many minutes to continue to retry the operation. |
| `delete shadows`<br>`vssadmin delete shadows /all`<br>`vssadmin delete shadows`<br>`/for=x:`<br>`vssadmin delete shadows`<br>`/shadow={guid}`<br>`vssadmin delete shadows /all`<br>`c:\>vssadmin create shadow`<br>`/for=e:` | Deletes volume shadow copies. You can delete all the shadow copies on the system, all the shadow copies for a specific drive, or a specific shadow copy identified by the GUID. New shadow copies will continue to be created based on the schedule.<br><br>You can use this to reclaim space taken by shadow copies. |
| `list shadowstorage`<br>`c:\>vssadmin list`<br>`shadowstorage` | Lists volume shadow copy storage associations, including how much is used, how much is allocated, and the maximum that can be allocated. |
| `resize shadowstorage`<br>`vssadmin resize`<br>`shadowstorage /for=x:`<br>`/on=x: /maxsize=size`<br>`c:\>vssadmin resize`<br>`shadowstorage /for=d:`<br>`/on=e: /maxsize= 1 GB` | Resizes a volume shadow copy storage association.<br><br>The **/for** switch identifies which drive shadow copies are created for, and the **/on** switch identifies the location to store the shadow copies. You can specify the size as KB, MB, GB, TB, PB, and EB. |
| `add shadowstorage`<br>`vssadmin add shadowstorage`<br>`/for=x: /on=x: /maxsize=size`<br>`c:\>vssadmin add`<br>`shadowstorage /for=d:`<br>`/on=e: /maxsize= 1 GB` | Adds a new volume shadow copy storage association. The same switches used for **resize shadowstorage** are used on **add shadowstorage**. |
| `delete shadowstorage`<br>`vssadmin delete shadowstorage`<br>`/for=x: [/quiet]`<br>`c:\>vssadmin delete`<br>`shadowstorage /for=d: /quiet` | Deletes volume shadow copy storage associations. This effectively stops shadow copy creation on the specified volume. All shadow copies are deleted, returning the space to the system. The **/quiet** switch suppresses confirmation prompts, which is useful in a script. |

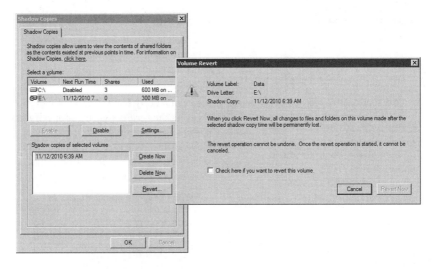

**Figure 3-2**   Reverting all previous versions for a specific volume

**TIP**   You can access the Shadow Copies tool shown in Figure 3-2 on a Windows Server 2008 system by entering **vssuirun** at an administrator prompt.

# Manipulating Shares with net share

You can create shares from the command prompt with the **net share** command. The basic syntax is

```
net share sharename = drive:path
```

**TIP**   You should be familiar with the **net share** tool when taking the 70-642 exam.

The following table describes some common uses with the **net share** command.

| net share Commands | Comments |
| --- | --- |
| View shares. <br><br> `c:\>net share` | Shows a listing of all shares on the local system. |
| Create a share. <br><br> `c:\>net share data=c:\data` | Creates a share named data from the folder named c:\data. The Everyone group is granted Read permission by default. <br><br> **NOTE**   This is another one of those commands that is particular about the equal sign (=). There shouldn't be any spaces before or after the equal sign. |

| net share Commands | Comments |
|---|---|
| Delete a share. <br><br> `/delete` <br> `c:\>net share data /delete` | The **/delete** switch deletes the named share. In this example, the share named data created in the previous step is deleted. |
| Create a share with specified permissions. <br><br> `/grant:user, [read \| change \| full ]` <br> `c:\>net share data=c:\data` <br> `/grant:darril,full` <br> `c:\>net share data=c:\data` <br> `/grant:"authenticated users",full` | You can modify the default permissions by using the **/grant** switch and specifying a user and the desired share permission. You can specify a user or a group. If the user or group name includes a space, it must be enclosed in quotes. <br><br> **NOTE**  Only the specified user or group is granted permissions. In other words, the default of Everyone being granted Read permission is not used. |

# Mapping Drives with net use

There might be times when you'll want to manipulate or access files on a remote share. You can use the Universal Naming Convention (UNC) of \\servername\sharename. However, some commands don't recognize the UNC path and need a drive letter, and sometimes it's just easier to use a drive letter instead of a full UNC path. You can use the **net use** command to map drive letters to UNC paths. The basic syntax is

`net use x: \\serverName\shareName`

You can use any drive letter that is not in use on the system, but if the drive letter is in use, the command will fail. Additionally, the UNC path must be reachable or you'll get an error.

| net use Command | Description |
|---|---|
| `c:\>net use` | You can view all currently mapped drives with this command. |
| `c:\>net use z: \\fs1\public` | This maps the driver letter z: to a share named public on a remote host named fs1. |
| `/delete` <br> `c:\>net use z: /delete` | The **/delete** switch deletes the mapped drive and frees up the mapped drive letter. |

| net use Command | Description |
|---|---|
| /persistent<br><br>`c:\>net use /persistent: No`<br><br>`c:\>net use /persistent: Yes` | The **/persistent** switch is used by itself and specifies whether the mapped drives are remembered at the next logon. When set to no, the **net use** command includes the following line: "New connections will not be remembered." This is the default.<br><br>When set to Yes, the **net use** command includes the following line: "New connections will be remembered." Mapped drives will survive reboots. |

**TIP**   If mapping a drive from a script that you want to survive reboots, it's best to enable persistent connections, map the drive, and then turn off persistent connections.

## Manipulating Users and Groups with the net Command

You can also use the **net** command to create, modify, and delete users and groups. The following table shows some of the common commands.

| net Command | Description |
|---|---|
| Create user.<br><br>`net user username password /add`<br>`c:\>net user Darril P@ssw0rd /add` | Creates a new user with the specified name and password. The password must meet the password requirements of the system.<br><br>If the command is executed on a local computer, it creates a local user account. If the command is executed on a domain controller, it creates an account in the Users container of Active Directory unless the **redirusr** command has changed the default location. |
| Create local group.<br><br>`net localgroup groupname /add`<br>`c:\>net localgroup ITPros /add` | Creates a local group with the group name. The group is created using the case specified in the command but can be identified later using any case. |
| Create group on domain controller.<br><br>`net group groupname /add`<br>`c:\>net group ITPros /add` | Creates a global security group using the group name. The group is added to the Users container.<br><br>**NOTE**   **group** works only on a domain controller and **localgroup** works only on a nondomain controller. |

| net Command | Description |
|---|---|
| Add user (or group) to group.<br><br>`c:\>net localgroup "event log readers" Darril /add`<br>`c:\>net localgroup "event log readers" ITPros /add` | You can use the **net localgroup** command to add a user or group to an existing group.<br><br>The examples add a user account (**Darril**) and a group (**ITPros**) to the preexisting **event log readers** group. |
| Delete user.<br><br>`net user username /delete`<br>`c:\>net user Darril /delete` | Deletes the specified user account. |
| Delete local group.<br><br>`net localgroup groupname /delete`<br>`c:\>net localgroup itpros /delete` | Deletes the specified local group. |
| Delete group on domain controller.<br><br>`net group groupname /delete`<br>`c:\>net group itpros /delete` | Deletes the specified domain group. |

## Modifying NTFS Permissions with icacls

You can modify file and folder permissions with the **icacls** command. The basic format is

`icacls file or folder /grant sid permission`

> **TIP** **icacls** modifies NTFS permissions for files and folders. The **net share** command modifies the permissions for shares.

The security identifier (**sid**) can be expressed as the actual sid of a user or group (with an asterisk as a prefix) or with the friendly name. For example, the following two commands both work:

`c:\>icacls c:\data /grant darrilgibson:f`
`c:\>icacls c:\data /grant *S-1-5-21-2165312475-2208171157-4291121935-1000:f`

The following table shows the basic codes used for permissions.

| Permission Code | Description |
|---|---|
| F | Full access |
| M | Modify access |
| Rx | Read and execute access |

| Permission Code | Description |
|---|---|
| R | Read-only access |
| W | Write-only access |

The following table shows some common usage of the **icacls** command. You can substitute the **f** permission code (for full access) with any of the permission codes listed in the previous table.

| icacl Command | Comments |
|---|---|
| Show permissions for a folder.<br><br>`c:\>icacls c:\data` | You can show the current permissions using only the command and the name of the folder. |
| Grant permission to a user.<br><br>`c:\>icacls c:\data /grant:r`<br>`darrilgibson:f`<br>`c:\>icacls c:\data /grant`<br>`darrilgibson:f` | You can append the permissions to any other explicitly added permissions or replace all explicitly added permissions. When you use **:r** in the **/grant** (**/grant:r**) switch, it replaces explicitly assigned permissions.<br><br>**TIP**   Inherited permissions are still inherited when **/grant:r** is used. |
| Include subfolders.<br><br>`c:\>icacls c:\data /grant:r`<br>`darrilgibson:f /t` | The **/t** switch includes all files and subfolders within the specified folder. |
| Deny permission to a user.<br><br>`c:\>icacls c:\data /deny`<br>`darrilgibson:f /t` | Instead of granting permissions, you can deny the permissions.<br><br>**TIP**   The deny permission always takes precedence. In other words, if a user is granted permission explicitly or as a member of a group and is also denied permission, the user is denied permission. |
| Remove permissions for a user.<br><br>`c:\>icacls c:\data /remove`<br>`darrilgibson:f /t` | Removes all ACL entries for the specified user. |

# CHAPTER 4

# Creating Batch Files

This chapter provides information and commands concerning the following topics:

- Using Notepad
- Giving feedback with **echo**
- Using parameters
- Calling another batch file with **call**
- Clearing the screen with **cls**
- Changing the order of processing with **goto**
- Checking conditions with **if**

## Using Notepad

Most students who have attended one of my classes on the command prompt, batch files, or PowerShell have heard me say this: "The difference between a good administrator and a great administrator is that great administrators have learned to script."

You don't even have to be a great scripter, but when you can automate some of your tasks, you can do much more than the good administrator who does tasks manually. You can start scripting by creating basic batch files in Notepad. One of the great things about the command prompt is that anything you can execute at the command prompt, you can embed as a script in a batch file, and anything you can script, you can automate.

Although there are more advanced tools you can use to create batch files, the simplest tool can meet most of your needs. Notepad is a simple text editor, and you can easily use it to create batch files. As a simple example, you can use the following steps to create a batch file in Notepad.

| Steps | Comments |
|---|---|
| 1. Type `c:\>md c:\scripts` | Creates a folder named scripts at the root of c:. |
| 2. Type `c:\>cd c:\scripts` | Changes the path to the c:\scripts folder. |
| 3. Type `c:\scripts>notepad sync.bat` | Launches Notepad and creates the batch file named sync.bat. When prompted to create the file, click **Yes**. |
| 4. Type the following line in the myfirstscript. bat file `repadmin /syncall` | Creates a one-line script in the batch file. |

| Steps | Comments |
|---|---|
| 5. Press Ctrl+S to save the batch file. | Saves the batch file. You can now execute it from the command line. |
| 6. Type `c:\scripts>sync` | Executes the script. The command **repadmin /syncall** forces replication between all domain controllers. This includes zone information in Active Directory Integrated zones. |

You can also create a batch file by just launching Notepad with the GUI or by typing **Notepad** without specifying the batch file name. The only difference is that when you save it, you need to ensure that you save it with a .bat extension. You do this by entering the filename as *scriptname*.**bat**. Notepad will still save it as a text file but with a .bat extension.

> **TIP**   If you don't add the .bat extension, Notepad defaults to a .txt extension and any file with a .txt extension does not execute as a batch file.

## Giving Feedback with echo

The **echo** command can be used to display messages to users from within a batch file. It's also useful to display the value of variables as shown in Chapter 2, "Basic Rules When Using the Command Prompt." For example, if you just want to know the path to the Program Files folder, you can use this command:

```
echo %programfiles%
```

However, **echo** has a quirk that can be confusing. If you use **echo** with a message from within a batch file, you'll see the **echo** command with the message and then the message again on the same line. For example, consider a file named synctest.bat with this line as you look at the following table:

```
echo This will synchronize DCs
```

| Batch File Contents | Result When Executed at Command Prompt | Comments |
|---|---|---|
| `echo This will synchronize DCs` | `c:\>synctest`<br>`c:\>echo This will synchronize DCs This will synchronize DCs` | Notice that the **echo** line shows, and then the result of the **echo** line shows. |
| `echo off`<br>`echo This will synchronize DCs` | `c:\>synctest`<br>`c:\>echo off`<br>`This will synchronize DCs` | The **echo off** command shows but the echo command isn't shown. |

| Batch File Contents | Result When Executed at Command Prompt | Comments |
|---|---|---|
| @echo off<br>echo This will<br>synchronize DCs | c:\>synctest<br>This will synchronize<br>DCs | The @echo off command turns off echo and also does not display the line. |
| @echo off<br>echo.<br>echo This will<br>synchronize DCs | c:\>synctest<br>This will synchronize<br>DCs | The echo. command displays a blank line (when a period is placed after the word echo as in echo.). |

**TIP**  If you enter **echo off** at the command prompt, the command prompt (c:\>) disappears, but you can still enter commands as normal. If you turn off **echo** from within a batch file, it does not affect the command prompt.

**NOTE**  If you want to include the pipe (|), the less-than character (<), the greater-than character (>), or the caret (^) symbol in an echo line, you need to precede the character with a caret (^). For example, if you want to send the output of the command to a text file with the > symbol, you would have to list it as ^>.

## Using Parameters

Windows Server 2008 supports the use of parameters in batch files. You define the parameter in the batch file, and then you can pass data to the batch file as a parameter. You can use as many as nine parameters, and they are defined as %1 through %9.

As an example, consider the **whoami** command. You can enter the following command to view the SID of the currently logged-on user:

```
whoami /user
```

You see information similar to the following:

```
USER INFORMATION
----------------

User Name     SID
============= =================================================
pearson\darril S-1-5-21-4285671909-4150961583-1987988917-1000
```

You can create a one-line batch file named who.bat with the following line:

```
whoami /%1
```

| who.bat Batch File Contents | Result When Executed at Command Prompt | Comments |
|---|---|---|
| `whoami /%1` | ```c:/>who user``` USER INFORMATION ---------------- User Name       SID ==================================== pearson\darril S-1-5-21-4285671909-4150961583-987988917-1000 | This command **(whoami /%1)** actually runs the following command by substituting **user** for **%1:whoami /user** |

Although the previous example is simplistic, it does show how a parameter is used. The following example shows a more usable batch file that can be used to set the IP address, subnet mask, and default gateway of a Windows Server 2008 Server Core system from the command line. Note that even though it runs to two lines in the text, it is entered on a single line.

```
netsh interface ipv4 set address name = "local area connection"
  static 10.10.0.10 255.0.0.0 10.10.0.1
```

The previous command sets the IP address to 10.10.0.10, the subnet mask to 255.0.0.0, and the default gateway to 10.10.0.1.

You can create a batch file named setip.bat with the following line using parameters. The batch file accepts three parameters identified as %1, %2, and %3:

```
netsh interface ipv4 set address name = "local area connection"
static %1 %2 %3
```

| setip.bat Batch File Parameters | Executing setip.bat at Command Prompt | Comments |
|---|---|---|
| `%1 %2 %3` | ```c:/>setip 10.10.0.10 255.0.0.0 10.10.0.1``` | This command sets the IP address, subnet mask, and default gateway using the setip.bat file. |

You can add a second line to your batch file to also set the address of the DNS server. Notice that the %4 parameter is the actual IP address of the DNS server.

```
netsh interface ipv4 set address name="Local Area Connection"
  static %1 %2 %3
netsh interface ipv4 set dnsserver "Local Area Connection" static %4
```

| setip.bat Batch File Parameters | Executing setip.bat at Command Prompt | Comments |
|---|---|---|
| %1 %2 %3 %4 | c:/>setip 10.10.0.10 255.0.0.0 10.10.0.1 10.10.0.5 | This command sets the IP address, subnet mask, default gateway, and DNS server address using the setip.bat file. |

## Calling Another Batch File with call

You can launch a batch file from within another batch file with the **call** command. The basic syntax is

```
call batchFileName
```

Figure 4-1 shows the order of processing when calling a batch file. Calltest.bat runs until it comes to the call calledbatch.bat line. It stops running and control is then passed to the called batch file, calledbatch.bat. After the called batch file runs, control passes back to the calling batch file.

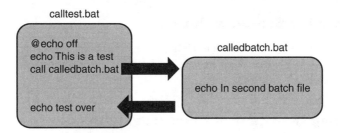

**Figure 4-1**    Order of processing when calling a batch file

Figure 4-2 shows the output when the batch file is run from the command prompt and calls the second batch file.

```
Administrator: Command Prompt
Microsoft Windows [Version 6.0.6001]
Copyright (c) 2006 Microsoft Corporation.  All rights reserved.

C:\Users\Administrator>cd \scripts

C:\scripts>calltest
This is a test
In second batch file
test over

C:\scripts>
```

**Figure 4-2**    Output of batch file calling another batch file

> **NOTE**   If the called batch file doesn't exist or somehow fails, control is still returned to the calling batch file. The call command works only from within a batch file. If you execute it directly from the command prompt, it is ignored.

The following table shows some use of the **call** command within a batch file.

| Using the call Command | Comments |
| --- | --- |
| `call newbatch.bat` | Calls the newbatch.bat batch file. The file must exist in the current path or in a path known by the system. |
| `call c:\scripts\newbatch.bat` | Calls the newbatch.bat batch file located in the c:\scripts folder. If the batch file doesn't exist, the call fails and control returns to the calling batch file. |
| `call newbatch.bat` *batch parameters* | If the called batch program accepts parameters, you can include them in the call. |
| `call newbatch.bat` *:Label* | Calls the batch program and starts execution at the specified label. |

## Clearing the Screen with cls

The **cls** command is useful within a batch file to clear the screen. It is entered simply as **cls** without any parameters. When entered, it clears the screen and puts the cursor at the top of the screen.

## Changing the Order of Processing with goto

You can use the **goto** statement to change the order of processing of a batch file. Normally, a batch file goes through the lines in the batch file from the first line to the last line. However, there are times you want to skip some areas of the batch file. The basic syntax of the **goto** statement in the batch file is

`goto` *label*

The label is listed elsewhere in the document as a string of characters beginning with a colon (:). For example, you can have a label at the end of the batch file named **:eof**. You can then include the following lines in the batch file:

| Using the goto Command | Comments |
| --- | --- |
| `goto eof` | The next command is at the **:eof** label. Notice that the label includes the colon (:), as in **:eof**, but the **goto** statement does not include the colon. |
| `repadmin /syncall` | This command never executes in this batch file because the **goto eof** statement always causes it to be skipped. |

| Using the goto Command | Comments |
|---|---|
| `:eof` | This is the **eof** label. |
| `echo Exiting batch file` | The **echo** command gives the user feedback. |

## Checking Conditions with if

When creating a batch file, you might occasionally want to check for specific conditions. If a condition exists, you do something. You use **if** statements frequently with **goto** statements.

The basic syntax of the command is

```
If condition command [else command ]
```

As a simple example, you can use the following **if** statement in a batch file:

```
if "%date%" == "Tue 11/20/2012" call magic.bat else Echo "Not yet"
```

The condition of the **if** command evaluates to either true or false. If the condition is true, it performs the command. If the condition is false, it does not perform the command. If an **else** clause is included, it is performed if the condition is false. In this example, the condition is a check to see whether today (%date%) is Tuesday, Nov 20, 2012. If so, it calls a batch file named magic.bat.

Although you can enter the entire **if** command on the same line, it is sometimes easier to read and understand when entered on separate lines. However, if you're using multiple lines, you must use parentheses around certain areas.

```
if condition (
  command
) else (
  command )
```

For example, the **if** command shown earlier would look like this:

```
if "%date%" == "Tue 11/16/2010" (
  call magic.bat
) else (
  echo "Not yet"
  )
```

There are certain conditions you can use, as shown in the following table.

| Condition | Example | Comments |
|---|---|---|
| `Exist` | `if exist log.txt copy`<br>`log.txt archive.txt` | Checks for the existence of the log.txt file and if it is there, it copies it to the archive.txt file. |
| `Errorlevel` | `if errorlevel 4 goto eof`<br>`This assumes a label of`<br>`:eof exists in the batch`<br>`file.` | Checks for the value of the **%errorlevel%** variable. If the value is 4, the batch goes to the **eof** label and presumably ends.<br><br>It's common to use this check to redirect the order of the batch file processing with the **goto** statement. |
| `string comparison`<br>`string1==string2` | `if %1 == Yes echo "User`<br>`entered Yes"` | Checks the value of one string against another. Notice that two equal signs (==) are required. |
| `not` | `if not exist log.txt copy`<br>`log.txt archive.txt`<br>`if not errorlevel 4 goto`<br>`end`<br>`if not %1 == Yes echo`<br>`"User did not enter Yes"` | The **not** condition negates the result of the conditional check. If the check results in true, the **not** condition changes it to false. If the check results in false, the **not** condition changes it to true. |

**NOTE**   You can use any valid command that you want after the condition. In other words, you aren't limited to using only certain commands when you use certain conditions. If it's a valid command from the command line, it's a valid command in the **if** statement.

When using comparison operators, you have several to choose from, as shown in the following table.

| Comparison Operator | Remarks |
|---|---|
| `==`<br>`if `*string1*` == `*string2*<br>`if abc ==  abc`<br>`if %1 == abc`<br>`if %1 == %myvar%` | Evaluates to true if string1 and string2 are the same. These values can be literal strings or batch variables, such as **%1** or **%myvar%**. You do not need to enclose literal strings in quotation marks.<br><br>For example, you can check to see what the user entered as a parameter using **%1**, and even check to see whether it's equal to a variable you created with a statement such as **set myvar= abc.** |

| Comparison Operator | Remarks |
|---|---|
| **if /i** *string1* **==** *string2* | If you want to ignore the case of the two strings, use the **/i** switch immediately after the **if** statement. |
| equ<br>**if** *value1* **equ** *value2* | Equal to.<br><br>Evaluates to true if the two values are equal. |
| neq<br>**if** *value1* **neq** *value2* | Not equal to.<br><br>Evaluates to true if the two values are not equal. |
| lss<br>**if** *value1* **lss** *value2* | Less than.<br><br>Evaluates to true if value1 is less than value2. |
| leq<br>**if** *value1* **leq** *value2* | Less than or equal to.<br><br>Evaluates to true if value1 is less than or equal to value2. |
| gtr<br>**if** *value1* **gtr** *value2* | Greater than.<br><br>Evaluates to true if value1 is greater than value2. |
| geq<br>**if** *value1* **geq** *value2* | Greater than or equal to.<br><br>Evaluates to true if value1 is greater than or equal to value2. |

It's common to use **if** statements in combination with **goto** statements and labels. For example, the batch file can accept an input and then check for the value of the input. Based on the input, it can take one of several actions. The following sample shows how to do this accepting a single parameter as **%1**:

```
@echo off
if %1#==# goto null
if %1==1 goto sync
if %1==2 goto show
if %1==3 goto summary
if %1 gtr 3 goto outofrange
:Null
echo "No Command entered."
goto eof
:outofrange
echo "Only values 1, 2, and 3 are valid."
goto eof
:sync
repdmin /syncall
:show
repadmin /showrepl
:summary
repadmin /replsummary
:eof
```

You can enter all of these commands in a batch file named repl.bat. You can then start the batch file with **repl 1** (to run **repladmin /syncall**), **repl 2** (to run **repadmin /show-repl**), or **repl 3** (to run **repadmin /replsummary**).

For clarification, the commands used in the previous batch file are explained in the following table.

> **NOTE**   Even though the example shows only one command in each of the labels, you can have as many commands as you like.

| Batch File Command | Comments |
|---|---|
| `@echo off` | Turns off **echo** so that the batch file commands don't show. |
| `if %1#==# goto null` | Checks for a null value. In other words, if the batch file is entered without a parameter, this evaluates to true and the batch file goes to the **:null** label. |
| `if %1==1 goto sync`<br>`if %1==2 goto show`<br>`if %1==3 goto summary`<br>`if %1 gtr 3 goto outofrange` | Checks for the value of the input. If it is any number, it uses the **goto** statement to process the command. |
| `:null`<br>`echo "No Command entered."`<br>`goto eof` | The **:null** label provides feedback if a parameter isn't provided. It gives feedback to the user and goes to the end of the file. |
| `:outofrange`<br>`echo "Only values 1, 2, and 3 are valid."`<br>`goto eof` | The **:outofrange** label provides feedback on valid numbers. If a value greater than 3 is entered, it gives feedback to the user and goes to the end of the file. |
| `:sync`<br>`repdmin /syncall` | The **:sync** label includes the **repadmin /syncall** command to force replication of objects between domain controllers (including those in different sites). |
| `:show`<br>`repadmin /showrepl` | The **:show** label includes the **repadmin /showrepl** command, which shows key information on replication. |
| `:summary`<br>`repadmin /replsummary` | The **:summary** label includes the **repadmin /replsummary** command, which includes a summary of replication events. |
| `:eof` | The **:eof** file label is placed at the end of the file and doesn't have any commands after it. The batch file then exits. |

# CHAPTER 5

# Using dnscmd

This chapter provides information and commands concerning the following topics:

- Retrieving DNS information
- Exporting DNS data
- Forcing zone transfers
- Clearing the DNS cache
- Working with DNS partitions
- Adding DNS zones
- Creating and deleting DNS records

**NOTE** Commands in this chapter are run on a domain controller named DC1 in the pearson.pub domain. The server is a DNS server with an Active Directory integrated (ADI) DNS zone named pearson.pub.

**TIP** You should be familiar with **dnscmd** when preparing for the 70-640 and 70-642 exams.

## Retrieving DNS Information

**dnscmd** includes several commands you can use to retrieve information about the server, zones, and records. The following table shows these commands.

| dnscmd Commands to Retrieve Information | Comments |
|---|---|
| Retrieve information on the DNS server.<br><br>/info<br>dnscmd *[server]* /info<br>c:\>dnscmd /info<br>c:\>dnscmd dc1 /info | Retrieves information on the DNS server including server-level properties.<br><br>You can include the name of a remote server by adding the name of the server, or you can execute it on a local DNS server and omit the server name. |
| List zones.<br><br>/enumzones<br>dnscmd *[server]* /enumzones<br>c:\>dnscmd /enumzones<br>c:\>dnscmd dc1 /enumzones | You can enumerate (or list) zones on a DNS server with the **/enumzones** switch. |

| dnscmd Commands to Retrieve Information | Comments |
|---|---|
| Retrieve performance statistics. `/statistics` `dnscmd` *[server]* `/statistics` `c:\>dnscmd /statistics` `c:\>dnscmd dc1 /statistics` | The **/statistics** switch shows performance statistics for the DNS server. |
| Retrieve information on a zone. `/zoneinfo` `dnscmd /zoneinfo` *zonefqdn* *filename* `c:\>dnscmd /zoneinfo` **pearson.pub** | The **/zoneinfo** switch retrieves information on a specific zone, including the properties of the zone. Much of this information is coded. For example, a zone type of 1 indicates it is a primary zone and a 1 for DS integrated indicates it is Active Directory integrated (ADI). Figure 5-1 shows the output of this command. |
| List records in zone. `/enumrecords` `dnscmd server /enumrecords` `zonename zonenode` `c:\>dnscmd dc1 /enumrecords` **pearson.pub @** | You can list all records in a zone with the **/enumrecords** switch. The @ symbol specifies that all the records from the zone root are listed. TIP  The output can be quite extensive. You can redirect the output to a text file with the redirect symbol (>) and the name of a file like this: **dnscmd dc1 /enumrecords pearson.pub @ > dns.txt** |

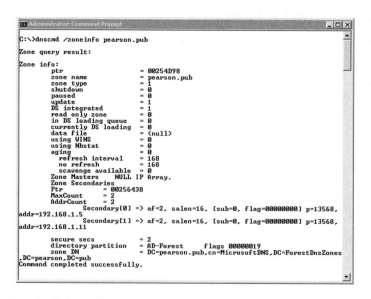

**Figure 5-1**  Retrieving DNS zone information with dnscmd

## Exporting DNS Data

You might occasionally want to create text files that include all the data from a zone. You can create them with the **/zoneexport** switch.

| Using /zoneexport | Comments |
|---|---|
| /zonexport<br><br>**dnscmd /zoneexport** *zonefqdn*<br>*filename*<br><br>c:\>**dnscmd /zoneexport**<br>**pearson.pub pearsonzone.txt** | Creates copies of the zone data as a file. The file can then be kept for archiving purposes or shared with other IT professionals (such as auditing and security personnel). |

**NOTE**   The exported file is created in the windows\system32\dns folder by default.

## Forcing Zone Transfers

Zone transfers occur on a regular schedule. When primary and secondary DNS servers are used, zone transfer schedules are based on settings in the Start of Authority (SOA) record. When ADI zones are used, zone transfers occur when Active Directory replication occurs. However, you can force zone transfers at different times.

| Forcing Zone Transfer Commands | Comments |
|---|---|
| Update secondary DNS server.<br><br>/zonerefresh<br>**dnscmd** *server* **/zonerefresh** *zone*<br>c:\>**dnscmd dc1 /zonerefresh**<br>**pearson.pub** | Forces a zone transfer from a primary DNS server to a secondary DNS server. You need to specify the server hosting the primary zone and the zone to transfer. In this example, the DC1 is the DNS server and the zone name is pearson.pub. |
| Update ADI zone data.<br><br>/zonereupdatefromds<br>**dnscmd** *server* **/ zoneupdatefromds**<br>*zone*<br>c:\>**dnscmd dc1 /zoneupdatefromds**<br>**pearson.pub** | Forces a zone transfer from directory services (for an ADI zone). This works for any ADI zone, including those hosted on read-only domain controllers (RODC).<br><br>**TIP**   When performing a zone transfer to update an RODC, run the command on a server that is not RODC. |

## Clearing the DNS Cache

When a DNS server queries a forwarder, it keeps the result in the DNS cache for the time to live (TTL) specified in the DNS record. You can use **dnscmd** to clear this DNS cache.

| Clear Cache Commands | Comments |
|---|---|
| Clear the DNS server cache.<br><br>`/clearcache`<br>**dnscmd** *server* **/clearcache**<br>`c:\>`**dnscmd /clearcache**<br>`c:\>`**dnscmd dc1 /clearcache** | If executed without a server name, it clears the DNS cache on the current server (assuming it's a DNS server). You can also specify a remote DNS server for the command.<br><br>Figure 5-2 shows how this is done from the DNS console. |
| Clear the host cache.<br><br>`c:\>`**ipconfig /flushdns** | You can clear the host cache on any computer using the **ipconfig /flushdns** command.<br><br>**NOTE**  Although you can clear the host's cache using the **ipconfig /flushdns** command on any computer, this is not the same as clearing the cache with the **dnscmd** or in the DNS console. |

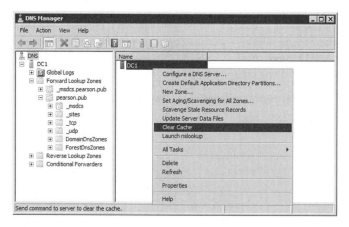

**Figure 5-2** Clearing the DNS cache from the DNS console

# Working with DNS Partitions

You might want to replicate data only between specific domain controllers. You can do this by creating directory partitions and having DNS servers enlist the partitions.

| DNS Partition Commands | Comments |
|---|---|
| Create a DNS application partition. `/createdirectorypartition` **dnscmd** *server* **/createdirectorypartition partitionFQDN** `c:\>`**dnscmd dc1 /createdirectorypartition pcgpartition.pearson.pub** | Data in the partition is replicated as part of Active Directory replication, and any severs that are configured with the partition. **TIP** A primary purpose of creating a directory partition is to control replication between a specific group of domain controllers (DC). Figure 5-3 shows how the created partition can be picked and how an ADI DNS zone can be configured to replicate with the partition. |
| List directory partitions. `/enumdirectorypartitions` **dnscmd** *server* **/enumdirectorypartitions** `c:\>`**dnscmd dc1 /enumdirectorypartitions** | This lists directory partitions for the specified server. By default, there are two partitions: **DomainDnsZones** and **ForestDnsZones**. This command also lists any partitions created with the **/createdirectorypartition** command. |
| Add a partition to a DNS server. `/enlistdirectorypartition` **dnscmd** *server* **/enlistdirectorypartition** *FQDNofPartition* `c:\>`**dnscmd dc1 /enlistdirectorypartition pcgpartition.pearson.pub** | Adds a DNS server to the replication set of the specified partition. **NOTE** This command is not needed on the DNS server where the directory partition was created. |
| Remove a directory partition. `/deletedirectorypartition` **dnscmd** *server* **/deletedirectorypartition** *FQDNofPartition* `c:\>`**dnscmd dc1 /deletedirectorypartition pcgpartition.pearson.pub** | Deletes an existing DNS application directory partition from the specified DNS server. If this is the last server where it exists, the partition is permanently deleted. |

## Adding DNS Zones

You can add DNS zones with **dnscmd**. The basic format is

```
dnscmd server /zoneadd zonename /zonetype
```

Configuring replication

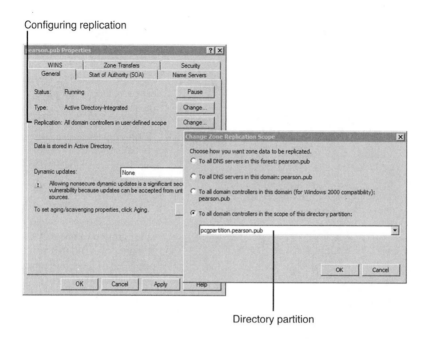

Directory partition

**Figure 5-3**   Configuring a server to replicate with a directory partition

The following table shows valid zone types you can create with the **/zoneadd** command.

| Valid Zone Types for /zoneadd | Comments |
|---|---|
| /dsprimary<br>dnscmd *server* /zoneadd *zonename*<br>/dsprimary<br>c:\>dnscmd dc1 /zoneadd<br>pcg.pearson.pub /dsprimary | Adds an ADI zone named pcg.pearson.pub. If the server has a pearson.pub zone, this command adds the pcg zone in the pearson. pub zone (as pcg.pearson.pub). |
| /primary<br>dnscmd *server* /zoneadd *zonename*<br>/primary /file *filename*<br>c:\>dnscmd dc1 /zoneadd<br>learning.pearson.pub /primary<br>/file learning.dns | You can create a nonADI primary DNS zone with the **/primary** switch. You must specify only the server, the zone name, and the name of the file to hold the DNS zone data. |
| /secondary<br>dnscmd *dc1* /zoneadd *zonename*<br>/secondary *masterIPaddress*<br>c:\>dnscmd dc1 /zoneadd<br>second.pearson.pub /secondary<br>192.168.1.150 | If you have a primary DNS server in your network, you can use the **/second- ary** switch to create a secondary zone. You must specify the server where you're creating the zone, the zone name, and the IP address of the master or primary DNS server. |

Figure 5-4 shows the result of executing the commands in the previous table. Notice that each zone has been added as an additional zone.

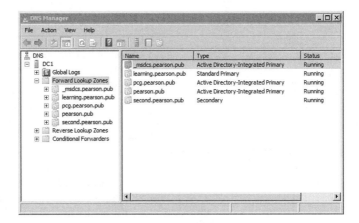

**Figure 5-4**   Zones created with the **/zoneadd** command

**NOTE**   In the Figure 5-4, the _msdcs.pearson.pub zone includes the SRV records for the domain, and the pearson.pub zone is the primary ADI zone for the domain. Only the other three zones were created from the previous table.

You can delete the zones created in the previous table with the following commands:

```
dnscmd dc1 /zonedelete pcg.pearson.pub /f /dsdel
dnscmd dc1 /zonedelete learning.pearson.pub /f
dnscmd dc1 /zonedelete second.pearson.pub /f
```

**NOTE**   The **/f** switch suppresses confirmation prompts, which is useful in a script. If the zone is an ADI zone (such as pcg.pearson.pub), you need to include the **/dsdel** switch to delete it from Active Directory.

# Creating and Deleting DNS Records

It's also possible to create and delete records in a DNS zone. The following table shows how this is done.

| Commands to Create and Delete DNS Records | Comments |
|---|---|
| Create DNS records.<br><br>`/recordadd`<br>**`dnscmd /recordadd`** *`zonename hostname`*<br>*`recordtype IPaddress`*<br>`c:\>`**`dnscmd /recordadd pearson.pub Web2`**<br>**`A 192.168.1.11`**<br>`c:\>`**`dnscmd /recordadd pearson.pub Web2`**<br>**`ptr 192.168.1.11`** | You can add different types of records with the **/recordadd** switch.<br><br>The example commands add an A record and a **ptr** record to the pearson.pub zone. |
| Delete DNS records.<br><br>`/recorddelete`<br>**`dnscmd`** *`dnsserver`* **`/recorddelete`** *`zonename`*<br>*`hostname record type`* **`/f`**<br>`c:\>`**`dnscmd dc1 /recorddelete`**<br>**`pearson.pub web2 a /f`**<br>`c:\>`**`dnscmd dc1 /recorddelete`**<br>**`pearson.pub web2 ptr /f`** | DNS records can be deleted with the **/recorddelete** switch. You must specify the server hosting the zone, the name of the zone, the name of the host, and the record type (such as **A** or **ptr**).<br><br>**NOTE**   The **/f** switch suppresses the confirmation. |

# CHAPTER 6

# Using nslookup

This chapter provides information and commands concerning the following topics:

- Verifying records with **nslookup**
- Configuring DNS for **nslookup**
- Using **nslookup** without PTR records
- Using **nslookup** without a reverse lookup zone

**NOTE** Commands in this chapter are run on a domain controller named DC1 in the pearson.pub domain. The server is a DNS server with an Active Directory integrated (ADI) DNS zone named pearson.pub.

**TIP** You should be familiar with **dnscmd** when preparing for the 70-646 and 70-647 exams.

## Verifying Records with nslookup

You can use the **nslookup** command to query the Domain Name System (DNS) server and diagnose different issues with DNS. The most common reason to use **nslookup** is to check for records. For example, you can use it to determine whether an A or Host record exists for a specific hostname. If the record exists, DNS can resolve it to an IP address. The basic syntax is

nslookup *Hostname*

Figure 6-1 shows the results of two simple **nslookup** queries. The first query looks for an A record for a server named Web1 to resolve it to an IP address. The second query looks for a PTR (pointer) record to resolve the IP address to a host name. Both queries succeed and return the desired information. Notice that the DNS server that responded is dc1.pearson.pub, identified by name and IP address in the first two lines after each query.

The following table outlines what is shown in Figure 6-1.

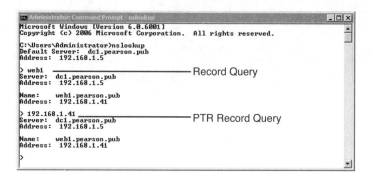

**Figure 6-1** Querying DNS with **nslookup**

| Using nslookup to Verify Records | Comments |
|---|---|
| `c:\>nslookup`<br>`Default Server: dc1.pearson.pub`<br>`Address: 192.168.1.5` | This puts **nslookup** into interactive mode as a shell. It's also possible to enter the complete **nslookup** command without entering interactive mode. It also identifies the name and IP address of the DNS server. |
| `> web1`<br>`Server: dc1.pearson.pub`<br>`Address: 192.168.1.5` | The first part of the response is only related to DNS. Because the system is configured with 192.168.1.5 as the IP address of the DNS server, **nslookup** shows that IP address. **nslookup** also tries to do a reverse lookup to determine the name of the system with that IP address.<br><br>If a PTR record exists in the reverse lookup zone, the query is successful (as shown here), and it displays the name of the DNS server (dc1.pearson.pub in the example). |
| `Name: web1.pearson.pub`<br>`Address: 192.168.1.41` | The next part of the response queries DNS for an A or host record for the host (web1 in this example). If a record exists, DNS gives the IP address of the host. |
| `> 192.168.1.41`<br>`Server: dc1.pearson.pub`<br>`Address: 192.168.1.5` | The next example gives the IP address of a computer with the goal of getting the name.<br><br>As before, the first two lines provide information on the server that is answering. |

| Using nslookup to Verify Records | Comments |
|---|---|
| Name:    web1.pearson.pub<br>Address: 192.168.1.41 | Because the DNS server includes a PTR record for the server, the response shows the IP address. |

Figure 6-2 shows the DNS console for the pearson.pub domain. Notice that an A (Host) record exists for web1.pearson.pub.

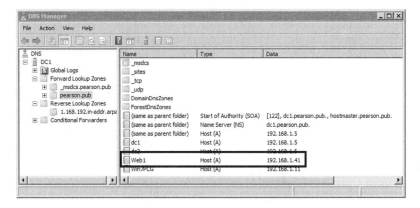

**Figure 6-2**  DNS console forward lookup zone in pearson.pub

Pointer (PTR) records exist in the reverse lookup zone of a DNS console, and Figure 6-3 shows the reverse lookup zone in the pearson.pub domain. Notice the PTR record for dc1.pearson.pub exists. This allows the **nslookup** query to identify the name of the DNS server's IP address.

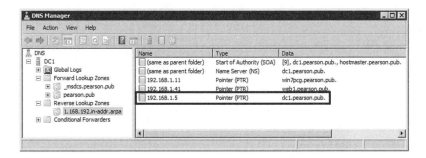

**Figure 6-3**  DNS console reverse lookup zone in pearson.pub

**NOTE**  The reverse lookup zone is optional, and pointer records are optional. You'll see different results depending on whether the reverse lookup zone exists and the PTR record exists within the reverse lookup zone.

In contrast, the following listing shows the result if an A record doesn't exist and if a PTR record doesn't exist.

```
C:\Users\Administrator>nslookup
Default Server:  dc1.pearson.pub
Address:  192.168.1.5

> web2
Server:  dc1.pearson.pub
Address:  192.168.1.5

*** dc1.pearson.pub can't find web2: Non-existent domain
> 192.168.1.42
Server:  dc1.pearson.pub
Address:  192.168.1.5

*** dc1.pearson.pub can't find 192.168.1.42: Non-existent domain
```

## Configuring DNS for nslookup

Although you can do some basic checking of records with **nslookup**, some attempts to transfer zone data will fail unless the DNS server is configured to allow zone transfers.

As an example, consider the following code listing. The **ls -d pearson.pub** command queries the DNS server for a listing of all records in the pearson.pub domain. However, it fails because zone transfers are not allowed to the computer where the **nslookup** command is issued from.

```
C:\>nslookup
Default Server:  dc1.pearson.pub
Address:  192.168.1.5

> ls -d pearson.pub
[dc1.pearson.pub]
*** Can't list domain pearson.pub: Query refused
The DNS server refused to transfer the zone pearson.pub to your
computer. If this is incorrect, check the zone transfer security
settings for pearson.pub on the DNS server at IP address 192.168.1.5.
```

> **TIP**   The words "Query refused" are a direct indication that zone transfers aren't allowed for this computer.

You can resolve this issue by adding the computer to the list of servers where zone transfers are allowed. Figure 6-4 shows the screen where you can add a computer to this list. In the figure, a computer named win7pcg has been added. **nslookup** zone transfer commands issued from this computer will now succeed.

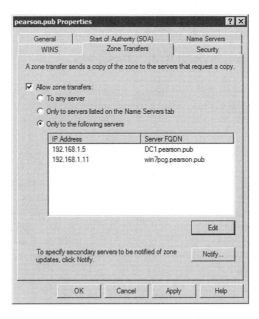

**Figure 6-4**   Adding a computer to the list for authorized zone transfers

You can access the screen shown in Figure 6-4 with these steps:

| Steps | Comments |
|---|---|
| 1. Launch the DNS console from the **Administrative Tools** menu. | Click **Start**, **Administrative Tools**, **DNS**. |
| 2. Expand the server and Forward Lookup Zones. Right-click the zone you want to modify and select **Properties**. | The DNS console remembers the last view so this might be expanded already. |
| 3. Select the **Zone Transfers** tab. | The view will be similar to Figure 6-4. |
| 4. Ensure **Allow Zone Transfers** is selected. | You can choose to allow zone transfers to any server (not recommended for security reasons), only to servers on the **Name Servers** tab (DNS servers with an NS record), or to servers that you add. Click the **Edit** button to add servers if you choose the last option. |

## Using nslookup Without PTR Records

If the DNS server doesn't have a PTR record for the DNS server, you receive an error when using **nslookup**. Although this looks serious, it isn't. You're still able to determine whether records exist on the DNS server with **nslookup**.

The following table shows what you see if the DNS server doesn't include a record for the DNS server but does include an A record for a queried host.

| nslookup Responses Without PTR Records | Comments |
|---|---|
| `C:\Users\Administrator>`**`nslookup`**<br>`Default Server:  UnKnown`<br>`Address:  192.168.1.5` | In this example, the PTR record for dc1. pearson.pub is deleted. Although the IP address of the DNS server (192.168.1.5) is still known, it can't resolve the IP address to the name of the DNS server, so the default server is listed as UnKnown. |
| `> `**`web1`**<br>`Server:   UnKnown`<br>`Address:  192.168.1.5`<br>`Name:     web1.pearson.pub`<br>`Address:  192.168.1.41` | However, DNS can still resolve the name (Web1) to an IP address. The results of the **Web1** query again show that the name of the DNS server is unknown, but it successfully shows the correct IP address (1921.68.1.41) of the Web1 server.<br><br>If you're focused only on seeing whether DNS can resolve Web1 to an IP address, this Unknown response can be ignored. If you're managing the DNS server, you might want to create the PTR record for the DNS server. |

# Using nslookup Without a Reverse Lookup Zone

**nslookup** works if a reverse lookup zone doesn't exist on the DNS server, but it gives some errors. The following table shows what you can expect if the DNS server doesn't have a reverse lookup zone.

| nslookup Responses Without a Reverse Lookup Zone | Comments |
|---|---|
| `C:\Users\Administrator>`**`nslookup`**<br>`DNS request timed out.`<br>`    timeout was 2 seconds.`<br>`Default Server:  UnKnown`<br>`Address:  192.168.1.5` | This DNS request timed out looks like you have serious problems, but it just indicates that the reverse lookup zone is deleted. Because reverse lookup zones are optional, this time out message can be ignored.<br><br>Your system still has an IP address of the DNS server (192.168.1.5 in the example), but it can't resolve it to a name because the reverse lookup zone (and its associated PTR record) does not exist. |

| nslookup Responses Without a Reverse Lookup Zone | Comments |
|---|---|
| ```<br>> web1<br>Server:   UnKnown<br>Address:  192.168.1.5<br><br>Name:     web1.pearson.pub<br>Address:  192.168.1.41<br>``` | However, even if the reverse lookup zone doesn't exist, DNS still resolves the name of hosts to IP addresses (as long as it has the associated A records).<br><br>This example shows that the name of the DNS server is unknown but it still resolves web1 to the correct IP address. |

# CHAPTER 7

# Using Basic ds Commands

This chapter provides information and commands concerning the following topics:

- Understanding distinguished names
- Adding objects with **dsadd**
- Modifying accounts with **dsmod**
- Moving accounts with **dsmove**
- Removing objects with **dsrm**

**NOTE** Commands in this chapter are run on a domain controller named DC1 in the pearson.pub domain.

**TIP** You should be familiar with basic ds commands when preparing for the 70-640 exam.

## Understanding Distinguished Names

Active Directory Domain Services (AD DS) uses the Lightweight Directory Access Protocol (LDAP). Every object in AD DS is uniquely identified with a distinguished name (DN). The DN identifies the object, domain, and Organizational Unit (OU) or container where it's located.

Figure 7-1 shows the Active Directory Users and Computers (ADUC) console with the properties of a user account in the pearson.pub domain. It's in the East OU, which is in the Sales OU.

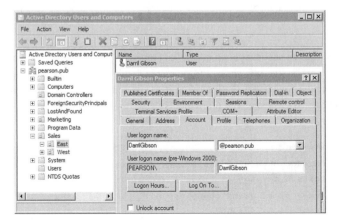

**Figure 7-1** ADUC showing user account

The DN for the user account shown in the figure is

```
cn=Darril Gibson, ou=East, ou=Sales, dc=pearson, dc=pub
```

> **NOTE**  DNs are not case sensitive. You can use the same case shown in ADUC, or any combination of upper- and lowercase characters. For example, the following DN is the same, even though it doesn't match the case shown in ADUC:
>
> ```
> cn=darril gibson, ou=east, ou=sales, dc=pearson, dc=pub
> ```

DS commands (such as **dsadd**, **dsmod**, and so on) need the DN to identify the object to create, modify, or delete. When the DN is used within a command, it must be enclosed within quotes if it includes spaces. The following table shows the common components of a DN used with DS commands.

| DN Component | Description |
|---|---|
| CN | CN is short for common name. It's used to indicate the common name of an object (such as the user's account name) or the name of a container (such as the Users or Computers containers). Notice in Figure 7-1 that the account name is Darril Gibson (with a space) but the user logon name is DarrilGibson (with no space). |
| OU | OU is short for Organizational Unit. When multiple OUs are listed, the top level is listed last. For example, the Sales OU is the top-level OU in Figure 7-1 and is listed as the last OU and closest to the domain.<br><br>**NOTE**  Nested OUs often give people the most trouble when building the DN. An easy check is to see whether the top-level OU is next to the domain component (dc) and the last child OU is listed first. |
| DC | DC is short for domain component. Notice that each portion of the DC must be separate. This is incorrect and results in an error: dc=pearson.pub. It must be separated as dc=pearson, dc=pub. |

> **NOTE**  Although there are many more DN components that can be used with LDAP, the three shown in the preceding table are the ones you need to know for the DS commands.

You can use spaces in some places in the DN command or omit them. For example, you can use spaces after the commas to separate the DN components. You also can use spaces before the equal signs (but not after the equal signs in some commands). They will be interpreted the same. The following table shows both valid usage of spaces and one example, which causes errors.

| Valid? | DN Component | Description |
|---|---|---|
| Valid | `"cn=Joe,ou=east,ou=sales,dc=pearson,dc=pub"` | No spaces |
| Valid | `"cn=Joe, ou=east, ou=sales, dc=pearson, dc=pub"` | Spaces after the commas |

| Valid? | DN Component | Description |
|---|---|---|
| Valid | `"cn =Joe, ou =east,`<br>`ou =sales, dc =pearson,`<br>`dc =pub"` | Spaces after the commas and before the equal (=) signs |
| Error | `"cn = Joe, ou = east,`<br>`ou = sales, dc = pearson,`<br>`dc = pub"` | Spaces after the equal (=) sign results in errors in many commands |

**TIP**  Avoid commas before and after the equal (=) sign to prevent potential problems. However, it's common to use spaces after the commas for readability. Just remember that if any spaces are used, the entire DN must be enclosed in quotes.

# Adding Objects with dsadd

You can add objects with the **dsadd** command. The basic syntax is

```
dsadd object-type DN
```

Some common object types you can add are users, computers, groups, and OUs. The following table shows the syntax to create specific accounts. Each of these commands creates an account in the pearson.pub domain, in the East OU nested in the Sales OU.

**NOTE**  The **dsadd** command creates accounts using the same case you use in the command. In other words, you can create an account named joe or an account named Joe, depending on the case you use in the DN. If the DN is lowercase, the account is built with lowercase.

| dsadd Command | Comments |
|---|---|
| Add a user.<br><br>`dsadd user dn [-pwd password]`<br>`C:\>dsadd user "cn=Joe,`<br>`ou=east,ou=sales,dc=pearson,`<br>`dc=pub"`<br>`C:\>dsadd user "cn=joe2,`<br>`ou=east,ou=sales,dc=pearson,`<br>`dc=pub" -pwd P@ssw0rd` | Adds a user account. The example adds a user account named Joe to the sales\east OU.<br><br>If you don't include a password, the account is disabled by default. If you include the password, but it doesn't meet the password complexity requirements, the account is disabled.<br><br>However, if you include the password and it meets complexity requirements, the account is enabled (as shown in Figure 7-2). |

| dsadd Command | Comments |
|---|---|
| Add a group.<br><br>`dsadd group dn -secgroup`<br>`{yes \| no} -scope { 1 \| g \|`<br>`u }`<br>`C:\>dsadd group "cn=IT Admins,`<br>`ou=east,ou=sales,dc=pearson,`<br>`dc=pub" -secgrp yes -scope g`<br>`C:\>dsadd group "cn=IT`<br>`Admins2, ou=east, ou=sales,`<br>`dc=pearson, dc=pub"`<br>`C:\>dsadd group "cn=dl_`<br>`printer, ou=east, ou=sales,`<br>`dc=pearson, dc=pub" -scope l` | You can add security groups (with **-secgroup yes**) or distribution groups (with **-secgroup no**). You add different scopes with the **-scope** switch. Create domain local groups (with **-scope l**), create global groups (with **-scope g**), and create universal groups (with **-scope u**).<br><br>**TIP**  The **dsadd** group command defaults to a global security group so you can omit the **-secgroup** and **-scope** switches.<br><br>The examples add two global security groups (IT Admins and IT Admins2) and one domain local security group (dl_printer). |
| Add a computer.<br><br>`dsadd computer dn`<br>`C:\>dsadd computer "cn=PC-1,`<br>`ou=east, ou=sales,`<br>`dc=pearson, dc=pub"` | The example command creates a computer named PC-1 in the sales\east OU. |

**TIP**  You can also identify different properties for any of these objects. For a full listing of the properties for any of the objects, use the help command as **dsadd user /?**, **dsadd group /?**, or **dsadd computer /?**.

Figure 7-2 shows ADUC with the accounts created in the previous table. Notice that the Joe account is disabled because a password wasn't given. The down arrow icon in the user icon indicates that it is disabled. Also, notice that Joe starts with an uppercase J because that's how the command was entered, and the joe2 account starts with a lowercase j.

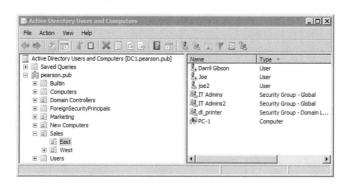

**Figure 7-2**  ADUC showing accounts created with the **dsadd** command

## Modifying Accounts with dsmod

You can modify account properties from the command prompt with the **dsmod** command. The basic syntax is

```
dsmod object-type dn-property property-value
```

The common object-types you modify with the **dsmod** command are the same ones you create with the **dsadd** command: users, computers, groups, and OUs.

> **TIP**   You can also identify different properties for any of these objects with the help command. Useful help commands are **dsmod user /?**, **dsmod group /?**, or **dsmod computer /?**.

The following table shows some common uses of the **dsmod** command when working with users and computers.

| dsmod Commands for Users and Computers | Comments |
|---|---|
| Change a user password.<br><br>`dsmod user dn -pwd * \| password`<br>`C:/>dsmod user "cn=joe,ou=east,`<br>`ou=sales,dc=pearson,dc=pub" -pwd`<br>`*`<br>`C:/>dsmod user "cn=joe,ou=east,`<br>`ou=sales,dc=pearson,dc=pub" -pwd`<br>`P@ssw0rd` | You can change a user's password with the **-pwd** switch. You can either specify the password or use the asterisk (*). If you use the asterisk, you will be prompted to enter the new password. |
| Enable or disable a user account.<br><br>`dsmod user dn -disabled yes \| no`<br>`C:\>dsmod user "cn=joe,ou=east,`<br>`ou=sales,dc=pearson,dc=pub"`<br>`-disabled no` | You can enable or disable a user account with the **-disabled** switch. To disable it, use **-disabled yes** and to enable it, use **-disabled no**. |
| Enable or disable a computer account.<br><br>`dsmod computer dn -disabled yes`<br>`\| no`<br>`C:\>dsmod computer "cn=PC-1,`<br>`ou=east, ou=sales, dc=pearson,`<br>`dc=pub" -disabled yes` | You can also enable or disable a computer account with the **-disabled** switch. To disable it, use **-disabled yes** and to enable it, use **-disabled no**. |

The following table shows some common uses of the **dsmod** command when working with groups.

| dsmod Commands for Groups | Comments |
|---|---|
| Change a group type.<br><br>`Dsmod group DN -secgrp yes \| no`<br>`C:\>dsmod group "cn=IT Admins,`<br>`ou=east, ou=sales, dc=pearson,`<br>`dc=pub" -secgrp no`<br>`C:\>dsmod group "cn=IT Admins,`<br>`ou=east, ou=sales, dc=pearson,`<br>`dc=pub" -secgrp yes` | You can designate a group as a security group with **-secgrp yes**, or as a distribution group with **-secgrp no**.<br><br>**NOTE**   Security groups can have permissions assigned and be used for email lists. Distribution groups can only be used for email lists. |
| Change a group scope.<br><br>`Dsmod group DN -scope l \| g \| u`<br>`C:\>dsmod group "cn=IT Admins,`<br>`ou=east, ou=sales, dc=pearson,`<br>`dc=pub" -scope u`<br>`C:\>dsmod group "cn=IT Admins,`<br>`ou=east, ou=sales, dc=pearson,`<br>`dc=pub" -scope l`<br>`C:\>dsmod group "cn=IT Admins,`<br>`ou=east, ou=sales, dc=pearson,`<br>`dc=pub" -scope u`<br>`C:\>dsmod group "cn=IT Admins,`<br>`ou=east, ou=sales, dc=pearson,`<br>`dc=pub" -scope g` | Group scopes include global, domain local, or universal in a domain. You can use the **-scope** group to change the scope from one to another. The examples change the scope of the IT Admins group from global to universal, then to domain local, back to universal, and then back to global.<br><br>**NOTE**   You can't convert a global group directly to a domain local group, and you can't convert a domain local group directly to a global group. However, you can convert it to a universal group first, and then convert it to a domain local or global group. |
| Add a user to a group.<br><br>`Dsmod group group-DN -addmbr`<br>`user-DN`<br>`C:\>dsmod group "cn=IT Admins,`<br>`ou=east, ou=sales, dc=pearson,`<br>`dc=pub" -addmbr "cn=Joe,ou=east,`<br>`ou=sales,dc=pearson,dc=pub"`<br>`C:\>dsmod group "cn=IT Admins,`<br>`ou=east, ou=sales, dc=pearson,`<br>`dc=pub" -addmbr "cn=Joe,ou=east,`<br>`ou=sales,dc=pearson,dc=pub"`<br>`"cn=Sally,ou=east,ou=sales,`<br>`dc=pearson,dc=pub"` | You can add or remove users to a group with the **-addmbr** switch.<br><br>The first example adds the user named Joe (created previously) to the IT Admins group and the second example adds both the user Joe and another user named Sally to the group.<br><br>**TIP**   You can add as many members as desired in the same command by adding additional DNs. You need only a space between DNs, not a comma. |
| Remove a user from a group.<br><br>`Dsmod group group-DN -rmmbr`<br>`user-DN`<br>`C:\>dsmod group "cn=IT Admins,`<br>`ou=east, ou=sales, dc=pearson,`<br>`dc=pub" -rmmbr "cn=Joe, ou=east,`<br>`ou=sales, dc=pearson, dc=pub"` | You can remove a user from a group with the **-rmmbr** command. The example removes the Joe user account from the IT Admins group.<br><br>Figure 7-3 shows the IT Admins **Members** tab after the user is added. |

| dsmod Commands for Groups | Comments |
|---|---|
| Add a domain local group to a global group.<br><br>Dsmod group domain-local-*DN*<br>-addmbr *global-group-DN*<br>C:\>dsmod group "cn=dl_printer,<br>ou=east, ou=sales, dc=pearson,<br>dc=pub" -addmbr "cn=IT Admins,<br>ou=east, ou=sales, dc=pearson,<br>dc=pub" | This example shows how to add a global group (IT Admins) to a domain local group (named dl_printer) with the **-add-mbr** switch.<br><br>In the IT Admins Member Of tab, you see the dl_printer added after executing this command. |
| Remove a group from another group.<br><br>Dsmod group domain-local-*DN*<br>-rmmbr *global-group-DN*<br>C:\>dsmod group "cn=dl_printer,<br>ou=east, ou=sales, dc=pearson,<br>dc=pub" -rmmbr "cn=IT Admins,<br>ou=east, ou=sales, dc=pearson,<br>dc=pub" | This example removes the global group (IT Admins) from the domain local group (named dl_printer) with the **-rmmbr** switch. |

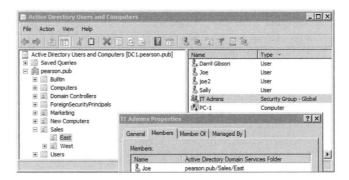

**Figure 7-3**   ADUC showing properties of the IT Admins group with member added

**TIP**   You can view a listing of all the properties you can change with the **dsmod** command on Microsoft's TechNet site: http://technet.microsoft.com/library/cc732406.aspx.

# Moving Accounts with dsmove

You can move accounts to different OUs or containers with the **dsmove** command. The difficult part about this task is building the DN, but if you've mastered the DN, the command is simple.

**NOTE**   You can also move objects with the Active Directory Migration Tool (ADMT) and with the **ldifde** command.

| dsmove Command | Comments |
|---|---|
| Move an object from one OU to another OU.<br><br>`Dsmove dn -newparent parentdn`<br>`C:\>dsmove "cn=joe,ou=east,ou=sales,dc=pearson,dc=`<br>`pub" -newparent "ou=west,ou=sales,dc=pearson,dc=pub"`<br>`C:\>dsmove "cn=joe,ou=west,ou=sales,dc=pearson,dc=`<br>`pub" -newparent "ou=east,ou=sales,dc=pearson,dc=pub"` | This example moves a user account from the sales\east OU to the sales\west OU and then back. |

**TIP**  You can view a listing of all the capabilities of the **dsmove** command on Microsoft's TechNet site: http://technet.microsoft.com/library/cc731094.aspx.

# Removing Objects with dsrm

Finally, you can remove objects with the **dsrm** command. The basic syntax is shown in the following table.

| dsrm Command | Comments |
|---|---|
| Delete an object.<br><br>`Dsmove dn -newparent parentdn [-noprompt]`<br>`C:\>dsrm "cn=joe,ou=east,ou=sales,dc=pearson,dc=pub"`<br>`C:\>dsrm "cn=joe,ou=east,ou=sales,dc=pearson,dc=pub"`<br>`-noprompt` | This example removes the specified user account. You are prompted to confirm the removal, but you can suppress the prompt with the **-noprompt** switch. |

**TIP**  You can view a listing of all the capabilities of the **dsrm** command on Microsoft's TechNet site at http://technet.microsoft.com/library/cc731865.aspx.

# CHAPTER 8

# Using Advanced ds Commands

This chapter provides information and commands concerning the following topics:

- Retrieving information about objects with **dsquery**
- Retrieving information about objects with **dsget**
- Viewing and modifying AD permissions with **dsacls**

**NOTE** Commands in this chapter are run on a domain controller named DC1 in the pearson.pub domain.

**TIP** You should be familiar with the advanced **ds** commands when preparing for the 70-640 and 70-646 exams.

## Retrieving Information about Objects with dsquery

You can use the **dsquery** command to retrieve information about objects in Active Directory (AD). A benefit of **dsquery** is that you can retrieve multiple objects at the same time by specifying filter criteria. The basic syntax of the **dsquery** command is

```
dsquery dn-property property-value
```

The following table shows some examples of how to use the **dsquery** command to retrieve multiple objects.

| dsquery Command | Comments |
|---|---|
| Retrieve all the groups in an Organizational Unit (OU). <br><br> `dsquery group dn` <br> `C:\>dsquery group "ou=east,` <br> `ou=sales, dc=pearson, dc=pub"` | Retrieves a list of all the groups in the sales\east OU. <br><br> **NOTE** The only thing you need to add is the distinguished name (DN). |
| Retrieve all the groups in an OU matching a specific name. <br><br> `dsquery group dn` <br> `C:\>dsquery group "ou=east,` <br> `ou=sales, dc=pearson, dc=pub" -name` <br> `IT*` | You can use the **-name** switch to identify all the groups with specific names, and you can also use the asterisk (*) wildcard. <br><br> This example retrieves a list of all the groups in the sales\east OU that have a name that starts with "IT." |

| dsquery Command | Comments |
|---|---|
| Retrieve a listing of all users in the domain or in an OU.<br><br>`dsquery user` *dn*<br>`C:\>dsquery user "dc=pearson, dc=pub"`<br>`C:\>dsquery user "ou=sales,dc=pearson, dc=pub"`<br>`C:\>dsquery user "ou=sales,dc=pearson, dc=pub" -scope base` | Retrieves a listing of all objects, such as all users or all computers. The *dn* identifies the search range.<br><br>The first example lists all users in the domain. The second example lists all users in the Sales OU and child OUs. The third example limits the scope to the base OU (Sales) and lists all users in the Sales OU only (not child OUs). |
| Identify inactive accounts.<br><br>`dsquery` *object-type dn* `-inactive` *number-of-weeks*<br>`C:\>dsquery user "dc=pearson,dc=pub" -inactive 4`<br>`C:\>dsquery computer "dc=pearson,dc=pub" -inactive 4` | The **-inactive** switch identifies inactive accounts.<br><br>These examples retrieve any user accounts and computer accounts that have not been logged on to in the past four weeks. |
| Identify accounts with stale passwords.<br><br>`dsquery user` *dn* `-stalepwd` *number-of-days*<br>`C:\>dsquery user "dc=pearson,dc=pub" -stalepwd 45` | A stale password hasn't been changed in a specific number of days.<br><br>**TIP**  Use this to locate service accounts that have the Password Never Expires setting enabled and haven't had their passwords changed within a given time. |
| Locate disabled accounts.<br><br>`dsquery user` *dn* `-disabled`<br>`C:\>dsquery user "dc=pearson,dc=pub" -disabled` | Locates all disabled accounts. |

**TIP**  You can view a listing of all the capabilities of the **dsquery** command on Microsoft's TechNet site: http://technet.microsoft.com/library/cc732952.aspx.

An added benefit of the **dsquery** command is that you can use it to modify multiple objects at the same time. You can pipe the results of the **dsquery** command to another command such as the **dsmod** command. The basic format is

`dsquery` *command* `| dsmod` *command*

**NOTE**  Piping or pipelining is done by adding a pipe character (|) between the commands. The output of the first command becomes the input of the second command.

The following table shows a few examples where you can pipe the results of a **dsquery** command to a **dsmod** command.

| dsquery Command | Comments |
|---|---|
| Disable inactive accounts.<br><br>dsquery *object-type* dn -inactive *number-of-weeks*  \| dsmod user -disabled yes<br>C:\>dsquery user "dc=pearson,dc=pub" -inactive 4 \| dsmod user -disabled yes | This example (shown in Figure 8-1) uses a query to identify accounts that are inactive, and then passes the list to the **dsmod** command. The **dsmod** command then disables all accounts in the list. |
| Modify a property for a group of users.<br><br>dsquery user *dn* \| dsmod user -office *value*<br>C:\>dsquery user "ou=east, ou=sales,dc=pearson,dc=pub" \| dsmod user -office "East Sales" | This example first retrieves a list of all users in the sales\east OU and passes this list to the **dsmod** command. The **dsmod** command uses the **-office** switch to change the **-office** name to Virginia Beach for each of the users.<br><br>**NOTE**   Because the office name of Virginia Beach has a space, it must be enclosed in quotes. |

**TIP**   In Figure 8-1, the first command is the **dsquery** command by itself. This is a good practice so that you know what you will modify before actually modifying it.

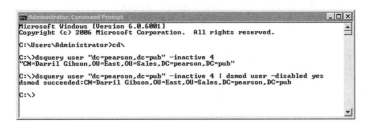

**Figure 8-1**   Piping the Results of a **dsquery** to **dsmod**

# Retrieving Information About Objects with dsget

You can use the **dsget** command to retrieve information about objects. The **dsget** command is useful when you want to get a list of group members or user group membership.

**TIP**   The primary difference between **dsquery** and **dsget** is that **dsquery** retrieves multiple objects that meet a given criteria, while **dsget** retrieves information about a single object.

| dsget Command | Comments |
|---|---|
| Get a list of members for a group.<br><br>`dsget group DN -members`<br><br>`C:\>dsget group "cn=it admins,`<br>`ou=east, ou=sales, dc=pearson,`<br>`dc=pub" -members` | Retrieves a list of members of the IT Admins group in the sales\east OU.<br><br>Figure 8-2 shows the result of this command. |
| List group membership for a user.<br><br>`dsget user dn [-memberof`<br>`-expand]`<br><br>`C:\>dsget user "cn=joe,`<br>`ou=east, ou=sales, dc=pearson,`<br>`dc=pub" -memberof`<br>`C:\>dsget user "cn=joe,`<br>`ou=east, ou=sales, dc=pearson,`<br>`dc=pub" -memberof -expand` | The **-memberof** switch shows the direct group membership for a user. The **-expand** switch includes nested group membership.<br><br>For example, consider the Domain Users group, which is a member of the Users group. If a user is added to the Domain Users group, the user is indirectly a member of the Users group.<br><br>The **-memberof** switch shows the Domain Users group but not the Users group, unless the **-expand** switch is also included.<br><br>Figure 8-3 shows the result of this command. |

**TIP**  You can view a listing of all the capabilities of the **dsget** command on Microsoft's TechNet site: http://technet.microsoft.com/library/cc755162.aspx.

**Figure 8-2**  Using **dsget** to view group members

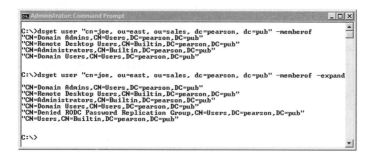

**Figure 8-3**  Using **dsget** to view user group membership

## Viewing and Modifying AD Permissions with dsacls

Every object in Active Directory Domain Services (AD DS) has an access control list (DS ACL), which is a list of access control entries (ACE). Each ACE includes the security identifier (SID) of an account and the permission. This is the same as in the **Security** tab of any AD DS object within Active Directory Users and Computers (ADUC), as shown in Figure 8-4.

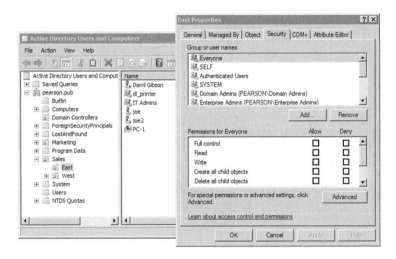

**Figure 8-4**   Viewing permissions in ADUC

Figure 8-4 shows the permissions assigned to the East OU. Even though these permissions are assigned by SID, ADUC does a lookup into ADUC to identify and display the user and group names.

> **TIP**   The **Security** tab does not show by default. If it isn't showing, select **View** and **Advanced Features** to enable the **Security** tab (and other advanced features).

| dsacls Command | Comments |
|---|---|
| Show permissions for an object.<br><br>`dsacls dn`<br>`C:\>dsacls "ou=east,ou=sales,`<br>`dc=pearson,dc=pub"` | You can view the permissions on any AD DS object simply by entering *dn* after **dsacls**. The example shows the permission on the sales\east OU. |
| Reset default permissions.<br><br>`dsacls dn -resetdefaultdacl`<br>`C:\>dsacls "ou=east,ou=sales,`<br>`dc=pearson,dc=pub" -resetdefaultdacl` | If you made a mistake when modifying permissions on an object, you can always return it to the original permissions with the **-resetdefaultdacl** switch. |

**NOTE**    You can do much more with the **dsacls** command, but it's rare that you need to do so with a script. For example, you can use an in-depth command to grant a group permission to change passwords for users in an OU. However, it's much easier to do so using the Delegation of Control wizard access in ADUC by right-clicking over any OU and selecting **Delegate Control**.

# CHAPTER 9

# Promoting and Demoting a Domain Controller (DC)

This chapter provides information and commands concerning the following topics:

- Promoting a DC with **dcpromo**
- Demoting a DC with **dcpromo**
- Using **dcpromo** with an unattend file
- Promoting a DC to an RODC with an existing account
- Using **dcpromo** to install from media
- Forcing removal of Active Directory

**TIP**  You should be familiar with **dcpromo** commands and capabilities when preparing for the 70-640 and 70-647 exams.

## Promoting a DC with dcpromo

You use the **dcpromo** wizard to promote a Windows Server 2008 server to a domain controller (DC). The **dcpromo** wizard is a rich wizard that enables you to promote a server to a DC. The following steps show how to run **dcpromo** to promote a server as the first DC in the first domain of a forest. In these steps, the domain is named pearson.pub.

**TIP**  The server should have a statically assigned IP address. Also, it's best to ensure that you have named the server before starting the process. You can rename the server after it's promoted, but this occasionally causes problems. It's easier to avoid the problems by renaming it before promoting it.

| Step | Action |
|------|--------|
| 1. | Launch a command prompt with administrative permissions. |
| 2. | Type **dcpromo** at the command prompt and press **Enter**. |
| 3. | When the **Welcome** screen appears, click **Next**. |
| 4. | Review the information on the **Operating System Compatibility** page and click **Next**. |
| 5. | Select **Create a New Domain in a New Forest**, and then click **Next**. |
| 6. | Type **pearson.pub** (or whatever name you like), and then click **Next**. |
| 7. | Review the information on the **Set Forest Functional Level** page. Select at least **Windows Server 2003** and click **Next**. |
| 8. | Review the information on the **Set Domain Functional Level** page. Select at least **Windows Server 2003**, and then click **Next**. |

| Step | Action |
|------|--------|
| 9. | On the **Additional Domain Controller Options** page, ensure that **DNS Server** is selected. Global Catalog will also be selected, but you can't deselect it because the domain must have at least one Global Catalog server. Click **Next**.<br><br>**NOTE** dcpromo automatically configures DNS for the domain. |
| 10. | If you have IPv6 enabled and you don't have a statically assigned IPv6 address, you'll see a warning similar to Figure 9-1. You see this warning even if you have a statically assigned IPv4 address. You can continue without assigning static IP addresses, but you should at least assign an IPv4 address.<br><br>Click **Yes. This Computer has Dynamically Assigned IP Address(es)**. |
| 11. | A warning displays, indicating that a delegation for the DNS cannot be created. This is normal. Click **Yes** to continue. |
| 12. | On the Location for Database, Log Files, and SYSVOL dialog box, accept the defaults and click **Next**. |
| 13. | Type a password (such as P@ssw0rd) in the **Password** and **Confirm Password** text boxes. This is needed for Directory Services Restore Mode. Click **Next**. |
| 14. | Review the information on the **Summary** page as shown in Figure 9-2. Click **Next**.<br><br>**TIP** You can click the **Export Settings** button to export your answers to an answer file. You can then use this answer file to run **dcpromo** from the command prompt without launching the wizard. |
| 15. | Select the **Reboot on Completion** checkbox. When **dcpromo** completes, the server will be a domain controller. |

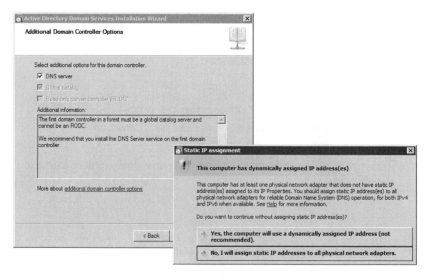

**Figure 9-1** Warning to assign a static IP address

**Figure 9-2  dcpromo** Summary page

# Demoting a DC with dcpromo

If you run **dcpromo** on a DC, it recognizes that the computer is already a DC hosting Active Directory. It then prompts you to remove Active Directory. The following steps show how to remove Active Directory from the last domain controller in a domain.

| Step | Action |
|------|--------|
| 1. | Launch a command prompt with administrative permissions. |
| 2. | Type **dcpromo** at the command prompt and press **Enter**. |
| 3. | When the **Welcome** screen displays, click **Next**. |
| 4. | A warning appears indicating the server is a Global Catalog server and recommending you ensure that you have at least one Global Catalog server in the domain. Click **OK**. |
| 5. | On the **Delete the Domain** page, select the checkbox to delete the domain, as shown in Figure 9-3. Click **Next**. |
| 6. | If the DC uses Active Directory Integrated DNS, a dialog box displays, indicating what partitions are installed on the DC and letting you know they'll be removed. Click **Next**. |
| 7. | On the **Confirm Deletion** page, select the checkbox to **Delete All Application Directory Partitions on this Active Directory Domain Controller**. Click **Next**. |
| 8. | Type the password for the local Administrator account in the **Password** and **Confirm Password** text boxes. Click **Next**. |
| 9. | Review the information on the **Summary** page and click **Next**. Select the checkbox to **Reboot on Completion**. When **dcpromo** completes, it automatically reboots as a standalone server. |

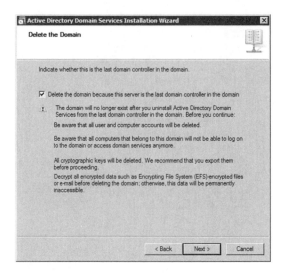

**Figure 9-3**    Using **dcpromo** to remove the last DC in the domain

# Using dcpromo with an unattend File

One benefit of launching **dcpromo** from the command line is that you can automate the installation with an unattend file. The easiest way to create an answer file is with the **dcpromo** wizard. You can run it on any non-DC server but when you get to the **Summary** page, click the **Export Settings** button to create the answer file (as shown in Figure 9-2).

The following code shows the contents of an answer file created from the earlier installation.

> **NOTE**    You can create this file from scratch within Notepad, but it is much easier to let the wizard create it for you.

```
; DCPROMO unattend file (automatically generated by dcpromo)
; Usage:
;    dcpromo.exe /unattend:C:\data\unattend.txt
;
[DCInstall]
; New forest promotion
ReplicaOrNewDomain=Domain
NewDomain=Forest
NewDomainDNSName=pearson.pub
ForestLevel=2
DomainNetbiosName=PEARSON
DomainLevel=2
InstallDNS=Yes
ConfirmGc=Yes
```

```
CreateDNSDelegation=No
DatabasePath="C:\Windows\NTDS"
LogPath="C:\Windows\NTDS"
SYSVOLPath="C:\Windows\SYSVOL"
; Set SafeModeAdminPassword to the correct value prior to
  using the unattend file
SafeModeAdminPassword=
; Run-time flags (optional)
; RebootOnCompletion=Yes
```

> **NOTE**   Comments in the unattend file are annotated with a semicolon (;). These lines
> are ignored by the **dcpromo** wizard.

Notice that the command to use it is embedded as a comment on the third line. This line
points to the location where the unattend.txt file was saved (**c:\data** in this example).

You must change the **SafeModeAdminPassword=** line by adding the password you
want to assign for Directory Services Restore Mode:

**SafeModeAdminPassword=P@ssw0rd**

After you add the password and save the file, you can use the following command to run
**dcpromo** with the answer file:

**dcpromo.exe /unattend:C:\data\unattend.txt**

> **NOTE**   You might need to use a different path depending on where the unattend.txt file
> is located.

No other user interaction is necessary. **dcpromo** completes and reboots the server. When
it reboots, it will be a domain controller.

## Promoting a DC to an RODC with an Existing Account

Read-only domain controllers (RODC) are an important addition to Windows Server
2008. An organization can increase security in a branch office by installing an RODC in
the branch office.

> **NOTE**   The RODC does not store administrator passwords on the server by default, so
> even if the RODC is stolen, the thief will not have access to critical data.

You can pre-create an RODC account from within Active Directory Users and
Computers (ADUC). This enables a user at the remote office to promote the server to an
RODC, without requiring the user to have elevated permissions.

Figure 9-4 shows the Domain Controllers OU with an RODC named VBRODC1 pre-
created. Also, the context menu accessed by right-clicking the mouse shows the selection
to pre-create an RODC account.

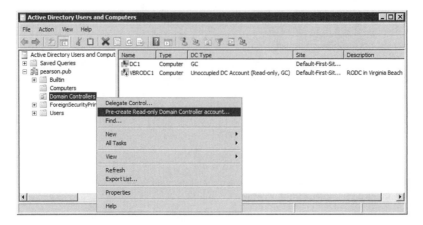

**Figure 9-4** Pre-creating an RODC account

The following steps show how to pre-create the account.

| Step | Action |
|------|--------|
| 1. | Launch **Active Directory Users and Computers** (ADUC) by clicking **Start**, **Administrative Tools**, **Active Directory Users and Computers**. |
| 2. | Expand the domain and right-click the **Domain Controllers** OU. Your display should look similar to Figure 9-4. |
| 3. | Review the information on the **Welcome** page and click **Next**. |
| 4. | Review the information on the **Operating System Compatibility** page and click **Next**. |
| 5. | On the **Network Credentials** page, select **Alternate Credentials** and click **Set**. Type the account credentials of a user that has permissions to run **dcpromo**. Click **OK**. Click **Next**.<br><br>You can use the same account that you launched ADUC with as long as the account has sufficient privileges to run **dcpromo**. |
| 6. | Type the name of the computer and click **Next**.<br><br>**NOTE** This is the name of the server at the remote location that will be promoted to an RODC. The computer can't be joined to the domain yet. |
| 7. | Select the appropriate site for the remote office and click **Next**. |
| 8. | The DNS server and Global Catalog server are selected by default. You can change these based on the needs of the remote office. Click **Next**.<br><br>**NOTE** Unless you have a DNS server in the remote office, you should leave the DNS server selected. If it's only a single domain forest, you should also leave the Global Catalog selected. |
| 9. | On the **Delegation of RODC Installation and Administration** page, click **Set**. Type the name of the user and click **Check Names**. Your display should look similar to Figure 9-5. Click **OK**. Click **Next**. |
| 10. | On the **Summary** page, click **Next**. Click **Finish**. |

At this point, the account is created. The user at the remote office, which you designated in the wizard, can run **dcpromo** to promote the server at the remote office to an RODC.

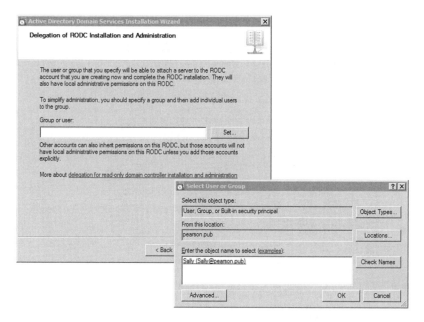

**Figure 9-5** Entering the account name of the user that will promote the RODC

## Using dcpromo to Install from Media

When you promote a server to a DC in a domain that already has a DC, it replicates all Active Directory data from an existing DC to the replica DC. If this is within a well-connected network, it's no problem. However, if the replication must occur over a slow wide area network (WAN) connection, it can cause problems. It can overwhelm the connection affecting other users or simply take an excessively long time to complete.

Instead, you can create a copy of the Active Directory data to replicate, send the media to the remote location, and then use the install from media (IFM) option.

The following steps show how to create the installation media with the **ntdsutil** command.

| Step | Action |
| --- | --- |
| 1. | Launch a command prompt with administrative permissions. |
| 2. | Type **ntdsutil** and press **Enter**. |
| 3. | Type **activate instance ntds** and press **Enter**. |
| 4. | Type **ifm** and press **Enter**. |
| 5. | Type **create rodc c:\ifm** and press **Enter**. When complete, the display looks similar to Figure 9-6. |

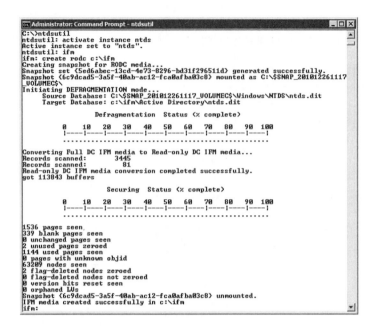

**Figure 9-6**   Creating installation media with **ntdsutil**

After you create the installation media, you can copy it to other media such as a CD or a flash USB drive, and then send it to the remote office. An administrator at the remote office can then start **dcpromo** with the following command:

```
dcpromo /adv
```

This launches **dcpromo** with advanced options. After selecting **Additional Domain Controller for an Existing Domain**, the **Copying Domain Information** page appears. The administrator can then specify the location of the media created with **ntdsutil**.

# Forcing Removal of Active Directory

There are occasions when you need to remove Active Directory from a system but **dcpromo** fails because the system can't connect to another DC. For example, imagine that a DC has a hardware failure and you have to seize the RID Master role while it is down. You shouldn't connect this DC back to the network as a DC because there is the potential of having two RID Masters and duplicate SIDs in your domain.

**NOTE**   If you seize the Schema Master, Domain Naming Master, or RID Master roles from a failed DC, you should not bring the original DC back online without first removing Active Directory. The potential for problems to the forest and domain can be catastrophic.

You can rebuild the failed DC from scratch, but it'd be much easier to simply run **dcrpromo** to remove Active Directory and then run **dcpromo** again to add Active Directory again.

You can force the removal of Active Directory with the following command:

```
dcpromo /forceremoval
```

Figure 9-7 shows one of the confirmation screens that might appear. In some situations, you see one of these for each of the master operations roles that the server holds. You also see a confirmation screen if the server is a DNS server, and another one if it's a global catalog server. After clicking **Yes** for each of these screens, the wizard starts. You can then follow the steps in the "Demoting a DC with **dcpromo**" section earlier in this chapter.

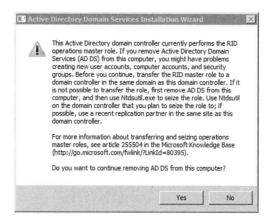

**Figure 9-7** Running **dcpromo /forceremoval**

# CHAPTER 10

# Working with the Schema

This chapter provides information and commands concerning the following topics:

- Modifying the schema with **adprep**
- Registering the Active Directory Schema snap-in

**TIP** You should be familiar with **adprep** commands when preparing for the 70-640 and 70-647 exams.

## Modifying the Schema with adprep

There are occasions when you need to modify the schema. For example, if you originally created your forest and domain by promoting a Windows Server 2003 server to a domain controller (DC), the forest and domain will not support Windows Server 2008 DCs. However, you can easily resolve this by modifying the schema with the **adprep** tool. The **adprep** tool is available on the installation DVD.

**TIP** The **adprep** executable file is stored in the \sources\adprep folder on the Windows Server 2008 installation DVD. It's stored in the \support \adprep folder on the Windows Server 2008 R2 installation DVD.

The following table shows common uses of the **adprep** command.

**NOTE** It's not necessary to run **adprep** if the forest was created on a Windows Server 2008 server. However, it doesn't cause any problems if you try.

| adprep Command | Comments |
|---|---|
| Prepare a forest for Windows Server 2008.<br><br>`C:\>d:\sources\adprep\`<br>`adprep /forestprep` | This command updates the schema information used for the forest. It must be run before the **adprep / domainprep** command.<br><br>**TIP** You must run this command on the server hosting the schema master role.<br><br>**NOTE** You must be a member of both the Enterprise Admins and Schema Admins groups to run this command.<br><br>In the example, the installation DVD is in the D: drive. If your installation DVD is in a different drive, you'll need to substitute the drive letter. |

| adprep Command | Comments |
|---|---|
| Prepare a domain for Windows Server 2008 DCs.<br><br>`C:\>d:\sources\adprep\`<br>`adprep /domainprep` | After **adprep /forestprep** is run, you can run this command. It prepares the domain for both Windows Server 2008 and Windows Server 2008 R2 domain controllers.<br><br>**TIP**    You should run this command on the DC hosting the Infrastructure Master role.<br><br>**NOTE**    You must be a member of the Domain Admins group to run this command. |
| `C:\>d:\sources\adprep\`<br>`adprep /domainprep`<br>`/gpprep` | This command is similar to the **adprep /domainprep** command, but it also provides updates to the schema for the Resultant Set of Policy (RSoP) tool.<br><br>**NOTE**    You must be a member of the Domain Admins group to run this command.<br><br>**TIP**    The **/gpprep** switch is needed if the current domain is running on a Windows 2000 domain controller. It's not needed if the current domain is running on Windows Server 2003 domain controllers. |
| Prepare the forest for RODCs.<br><br>`C:\>d:\sources\adprep\`<br>`adprep /rodcprep` | If you also want to add Read-only Domain Controllers (RODC), you need to run this command.<br><br>**NOTE**    You must be a member of the Enterprise Admins group to run this command. |

**TIP**    After running **adprep**, ensure that you give it enough time to replicate the changes to all domain controllers before making changes. For example, if you're running **adprep /domainprep** to prepare a Windows Server 2003 domain to host Windows Server 2008 domain controllers, give replication enough time to replicate the changes to all DCs in the domain.

# Registering the Active Directory Schema Snap-In

You can't access the Active Directory Schema snap-in by default. This is to provide an extra layer of protection so that someone doesn't accidentally modify the schema causing problems. You can access the schema only after you register the schmmgmt.dll for the Active Directory Schema snap-in.

The command to register the Active Directory Schema is

`regsvr32 schmmgmt.dll`

After you register the snap-in, the Active Directory Schema will be available as a snap-in that you can add to an MMC as shown in Figure 10-1.

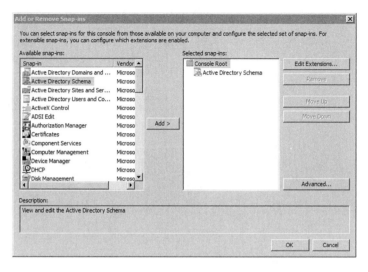

**Figure 10-1**    Adding the Active Directory Schema snap-in to an MMC

# CHAPTER 11

# Working with Active Directory Accounts

This chapter provides information and commands concerning the following topics:

- Using **ldifde** to export, import, and delete accounts
- Using **csvde** to export and import accounts
- Redirecting computer accounts
- Redirecting user accounts

**NOTE**   Commands in this chapter are run on a domain controller named DC1 in the pearson.pub domain.

**TIP**   You should be familiar with these commands when preparing for the 70-640 exam.

## Using ldifde to Export, Import, and Delete Accounts

The **ldifde** command works on line-delimited, or line-separated values within files. You can use it to import or export data into or out of Active Directory (AD). You execute these commands on a domain controller (while logged on with an account with administrative permissions).

**TIP**   The L in **ldifde** represents the Lightweight Directory Access Protocol, and dif represents data interchange format. The last two letters (de) represent directory exchange.

The following table shows some common switches used with **ldifde**.

| ldifde Switch | Comments |
|---|---|
| -i | Import mode. If not included, the default mode is export. |
| -k | Ignores errors. Enables the operation to continue even if there are errors. The lines with errors are not processed, but other lines are as long as they aren't dependent on the line that had an error. If omitted, the operation stops at the first error and none of the lines are processed. |
| -f *filename* | Filename. Identifies the name of the file to use for the import or export operation. |

| ldifde Switch | Comments |
|---|---|
| **-b** `user domain password` | Specifies the username, domain, and password of the account to run the operation. If not specified, the command runs under the context of the currently logged-on user. If the user has appropriate permissions, this switch is not needed. |
| **-j** `path` | Specifies the path for a log file.<br><br>**NOTE**  This is not the actual filename but instead just the path. The error log is named ldif.err and can be opened with Notepad. |
| `-v` | Enable verbose mode. This provides the most words in the output and is useful when troubleshooting problems with the command. |

Use the following command to export all the accounts from the domain into a file named export.txt:

```
ldifde -f ldexport.txt
```

**TIP**  You can learn a lot about the different attributes used with **ldifde** by browsing through the export.txt file created from this command.

When importing accounts, you need a file that includes the accounts in a line-delimited format. Each line identifies specific attributes of an account, and the formatting of this file is critical. The following table shows some of the elements you can add to the file.

| Input File Attributes | Comments |
|---|---|
| `# comments` | You can add comments with a hash mark. The **ldifde** command ignores comments. |
| `dn:  dn` | The distinguished name (**dn**) attribute identifies the account name and location using a distinguished name. |
| `changetype: {add | modify | delete}` | This identifies whether you'll be adding, modifying, or deleting accounts. |
| `objectclass: {user | computer | organizationalunit}` | You can create users, computers, organizational units, and more by identifying them in the **objectclass** attribute. |

| Input File Attributes | Comments |
|---|---|
| `samaccountname: name` | The SAM account name shows the account in the legacy (pre-Windows 2000) name format. Figure 11-1 shows the SAM account name for a user in the text box to the right of the text box labeled **PEARSON\**.<br><br>**NOTE**  The SAM account name is sometimes listed as domain-name\account-name; however, you need only the account name for the **Idifde** file. |
| `userprincipalname: upn` | The user principal name (**upn**) looks like an email address. It's created by combining the user logon name with a suffix that identifies the domain. In Figure 11-1, the UPN is DarrilGibson@pearson.pub. |
| `displayname: name` | This is the name listed in the **General** tab of the account properties in the **Display Name** text box. In Figure 11-1, it is Darril Gibson (with a space) in the Sales\East OU.<br><br>**NOTE**  This is not the name displayed in the Active Directory Users and Computers (ADUC) console. That name is derived from the common name (CN) attribute in the DN. |
| `givenname: firstname` | The first name is identified as given name. |
| `sn: lastname` | The last name is identified as **sn**. |
| `useraccountcontrol: {512 \| 514}` | You can specify that the account is enabled (**512**) or disabled (**514**) with the **useraccount-control** attribute.<br><br>**TIP**  If you don't specify the password, or if the password doesn't meet the complexity requirements, the command will fail unless you use **514** to disable the user. |

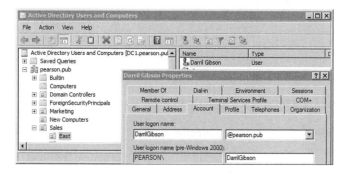

**Figure 11-1**  User account in ADUC

As an example, you can use the following data in a file named ldou.txt:

```
#create an OU
dn: ou=test,dc=pearson,dc=pub
changetype: add
objectclass: organizationalunit
```

You can then use the following command to create the Organizational Unit (OU) in the domain:

**ldifde -i -f lduser.txt -v -j c:\de**

The command specifies that it is an import (**-i**), from the file named ldou.txt (**-f lduser. txt**), with a verbose output (**-v**), and sends error to a log file in the c:\de folder (**-j c:\de**).

You can delete the OU by using the following data in a file named lddel.txt. Notice that the only difference is that the **changetype** is delete instead of add, and you don't need to specify the **objectclass**.

```
#create an OU
dn: ou=test,dc=pearson,dc=pub
changetype: delete
```

The following command deletes the OU:

**ldifde -i -f lddel.txt -v -j c:\de**

As another example, you can use the following data in a file named lduser.txt to create a user:

```
#Create a user
dn: cn=Marina,ou=sales,dc=pearson, dc=pub
changetype: add
objectclass: user
samaccountname: Marina
userprincipalname: marina@pearson.pub
displayname: Marina Jonason
givenname: Marina
sn: Jonason
useraccountcontrol: 514
```

You can then execute the following command to add the user to the domain:

**ldifde -i -f lduser.txt -v -j c:\de**

The command specifies that it is an import, from the file named lduser.txt, with a verbose output, and logs errors to a file in the c:\de folder.

Figure 11-2 shows the account created in ADUC.

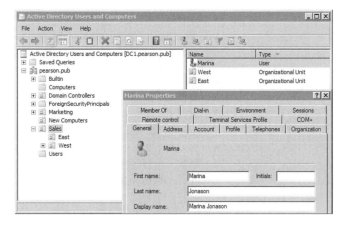

**Figure 11-2**   Marina user account created from ldifde

**NOTE   ldifde** has more depth than you see here. The TechNet website shows many more details: http://technet.microsoft.com/library/cc731033.aspx.

# Using csvde to Export and Import Accounts

The comma separated value directory exchange (**csvde**) command works on comma-separated value files. Each element in the csv file is separated by a comma, and you can use the **csvde** command to import or export objects for AD.

**TIP**   You can only import and export with **csvde**. You cannot delete objects or make any modifications to objects with **csvde**. You can import, export, delete, and modify objects with **ldifde**.

The following table shows some common switches used with **csvde**.

| ldifde Switch | Comments |
|---|---|
| -i | Import mode. If not included, the default mode is export. |
| -k | Ignores errors. Enables the operation to continue even if there are errors. The lines with errors are not processed, but other lines are as long as they aren't dependent on the line that had an error. If omitted, the operation stops at the first error and none of the lines are processed. |
| -f *filename* | Filename. Identifies the name of the file to use for the import or export operation. |

| ldifde Switch | Comments |
|---|---|
| `-b user domain password` | Specifies the username, domain, and password of the account to run the operation. If not specified, the command runs under the context of the currently logged-on user. If the user has appropriate permissions, this switch is not needed. |
| `-j path` | Specifies the path for a log file.<br><br>**NOTE** This is not the actual file name, but instead just the path. The error log will be named csv.err and can be opened with Notepad. |
| `-v` | Enables verbose mode. This provides the most words in the output and is useful when troubleshooting problems with the command. |

Use the following command to export all of the accounts from the domain into a file named export.txt:

```
csvde -f csexport.csv
```

> **TIP** The first line shows all of the possible attributes you can include in a csv input file. It also shows the format of a csv file. You can open this file in Microsoft Excel or Notepad.

You saw earlier that the **ldifde** input file is line delimited with a separate attribute on each line. In addition, each line identifies both the attribute and the attribute value (such as **changetype: add**). In contrast, **csvde** is a comma-delimited file with attributes separated by commas. A significant difference is that the attributes aren't specified on each line. Instead, the first line in the csv file is the header line and identifies the attributes in each of the following lines.

For example, consider the following three lines in a sample csv file. The first line is the header line and identifies what attributes are in each of the other lines. The second and third lines provide the data for the user accounts.

| Line | Contents of Each Line in csv File |
|---|---|
| Header line | `dn, objectclass, samaccountname, userprincipalname, displayname, useraccountcontrol` |
| First user | `"cn=Dawn, ou=west, ou=sales, dc=pearson, dc=pub", user, Dawn, Dawn@pearson.pub, Dawn Grzena, 514` |
| Second user | `"cn=Bob,ou=west,ou=sales,dc=pearson,dc=pub", user, Bob, Bob@pearson.pub, , 514` |

There are some important points you need to recognize:

- First, the order of the attributes in each line must follow the same order in the header line. For example, the DN is first, the **objectclass** is second, and so on.

- Second, because the DN includes commas, the entire DN must be enclosed in quotes; otherwise, each comma in the DN will be interpreted as a different attribute and the command will fail.

- Third, you can skip an attribute value by adding a comma without a value. For example, in the second user line, the **displayname** attribute is not included; instead, there is simply an extra comma.

If you have a file named csuser.csv with the three lines in the preceding table, you can use the following command to input the two users into the domain. The **-i** indicates it is an import, the **-f** indicates the file is csuser.csv, the **-v** specifies a verbose output, and the **-j** creates the error log in the c:\de folder.

```
csvde -i -f csuser.csv -v -j c:\de
```

Figure 11-3 shows the accounts created with the previous command.

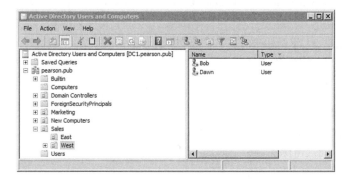

**Figure 11-3**  User accounts created from csvde

**NOTE**  **csvde** has more depth than you see here. The TechNet website shows many more details: http://technet.microsoft.com/library/cc732101.aspx.

# Redirecting Computer Accounts

When a computer joins a domain, the computer account is added to the Computers container by default; however, you can change the default behavior with the **redircmp** command. The basic syntax is

```
redircmp target-DN
```

**TIP**  The **target-DN** can be any container or OU but is typically an OU.

For example, if you want new computers to be placed into an OU you've created called New Computers (shown in Figure 11-4), you can use the following command:

```
redircmp "ou=new computers,dc=pearson,dc=pub"
```

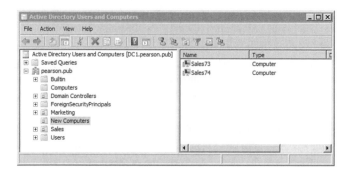

**Figure 11-4**   New Computers OU in ADUC

The primary reason to do this is to control the new computers with a Group Policy Object (GPO). You can create a GPO that configures security settings or install software for all new computers placed into this OU. As soon as a computer joins the domain, the GPO applies these settings.

> **TIP**   You can link a GPO to an OU but not to a container such as the Computers container or the Users container.

## Redirecting User Accounts

You can also redirect new user accounts that are created with the **net user** command. The basic syntax to redirect user accounts is

```
redirusr target-DN
```

> **TIP**   If the user account is created with a DN (such as with **dsadd**, **csvde**, or **ldifde**), the target DN is already specified. The **redirusr** command does not override these commands. However, because the **net user** command doesn't specify a DN, the **redirusr** command redirects these user accounts.

For example, the following command redirects all user accounts created with the **net user** command to the Sales OU:

```
redirusr "ou=sales,dc=pearson,dc=pub"
```

Most methods of creating user accounts identify the target location. For example, if you're using ADUC, you simply right-click over the target OU and select **New**, User. If you're using **csvde** or **ldifde**, the target OU is included in the DN.

It's not as common to create accounts with the **net user** command, but it can be done. The basic syntax is

```
net user username [password] /add
```

For example, the following command creates an account for a user named Maria:

```
net user Maria P@ssw0rd /add
```

> **TIP**   If you run the **net user** command on a DC, it adds the account to AD. If you run it on a member server or a standalone system, it adds it as a local account.

# CHAPTER 12

# Using ntdsutil

This chapter provides information and commands concerning the following topics:

- Resetting the directory services restore mode password
- Changing the garbage collection logging level
- Moving Active Directory to a different drive
- Defragmenting Active Directory
- Performing an authoritative restore
- Removing a domain controller from Active Directory
- Seizing an operations master role

**NOTE**   Commands in this chapter are run on a domain controller (DC) named DC1 in the pearson.pub domain.

**TIP**   You should be familiar with **ntdsutil** commands and capabilities when preparing for the 70-640, 70-646, and 70-647 exams.

## Resetting the Directory Services Restore Mode Password

The following steps show how to reset the Directory Services Restore Mode (DSRM) password.

| Step | Command |
|------|---------|
| 1. | Start a command prompt with administrative permissions on a domain con-troller. |
| 2. | Type **ntdsutil** and press **Enter**. |
| 3. | Type **set dsrm password** and press **Enter**. This accesses the Reset DSRM Administrator Password prompt. |
| 4. | Type **reset password on server** *servername* and press **Enter**. Substitute *servername* with the name of the domain controller. |
| 5. | Type a new password and press **Enter**. Type the same password and press **Enter** again. |
| 6. | Type **quit** and press **Enter**. Type **quit** and press **Enter** again. |

## Changing the Garbage Collection Logging Level

Garbage collection runs regularly in a DC and removes deleted (or tombstoned) objects from the database.

**NOTE**    This is also known as online defragmentation.

When objects are deleted, it frees up space in the database but the database file size does not change. In other words, if the database is 100 MB, and then you delete 100 objects, the database size will still be 100 MB but it will have more free space. However, if you do an offline defragmentation, you can reclaim the free space. Before you do this, figure out how much free space you'll gain by doing the offline defragmentation.

If you change the garbage collection logging level, the garbage collection process will log Event ID 1646 (as shown in Figure 12-1) in the Directory Service log. This log entry shows how much free space an offline defragmentation will reclaim (only 2 MB in Figure 12-1).

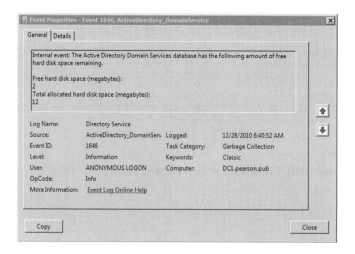

**Figure 12-1**    Event ID 1646 after changing the garbage collection logging level

**TIP**    Before modifying the registry, you should create a backup.

The following steps show how to reset the garbage collection logging level.

| Step | Command |
| --- | --- |
| 1. | Click **Start**, type **regedit**, and press **Enter** to launch the **Registry Editor**. |
| 2. | Browse to the **HKEY_LOCAL_MACHINE\SYSTEM\CurrentControlSet\ Services\NTDS\Diagnostics** entry. |
| 3. | Locate the **Garbage Collection** value and double-click it. Enter **1** as the value. Your display should look similar to Figure 12-2. |
| 4. | Click **OK**. Close the **Registry Editor**. |

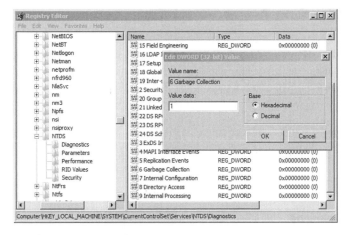

**Figure 12-2**   Changing the garbage collection logging level

# Moving Active Directory to a Different Drive

You can sometimes improve the performance of Active Directory (AD) by moving the database file (ntds.dit) to a different physical drive. This can also be useful if you are running out of hard drive space. You can use the following steps to move the ntds.dit database file to a different location.

| Step | Command |
|------|---------|
| 1. | Launch a command prompt. Back up system state data with the following command. This command uses the D: drive as the backup target, but you can choose a different target based on your system.**wbadmin start systemstate-backup -backuptarget:d: -quiet**<br><br>**NOTE**  The Windows Server Backup feature must be installed for this step to work.<br><br>**TIP**  Although this step is not required, it ensures that you can recover your DC if something goes wrong. It takes some time to complete. |
| 2. | At the command, type **net stop ntds** and press **Enter**. When prompted to stop additional services, press **Y** to confirm. This stops AD and related services. |
| 3. | Type **ntdsutil** and press **Enter**. |
| 4. | Type **activate instance ntds** and press **Enter**. |
| 5. | Type **files** and press **Enter**. |
| 6. | Type **move db to e:\ntds** and press **Enter**.<br><br>**NOTE**  You need to substitute the drive letter e: with a valid writable drive on your system. The folder doesn't need to exist because the **move** command creates it. |
| 7. | Type **quit**, and then press **Enter** twice to return to the command prompt. |
| 8. | Type **net start ntds** and press **Enter** to restart AD. After it starts, you can launch ADUC to verify that everything still works. |

## Defragmenting Active Directory

AD performs an online defragmentation every 12 hours by default. This is normally all that's required. However, the online defragmentation does not reduce the size of the ntds.dit database file. If you have significantly fewer objects in AD than you had previously, you can shrink the size of the ntds.dit file by performing an offline defragmentation.

> **TIP**  An offline defragmentation compacts the file, and you can compact the file only when AD is not running. You can stop the service with the **net stop ntds** command. It's not necessary to reboot into Directory Services Restore Mode.

You can use the following steps to compact the database.

| Step | Command |
|------|---------|
| 1. | Launch a command prompt. Back up system state data with the following command. This command uses the D: drive as the backup target, but you can choose a different target based on your system.**wbadmin start systemstate-backup -backuptarget:d: -quiet**<br><br>**NOTE**  The Windows Server Backup feature must be installed for this step to work.<br><br>**TIP**  Although this step is not required, it ensures that you can recover your DC if something goes wrong. It takes some time to complete. |
| 2. | At the command, type **net stop ntds** and press **Enter**. When prompted to stop additional services, press **Y** to confirm. This stops AD and related services. |
| 3. | Type **ntdsutil** and press **Enter**. |
| 4. | Type **activate instance ntds** and press **Enter**. |
| 5. | Type **files** and press **Enter**. |
| 6. | Type **compact to C:\compact** and press **Enter**. You can use any target folder desired (other than C:\compact). Your display should be similar to Figure 12-3. |
| 7. | Type **quit** and press **Enter**. Type **quit** and press **Enter** again. This returns you to the command prompt.<br><br>Although the following steps aren't required, they help ensure that you can return to the original configuration if something goes wrong.<br><br>a. Create a backup folder named ntdsbu in the root of C by typing **md C:\ntdsbu** and pressing **Enter**.<br><br>b. Type **copy C:\windows\ntds\ntds.dit C:\ntdsbu\ntds.dit** and press **Enter**.<br><br>**NOTE**  If you moved the ntds.dit file, you need to substitute the C:\windows\ntds folder for the actual location.<br><br>c. Type **copy C:\windows\ntds\*.log C:\ntdsbu** and press **Enter**.<br><br>**NOTE**  These steps create backup files of the ntds.dit AD database and the AD logs. If the ntds service is unable to restart, you can simply copy these files back to their original location. |

| Step | Command |
|------|---------|
| 8.   | Type **copy C:\compact\ntds.dit C:\windows\ntds\ntds.dit** and press **Enter**. When prompted to confirm the overwriting, type **Y** for yes. |
| 9.   | Type **del C:\windows\ntds\\*.log** and press **Enter**. |
| 10.  | Type **net start ntds**, and press **Enter**. This restarts the ntds service. After it starts, you can launch ADUC to verify that everything still works. |

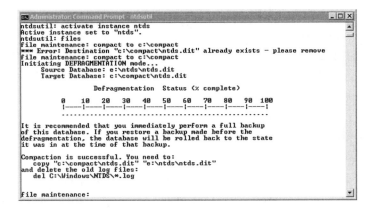

**Figure 12-3**    Performing an offline defragmentation

# Performing an Authoritative Restore

When you do a normal nonauthoritative restore in a domain with more than one DC, the restored DC will replicate with other DCs in the domain to update itself. The restored DC will quickly have all the changes that occurred since the last backup. However, there are times when you want to restore objects authoritatively. In other words, when the restored DC comes back up, you want objects restored on the DC to be replicated to other DCs. You want this DC to communicate to all the other DCs that its change is the authoritative change.

For example, if an administrator accidentally deletes a user object and you perform a nonauthoritative restore, the user object will be deleted again as soon as the DC replicates with other DCs. However, you can restore the user object authoritatively, and you can even restore entire OUs authoritatively.

You can use the commands in the following table to authoritatively restore AD objects from the authoritative restore prompt in **ntdsutil**.

| Restore Command | Comments |
|---|---|
| Restore OU.<br><br>`restore subtree` *dn*<br><br>authoritative restore:<br><br>`restore subtree`<br>`"ou=sales,dc=pearson,dc=pub"` | You can use this to restore an OU (including child OUs).<br><br>The example command restores the Sales OU. |
| Restore Object.<br><br>`restore object` *dn*<br><br>authoritative restore:<br><br>`restore object "cn=Sally,`<br>`ou=sales,dc=pearson,dc=pub"` | This enables you to restore an individual object.<br><br>The example command restores the Sally user object in the sales OU. |

The following table shows the overall steps to perform an authoritative restore.

| Step | Command |
|---|---|
| 1. | Reboot the DC and press **F8** to access **Advanced Boot Options**. |
| 2. | Select **Directory Services Restore Mode**. When prompted, log on with the user name of **.\administrator** and the DSRM password. |
| 3. | Restore AD nonauthoritatively from a backup. You can use the command-line backup tool, **wbadmin**, or any other method your organization has available. Do not reboot after the restore is complete.<br><br>**NOTE**   Chapter 27, "Using **wbadmin**," covers the use of **wbadmin** to perform backup and restores of system state data. |
| 4. | Launch a command prompt, type **ntdsutil**, and then press **Enter**. |
| 5. | Type **activate instance ntds** and press **Enter**. |
| 6. | Type **authoritative restore** and press **Enter**. |
| 7. | At this point, determine whether you're restoring an OU or an object. The previous table showed the syntax to restore either an OU or an object. Type the restore command and press **Enter**.<br><br>For example, to restore a user object, use the following format:<br><br>**restore object** *dn*<br><br>**restore object "cn=Sally,ou=sales,dc=pearson,dc=pub"**<br><br>Or, to restore an OU, use the following format:<br><br>**restore subtree** *dn*<br><br>**restore subtree "ou=sales,dc=pearson,dc=pub"**<br><br>**NOTE**   This increments the update sequence number (USN) so that all other DCs consider it the most recent change. |
| 8. | Type **quit** and press **Enter** twice to exit **ntdsutil**. |
| 9. | Restart the DC normally. |

## Removing a Domain Controller from Active Directory

If you run **dcpromo** on a DC to remove AD, the AD database will be updated to show that this server is no longer a DC. However, if a DC fails, you won't be able to run **dcpromo**.

If the DC has failed, AD still thinks it's an active DC. This causes a wide variety of errors that can be resolved if you remove the DC from AD, as shown in the following steps.

| Step | Command |
| --- | --- |
| 1. | Start a command prompt with administrative permissions. |
| 2. | Type **ntdsutil** and press **Enter**. |
| 3. | Type **metadata cleanup** and press **Enter**. This accesses the **metadata cleanup** prompt. |
| 4. | Type **connections** and press **Enter**. This accesses the connections prompt. |
| 5. | Connect to an active DC in the domain with the following command. Substitute the FQDN of an active DC in your domain. <br><br> **connect to server** *dc-fqdn* <br><br> **connect to server dc1.pearson.pub** |
| 6. | Type **quit** and press **Enter**. This brings you back to the **metadata cleanup** prompt. |
| 7. | Type **select operation target** and press **Enter**. This accesses the **select operation target** prompt. |
| 8. | Select the site where the damaged DC is located with the following commands. Substitute the number of the site in the second command based on the output of the **list sites** command. <br><br> Type **list sites** and press **Enter**. <br><br> Type **select site** *number* and press **Enter**. |
| 9. | Select the damaged DC with the following commands. Substitute the number of the server in the second command based on the output of the **list servers in site** command. <br><br> Type **list servers in site** and press **Enter**. <br><br> Type **select server** *number* and press **Enter**. |
| 10. | Type **quit** and press **Enter**. This brings you back to the **metadata cleanup** prompt. |
| 11. | Type **remove selected server** and press **Enter**. This removes the instance of the server from AD. |
| 12. | Type **quit** and press **Enter**. |

## Seizing an Operations Master Role

If a DC hosting a critical operations master role (previously called flexible single master operations role, [FSMO]) fails, you might need to have another DC take over the role. The best choice is to transfer the role while both servers are operational. However, if the role holder fails, you can seize the role using a DC that is operational.

> **TIP**   Seizing a role is a drastic operation. You should seize roles only when absolutely necessary. If you are seizing the Schema Master, the Domain Naming Master, or the RID Master roles, it's recommended that you don't bring the original DC back online in the domain.

The following steps show how to seize a role.

| Step | Command |
| --- | --- |
| 1. | Start a command prompt with administrative permissions on a domain controller. |
| 2. | Type **ntdsutil** and press **Enter**. |
| 3. | Type **roles** and press **Enter**. This accesses the **fsmo maintenance** prompt. |
| 4. | Type **connection** and press **Enter**. This accesses the **server connections** prompt. |
| 5. | Identify the fully qualified domain name (FQDN) of the operational DC. Substitute your DC's name in the following command:<br><br>**connect to server dc1.pearson.pub** |
| 6. | Type **quit** and press **Enter**. This brings you back to the **fsmo maintenance** prompt. |
| 7. | Identify the role you want to seize. These are identified in **ntdsutil** as Infrastructure Master, Naming Master, PDC, RID Master, and Schema Master. Use one of the following commands to seize the role:<br><br>**seize infrastructure master**<br><br>**seize naming master**<br><br>**seize pdc**<br><br>**seize rid master**<br><br>**seize schema master** |
| 8. | A confirmation dialog box appears similar to Figure 12-4. Review it and click **Yes** if you want to seize the role.<br><br>**NOTE**   ntdsutil first tries to do a logical transfer. If the other DC is up and operational, it is transferred normally. If it fails, it seizes the role. |
| 9. | Type **quit** and press **Enter** twice to exit **ntdsutil**. |

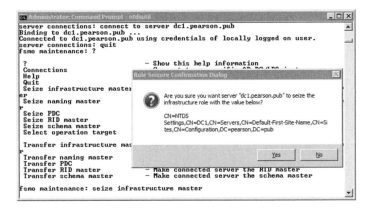

**Figure 12-4**  Seizing an operations role

# CHAPTER 13

# Using netdom

This chapter provides information and commands concerning the following topics:

- Identifying operations master roles
- Joining a computer to a domain
- Verifying trust relationships
- Querying and resetting secure channels with **netdom**

**NOTE** Commands in this chapter are run on a domain controller named DC1 in the pearson.pub domain.

**TIP** You should be familiar with **netdom** commands when preparing for the 70-640 exam.

## Identifying Operations Master Roles

There are many times when you need to know which server holds which operations master roles. You can get the answer from different graphical user interfaces. However, it's much easier from the command line with the **netdom** tool (as **netdom query fsmo**). The following text shows the output within a domain named pearson.pub:

```
C:\>netdom query fsmo
Schema master              DC1.pearson.pub
Domain naming master       DC1.pearson.pub
PDC                        DC1.pearson.pub
RID pool manager           DC1.pearson.pub
Infrastructure master      DC1.pearson.pub
The command completed successfully.
```

**NOTE** Operations master roles were previously called flexible single master operations (FSMO) roles.

## Joining a Computer to a Domain

You can join a computer to a domain from the command prompt using the **netdom join** command. The following table shows the different switches available with the **netdom**

**join** command. Each of these switches is used in the following command, which joins a computer named dc2 to a domain named pearson.pub:

```
C:\>netdom join dc2 /domain:pearson.pub
/userd:administrator@pearson.pub /passwordd:*
/ou:"ou=sales,dc=pearson,dc=pub" /reboot:60
```

| netdom Join Machine Switches | Comments |
|---|---|
| `netdom join computername`<br>`C:\>netdom join dc2 . . .`<br>`C:\>netdom join %computername% . . .` | The **computername** identifies the name of the computer joining the domain. The **%computername%** variable uses the local computer name. |
| `/domain:domain`<br>`/domain:pearson.pub` | Specifies the domain the computer will join. |
| `/userd:username`<br>`/userd:administrator` | The user account used to make the connection with the domain specified by the **/domain** switch. |
| `/passwordd:{password \| *}`<br>`/passwordd:P@ssw0rd` | The password of the user account specified by **/userd**. You can use an asterisk (*) and the command will prompt you to enter a password.<br><br>**NOTE**  The second "d" at the end of **/passwordd** looks like a typo, but it's valid. It specifies that this is the password for the **/domain** component. |
| `/ou:oudn`<br>`/ou:"ou=sales,dc=pearson,dc=pub"` | The organizational unit where you want the account created. You need to specify this as a distinguished name. The example specifies the Sales OU.<br><br>**TIP**  If you don't use the **/ou** switch, the account will be created in the default location. This is the Computers container by default, but can be redirected to another location with the **redircmp** command (covered in Chapter 11, "Working with Active Directory Accounts"). |
| `/reboot [:number-of-seconds-delay]`<br>`/reboot:10` | Reboots the computer after it's joined to the domain. The default delay is 30 seconds but you can change it. The example reboots the system 10 seconds after it joins the domain. |

| netdom Join Machine Switches | Comments |
|---|---|
| /securepasswordprompt | Uses a secure credentials popup to specify credentials. You can use this to supply smartcard credentials. This option is in effect only when the password value is supplied as *. |

## Verifying Trust Relationships

You can also use the **netdom** command to verify trust relationships. The basic syntax of the command is

**netdom trust** trusting_domain_name **/domain:**trusted_domain_name

Figure 13-1 shows the Active Directory Domains and Trusts console with a parent domain (pearson.pub) and a child domain (training.pearson.pub). There is a parent/child trust relationship between the two domains. Furthermore, the outgoing trust has been validated.

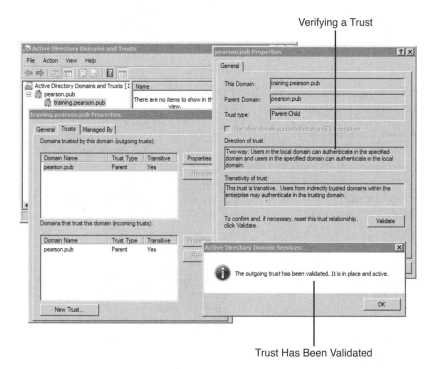

**Figure 13-1**   Verifying a trust with Active Directory Domains and Trusts

**NOTE**   There are two trusts between the domains. The parent trusts the child and the child trusts the domain. These trusts are displayed as an outgoing trust and an incoming trust in Figure 13-1.

You can perform the same check from the command line with the following command:

```
netdom trust training.pearson.pub /domain:pearson.pub
```

The concept of trusted and trusting domains and the terminology can be confusing. Figure 13-2 shows two domains with a one-way trust between them. Notice that the arrow is pointing to Domain B. When shown this way, it indicates that Domain A trusts Domain B, and users in Domain B can be granted access to resources in Domain A. In other words, Domain B is trusted by Domain A.

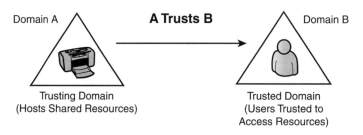

**Figure 13-2**   One-way trust relationship between two domains

The following table identifies many of the switches that can be used with the **netdom trust** command to validate a trust.

| netdom Trust Switches | Comments |
| --- | --- |
| `netdom trust trusting-domain`<br>`C:\>netdom training.pearson.pub` | Enter the name of the trusting domain first. In Figure 13-2, this is Domain A in the outgoing trust. |
| `/domain:domain`<br>`/domain:pearson.pub` | Specifies the name of the trusted domain or Non-Windows Realm.<br><br>**NOTE**   You can create trusts with UNIX Realms and test them with the **netdom** trust command. |
| `/userd:username`<br>`/userd:administrator` | The user account used to make the connection with the domain specified by the / **domain** switch. |
| `/passwordd:{password \| *}`<br>`/passwordd:P@ssw0rd` | The password of the user account specified by **/userd**. You can use an asterisk (*) and the command will prompt you to enter a password. |

| netdom Trust Switches | Comments |
|---|---|
| `/usero:`*`username`*<br>`/usero:administrator` | The user account for making the connection with the trusting domain.<br><br>**NOTE**   The "o" for **/usero** specifies that this is the user account for the *other* domain, or the trusting domain. |
| `/passwordo:{`*`password`* \| `*}`<br>`/passwordo:P@ssw0rd` | The password of the user account specified by **/usero**. You can use an asterisk (*) and the command will prompt you to enter a password. |
| `/verify` | Verifies that the trust is operating properly. |
| `/quarantine[:yes` \| `: no]` | This switch enables you to view, set, or disable the **/quarantine** attribute. When set to yes, only SIDs from the directly trusted domain are able to access resources, and other SIDS are filtered out. When set to no (the default), any accounts in the trusted domain are accepted.<br><br>**TIP**   This is relevant if the trusted domain includes migrated accounts. The migrated accounts are filtered if this is set to yes, and won't be able to access resources in the trusting domain.<br><br>Specifying **/quarantine** without yes or no displays the current state. |

Figure 13-3 shows the result of entering the following command using some of these switches:

```
C:\>netdom trust training.pearson.pub /domain:pearson.pub
/userd:administrator /passwordd:* /usero:administrator
/passwordo:* /verify
```

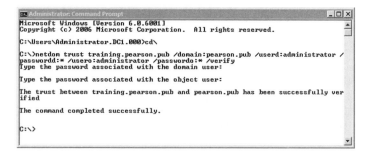

**Figure 13-3**   Verifying a trust with the **netdom** command

If it's a two-way trust, you can verify the trust from the other direction by swapping the trusted and trusting domains like the following command:

```
C:\>netdom trust pearson.pub /domain:training.pearson.pub
/userd:administrator /passwordd:* /usero:administrator
/passwordo:* /verify
```

> **TIP**   There is much more you can do with the **netdom** command than shown in this short chapter. If you want more information, check out the TechNet page:
>
> http://technet.microsoft.com/library/cc772217.aspx

## Querying and Resetting Secure Channels with netdom

You can use the **netdom** command to query and verify secure channels between computers in the domain. When needed, you can use the **netdom** command to reset these channels.

> **TIP**   Computers have passwords used to establish the secure channels. When the password kept on the system doesn't match the password kept in the domain, the secure channel is broken. This can happen when the computer has been turned off for a long time, or after restoring Active Directory.

The basic command to query and verify the secure channel with computers in the domain is

```
netdom query server /verify
```

The following output shows the partial result of this command:

```
C:\>netdom query server /verify
Verifying secure channel setup for domain members:
Machine                  Status/Domain        Domain Controller
=======                  =============        =================
\\SALES73                PEARSON              \\DC1.PEARSON.PUB
\\SALES74                PEARSON              \\DC1.PEARSON.PUB
\\WIN7PCG                ERROR! ( The network path was not found. )
\\DC2                    PEARSON              \\DC1.PEARSON.PUB
\\PC-1                   PEARSON              \\DC1.PEARSON.PUB
\\SC1                    PEARSON              \\DC1.PEARSON.PUB
The command completed successfully.
```

Notice that the majority of these systems show the domain and the domain controller where the secure channel (trust relationship) has been verified. However, the \\win7pcg computer has a problem.

> **NOTE**   Before resetting the trust, you should verify that the system is up and operational.

You can also check the channel with just a single computer using the following command:

```
netdom verify /d:domain computer-name
```

For example, the following listing shows how to verify the channel with a computer named dc2 in the pearson.pub domain, and the result:

```
C:\>netdom verify /d:pearson.pub dc2
The secure channel from DC2 to the domain PEARSON.PUB has been
verified.  The connection is with the machine \\DC1.PEARSON.PUB.

The command completed successfully.
```

If the command fails, you can reset the secure channel between the domain and the computer with the following command:

```
netdom reset /d:domain computer-name
```

The following listing shows how to reset the secure channel with the computer named dc2 in the pearson.pub domain:

```
C:\>netdom reset /d:pearson.pub dc2
The secure channel from DC2 to the domain PEARSON.PUB has been reset.
The connection is with the machine \\DC1.PEARSON.PUB.

The command completed successfully.
```

# CHAPTER 14

# Troubleshooting Replication

This chapter provides information and commands concerning the following topics:

- Checking replication with **repadmin**
- Forcing replication with **repadmin**
- Migrating to DFSR with **dfsrmig**

**NOTE** Commands in this chapter are run on a domain controller (DC) named DC1 in the pearson.pub domain.

**TIP** You should be familiar with **repadmin** and **dfsrmig** commands when preparing for the 70-640 exam.

## Checking Replication with repadmin

One of the primary command prompt commands you can use to troubleshoot Active Directory (AD) replication issues is **repadmin**. It's available on DC, and you can use it to view replication data, force replication events, and manually create the replication topology if things really go wrong.

**TIP** One of the primary symptoms that indicate a problem with replication is that new users are unable to log on. Their accounts are created in AD using one DC, but when they attempt to log on using a different DC, they receive an error message indicating the username or password is incorrect. After verifying they are using the correct username and password, it's time to break out **repadmin**.

**repadmin** includes several commands that you can use to view replication data as shown in the following table. When AD has problems with replication, these normally give clear indications that you have errors. When these come up error-free, you can be confident that your problem is not due to replication.

**NOTE** You must run **repadmin** with administrative permissions.

| repadmin Status and Data Commands | Comments |
|---|---|
| Show replication status.<br><br>`C:\>repadmin /showrepl` | Displays replication status for recent inbound replication attempts. It identifies replication partners, identifies when the last replication occurred, and determines whether it was successful. Figure 14-1 shows the output of this command. |
| Summarize status of replication.<br><br>`C:\>repadmin /replsummary` | This command summarizes the replication state and relative health of a forest. It lists the total number of replication attempts, the number of failures, and the percent of failures compared with the total. |
| Show highest update sequence numbers.<br><br>`repadmin /showutdvec` *dc-name*<br>*naming-context*<br>`C:\>repadmin /showutdvec dc1`<br>`dc=pearson,dc=pub` | Replication uses Update Sequence Numbers (USN) to determine whether a DC has the most up-to-date version of an object. You can view the highest USNs for a DC with the **/showutdvec** switch.<br><br>**NOTE**   The naming-context is the distinguished name of the directory partition. |
| View queued replications.<br><br>`C:\>repadmin /queue` | Shows a listing of inbound replication requests that the DC has in queue. This should normally be zero within a site (or certainly a low number). The number of items in queue between sites is dependent on the replication schedule between sites. If you replicate only once a day between sites, this queue will steadily build up into the scheduled replication time. |
| Show attributes of a DC.<br><br>`repadmin /showattr` *dc-name*<br>*naming-context*<br>`C:\>repadmin /showattr dc1`<br>`dc=pearson,dc=pub` | You can display the attributes of an object. This is sometimes useful when troubleshooting replication for a specific DC. The example shows the attributes of a DC named dc1 in the pearson.pub domain.<br><br>**NOTE**   This shows low-level AD data similar to what you can access using the **ldp** GUI tool. |
| Show replication metadata for a DC.<br><br>`repadmin /showobjmeta` *dc-name*<br>*naming-context*<br>`C:\>repadmin /showattr dc1`<br>`dc=pearson,dc=pub` | You can use the **/showobjmeta** switch to show replication metadata for a DC. The example command displays metadata for the DC named dc1 in the domain pearson.pub. Data includes the attribute ID, version number, originating and local USN, originating server's globally unique identifier (GUID), and a date and time stamp of the update. |

| repadmin Status and Data Commands | Comments |
|---|---|
| Show bridgehead servers.<br><br>`/bridgeheads [/v]`<br>`C:\>repadmin /bridgeheads /v` | Shows all the bridgehead servers for each site that includes a DC. The **/v** switch is used for a verbose output.<br><br>**NOTE**  If you have only DCs in a single site, you won't have any bridgehead servers assigned. |

**Figure 14-1**  Viewing the output of the **repadmin /showrepl** command

**NOTE**  **replmon** (available in Windows Server 2003) is not included in Windows Server 2008 or Windows Server 2008 R2.

# Forcing Replication with repadmin

**repadmin** has a few primary commands you can use to force replication as shown in the following table.

**TIP**  If you are having problems with replication and cannot force replication, check DNS. One important check is to ensure that DNS has created SRV records. You can stop and restart the **netlogon** service to re-create SRV records with the **net stop netlogon** and **net start netlogon** commands.

| repadmin Replication Commands | Comments |
|---|---|
| Synchronize a DC with all partners.<br><br>`C:\>repadmin /syncall` | Synchronizes a specified DC with all replication partners.<br><br>This should generate callback messages indicating replication is in progress, replication has completed, and that syncall finished. |
| Force replicate with a specific DC.<br><br>`repadmin /replicate target-DC`<br>`source-DC domain-DN`<br><br>`C:\>repadmin /replicate dc2`<br>`dc1 dc=pearson,dc=pub` | Triggers immediate replication of the specified directory partition to the destination DC from the source DC.<br><br>This performs the same actions as selecting **Replicate Now**, as shown in Figure 14-2. You can access this by clicking **Start, Administrative Tools, AD Sites and Services**. Additionally, it works the same way if the DCs are in different sites, as shown in Figure 14-3. |
| Recalculate replication topology.<br><br>`repadmin /kcc target-DC`<br>`C:\>repadmin /kcc dc1` | Forces the knowledge consistency checker (KCC) to recalculate the replication topology and re-create replication connections if needed. The KCC runs every 15 minutes by default. The example forces the KCC to run on the domain controller dc1.<br><br>**NOTE**   You can run this for each DC in your domain from a single DC. It doesn't need to be run locally. |

**Figure 14-2**   Forcing replication with another DC in the same site

**TIP**   **repadmin** has a rich set of commands that you can use to monitor and troubleshoot replication. This chapter doesn't attempt to show them all. However, if you want to dig deeper, check out the TechNet web page: http://technet.microsoft.com/library/cc770963.aspx.

**Figure 14-3**  Forcing replication with another DC in a different site

# Migrating to DFSR with dfsrmig

The **dfsrmig** tool is used to migrate the SYSVOL folder from New Technology File Replication Service (NT FRS) to Distributed File System Replication (DFSR). FRS was the first method, and it was used in all AD domains by default up to and including Windows Server 2008. Windows Server 2008 R2 is the first version that uses DFSR by default.

> **NOTE**  The SYSVOL folder hosts AD data that is shared between DCs. Changes to the SYSVOL folder on one DC are automatically replicated to other DCs. Data in the SYSVOL folder includes Group Policy objects, logon scripts, and more.

DFSR is more efficient than FRS, so many administrators want to switch over to DFSR from FRS in existing domains.

The primary requirement is that the domain functional level must be Windows Server 2008. You can raise the domain functional level from within Active Directory Users and Computers (ADUC) by right-clicking over the domain and selecting **Raise Domain Functional Level**. Figure 14-4 shows the screen that appears. The functional level is raised after you click **Raise** and click **OK**.

> **NOTE**  You cannot lower the domain functional level; you can only raise it. You can raise it to Windows Server 2008 only after all DCs in the domain are running at least Windows Server 2008. After raising it to Windows Server 2008, you cannot promote any Windows Server 2003 servers to DCs.

The process to migrate to DFSR uses several steps identified as global states. The primary goal is to ensure that problems in the migration do not take down the domain. You can verify that replication is working as expected after each of the steps.

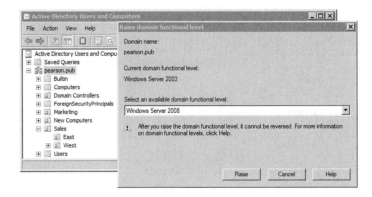

**Figure 14-4**   Raising the domain functional level

The following table identifies the four **dfsrmig** global states.

| dfsrmig Global State | Comments |
|---|---|
| 0 Start | SYSVOL replication is handled by FRS. |
| 1 Prepared | FRS still replicates the SYSVOL folder. |
| | DFSR also replicates a copy of the SYSVOL folder but the DFSR-replicated copy is not used by any DCs. |
| 2 Redirected | DFSR takes over replication of the SYSVOL folder and DCs use the DFSR-replicated copy. |
| | FRS continues to replicate the SYSVOL folder. |
| 3 Eliminated | DFRS continues to replicate the SYSVOL folder. |
| | The original SYSVOL folder used by FRS is deleted, and FRS no longer replicates the SYSVOL folder. |

The following table shows the **dfsrmig** switches and commands you use in the migration process.

| dfsrmig Switches | Comments |
|---|---|
| Get global state. `C:\>dfsrmig /getglobalstate` | Returns the current state of the migration as long as the migration has been started. |
| Get migration state. `C:\>dfsrmig /getmigrationstate` | Shows the progress of migration across all DCs in the domain. You can use this to verify that all of the DCs are ready to progress to the next global state in the migration process. |
| Set global state. `dfsrmig /setglobalstate` *state* `C:\>dfsrmig /setglobalstate 1` | Sets the global state. Valid states are 0, 1, 2, and 3. The example assumes the current state is 0 and changes it to 1. |

**TIP**   You should ensure that the FRS replication of the SYSVOL folder is running without any problems. The migration process will fail in some instances if FRS is not working correctly. One way to verify that FRS replication is working correctly is by checking the File Replication Service log in Event Viewer, as shown in Figure 14-5. Investigate any errors to determine whether it is running correctly.

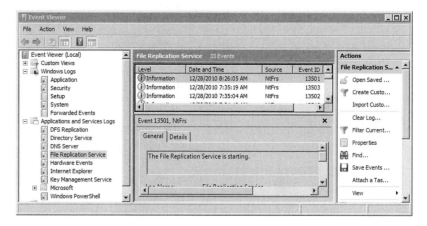

**Figure 14-5**   Checking the File Replication Service log

You can use the following steps to migrate from FRS to DFS for SYSVOL replication.

**TIP**   Ensure that you have a current backup of system state data before beginning this process.

| Step | Action | Comments |
|------|--------|----------|
| 1. | Ensure the domain is raised to Domain Functional Level 2008. | Figure 14-4 (shown previously) shows how this is done. |
| 2. | Type C:\>**dfsrmig /setglobalstate 0** | Sets the new DFSR global state to Start. |
| 3. | Type C:\>**dfsrmig /getglobalstate** | Verifies the global state is set to Start. |
| 4. | Type C:\>**dfsrmig /getmigrationstate** | When this indicates that all DCs have migrated successfully to the global state Start, you can continue. |
| 5. | Type C:\>**dfsrmig /setglobalstate 1** | Changes the new DFSR global state to Prepared.<br><br>**TIP**   This takes some time. In a production environment, it's easier to execute this on one day, and then continue the migration on the following day. |
| 6. | Type C:\>**dfsrmig /getglobalstate** | Verifies whether the global state is set to Prepared. |

| Step | Action | Comments |
|------|--------|----------|
| 7. | Type C:\>**dfsrmig /getmigrationstate** | When this indicates that all DCs have migrated successfully to the global state Prepared, you can continue.<br><br>**NOTE**   If you use this command at different times, you may see the state of other DCs change as the migration progresses. |
| 8. | Type C:\>**dfsrmig /setglobalstate 2** | Changes the new DFSR global state to Redirected. |
| 9. | Type C:\>**dfsrmig /getglobalstate** | Verifies whether the global state is set to Redirected. |
| 10. | Type C:\>**dfsrmig /getmigrationstate** | When this indicates that all DCs have migrated successfully to the global state Redirected, you can continue.<br><br>**NOTE**   This is much quicker than changing the state to Prepared. |
| 11. | Type C:\>**dfsrmig /setglobalstate 3** | Changes the new DFSR global state to Eliminated. |
| 12. | Type C:\>**dfsrmig /getglobalstate** | Verifies the global state is set to Eliminated. |
| 13. | Type C:\>**dfsrmig /getmigrationstate** | When this indicates that all DCs have migrated successfully to the global state Redirected, the migration is complete. |

# CHAPTER 15

# Group Policy Overview

This chapter provides information and commands concerning the following topics:

- Launching the Group Policy Management Console
- Understanding Group Policy order of precedence
- Filtering GPOs by modifying permissions
- Understanding Group Policy settings
- Blocking inheritance
- Enforcing GPOs
- Using loopback processing
- Running scripts with Group Policy

**TIP**   You should be familiar with Group Policy objects when preparing for any of the MCITP exams.

## Launching the Group Policy Management Console

The majority of the work with Group Policy starts with the Group Policy Management Console (GPMC). Figure 15-1 shows the GPMC with the Default Domain Policy selected and the Default Domain Controllers Policy showing.

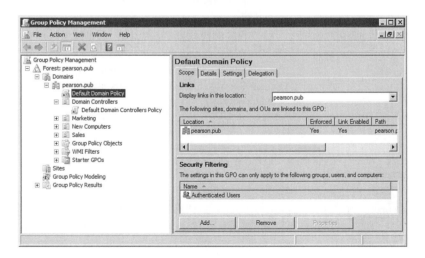

**Figure 15-1**   Group Policy Management Console with Default Domain Policy selected

**NOTE** The only two default Group Policy objects in a domain are the Default Domain Policy (linked to the domain) and the Default Domain Controllers Policy linked to the Domain Controllers OU.

You can launch the GPMC by clicking **Start**, **Administrative Tools** and selecting **Group Policy Management**. Expand the domain to view the Default Domain Policy. Expand the Domain Controllers OU to view the Default Domain Controllers Policy.

**TIP** You can create and link Group Policy objects (GPO) at the domain level, at any OU level, and at any site level within the GPMC. You also can back up and restore GPOs in the GPMC and analyze GPOs with the Group Policy Modeling and Group Policy Results tools.

## Understanding Group Policy Order of Precedence

The following table shows the different levels where Group Policy can be applied.

| Group Policy Scope | Comments |
|---|---|
| Local Computer Policy | This is applied first, and it applies only to the local computer. <br><br> Local computer policies are overwritten by any Group Policy settings in the domain. |
| Site | GPOs linked to a site apply to all computers and users in the site. <br><br> There aren't any default site policies in a domain. <br><br> **TIP** The most common use of site GPOs is to deploy applications on a per-site basis. |
| Domain | GPOs linked to a domain apply to all computers and users in the domain. Domains include a Default Domain Policy by default. |
| Organizational unit (OU) | GPOs linked to an OU apply to all computers and users in the OU. <br><br> The Default Domain Controllers Policy applies to the Domain Controllers OU. When a server is promoted to a domain controller, it is automatically placed in the Domain Controllers OU. |

**NOTE** Some use the initials LSDOU to help remember the order as Local, Site, Domain, and OU.

When multiple GPOs are applied to a single user or computer, the settings in each of the GPOs are applied. If there is a conflict between the GPOs, the last GPO applied wins in most situations.

**TIP**    The two exceptions to the "last GPO applied wins" rule are when a higher-level setting is enforced or loopback processing is enabled. Both of these exceptions are explained later in this chapter.

The order in which GPOs are applied is

- Local computer policy

- Site GPOs

- Domain GPOs

- OU GPOs (parent OUs first and child OUs last)

Consider the following table, where a computer named Sales1 is joined to a domain, located in the Virginia Beach site, and in a GPO named Sales. For simplicity sake, this table focuses only on the Control Panel setting and deploying a sales application.

| Group Policy Name | Linked To | Setting |
|---|---|---|
| Local Group Policy | Sales1 computer | Control Panel access is removed |
| Default Domain Policy | Domain | Control Panel access is granted |
| Sales GPO | Sales OU | Control Panel access is removed |
| Deploy Sales Application | Virginia Beach site | Deploys a Sales application |

Figure 15-2 shows the Sales OU with the precedence of both the Sales GPO and the Default Domain Policy.

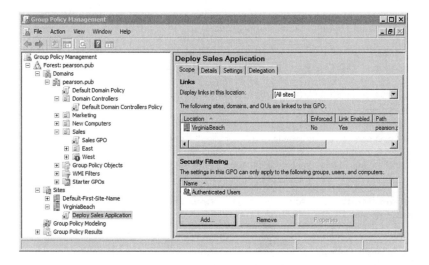

**Figure 15-2**    Group Policy Management Console showing precedence of GPOs

Notice that there's a conflict with the Control Panel setting for the Sales1 computer. The local policy removes access, the Default Domain Policy grants access, and the Sales GPO removes access again. Because the last setting for the Control Panel was applied by the Sales GPO, that's the setting that takes precedence.

**TIP**   The simplest rule to remember is that by default, the last GPO applied wins when there is a conflict. GPOs are applied in the following order: local, site, domain, OU.

**NOTE**   When a conflict doesn't exist, all GPO settings apply. For example, the Sales application deploys to all users in the Virginia Beach site.

The following table shows the result if a user logs on to the Sales1 computer.

| User Account Location | Result |
| --- | --- |
| User logs on locally. | Access to the Control Panel is removed.<br><br>If the user is logged on to the computer locally, domain Group Policy settings are not applied. |
| User logs on to Sales1 computer using a domain account. | Access to the Control Panel is removed.<br><br>Users in this OU have three GPOs applied. The local Group Policy removes the Control Panel. The Default Domain Policy grants access to the Control Panel, and the Sales GPO (the last GPO applied) removes it. |

In contrast, if a user logs on to a different computer in the domain (such as in the Computers container or another OU), the Control Panel would be present because access is granted through the Default Domain Policy.

## Filtering GPOs by Modifying Permissions

When you create a GPO, two primary permissions are applied to the Authenticated Users group as shown in the following table.

**TIP**   As soon as a user logs in to the domain, the user account is automatically added to the Authenticated Users group. In other words, all GPOs automatically apply to any user that logs in because the GPOs apply to the Authenticated Users group by default.

| Default Permissions for Authenticated Users Group | Comments |
| --- | --- |
| Read | Settings in the GPO can be read. |
| Apply Group Policy | Settings in the GPO are applied. |

Figure 15-3 shows the permissions for a GPO named **Deploy Sales Application** with the default permissions. When both **Read** and **Apply Group Policy** permissions are set to **Allow**, the policy applies.

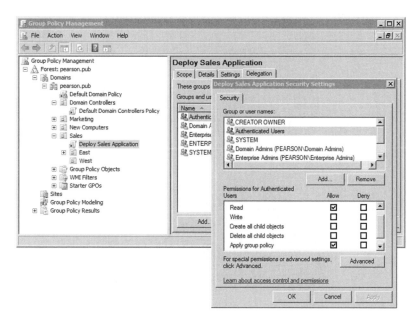

**Figure 15-3**   Default permissions for a new GPO

**TIP**   You can filter Group Policy by changing the **Apply Group Policy Allow** permission to **Apply Group Policy Deny** for any user or group. For example, if you don't want the policy to apply to members of the Administrators group, select the group and select **Deny** for the **Apply Group Policy** permission.

Figure 15-4 shows security filtering applied to a GPO. The **Apply Group Policy** setting is changed to **Deny** for the IT Admins group. Users in this group still have access to Read and Write (and more), but the policy does not apply to them.

**TIP**   Selecting **Deny** for the **Apply Group Policy** permission is also known as *security filtering*. As long as the permissions applied to the Authenticated Users group is not changed, the GPO will still apply to all other users in the domain.

There is another method of using security filtering to modify the application of a GPO. First, remove the Authenticated Users group. At this point, the GPO won't apply to anyone. Then add the group that you want the GPO to apply to, and configure the permissions. The following table shows the overall action steps to do this.

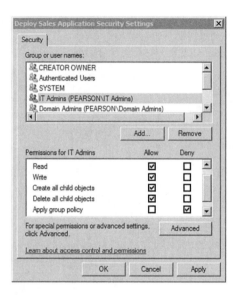

**Figure 15-4**   Filtering permissions for a new GPO

| Step | Action |
|------|--------|
| 1. | Launch the GPMC and browse to the Group Policy. |
| 2. | Select the **Delegation** tab. |
| 3. | Click **Advanced**. Select **Authenticated Users** group, and then click **Remove**. <br> **NOTE**   At this point, the GPO does not apply to any users. |
| 4. | Click **Add**. Enter the name of the group you want the GPO to apply to and click **OK**. |
| 5. | Allow is already selected for the **Read** permission. Select **Allow** for **Apply Group Policy**. Click **OK**. <br> **NOTE**   You might have to scroll down to see **Apply Group Policy**. |

# Understanding Group Policy Settings

Administrators use Group Policy to administer and manage users and computers within a domain. There are literally thousands of Group Policy settings. The goal isn't to know them all but instead to understand a few key Group Policy settings, how they're created, and how they apply. The following sections cover a few Group Policy settings.

## Enabling Auditing Through Group Policy

You can configure audit policy settings to ensure that certain activities in your organization are tracked.

Figure 15-5 shows the **Audit Policy** in the **Default Domain Policy** open, and the following table explains these audit policy settings.

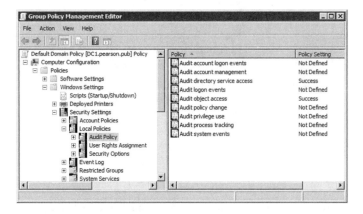

**Figure 15-5**   Audit Policy in the Default Domain Policy

| Audit Policy Settings | Comments |
| --- | --- |
| Audit account logon events. | Account logon events are generated when a domain user account is authenticated on a domain controller and the event is logged in the domain controller's security log. Account logoff events are not generated. |
| Audit account management. | Account management events include when a user account or group is created, changed, or deleted; a user account is renamed, disabled, or enabled; or a password is set or changed. |
| Audit directory service access. | Enables security logging for any Active Directory object (such as users, groups, and OUs) access in Active Directory that have security logging enabled. This setting is enabled by default for domain controllers.<br><br>**NOTE**   This setting only applies to domain controllers. It has no meaning for workstations and servers. |
| Audit logon events. | Logon events are generated when a local user is authenticated on a local computer. The event is logged in the local security log. |
| Audit object access. | Enables security logging for any object (such as files, folders, and printers) access in the domain that has security logging enabled. It is not enabled by default.<br><br>**TIP**   Enabling object access auditing is a two-step process. You must first enable the auditing through Group Policy. Then you must enable auditing for the individual object. For example, Figure 15-6 shows the **Auditing** tab of the Advanced Security Settings of a folder named Data. |

| Audit Policy Settings | Comments |
|---|---|
| Audit policy change. | Generates security log entries in response to changes in user rights assignment policies, audit policies, or trust policies. |
| Audit privilege user. | The use of elevated privileges generates a log in the security log. For example, if a user takes ownership of a file, it generates a log entry. |
| Audit process tracking. | Process tracking logs entries for events such as program activation, process exit, handle duplication, and indirect object access. |
| Audit system events. | System events include when a user restarts or shuts down the computer or when an event occurs that affects either the system security or the security log. |

**NOTE**  Both success and failure events can be logged for each of these Audit Policy settings. A success event occurs when the user succeeds in the action. A failure event occurs when the user attempts the action but is unsuccessful, such as when the user doesn't have permissions or rights to take the action.

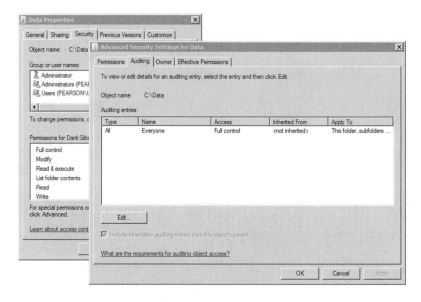

**Figure 15-6**  Enabling Object Access Auditing for a folder

## Enabling Advanced Auditing for Directory Services Changes

You can enable advanced auditing capabilities in Windows Server 2008 with the **audit-pol** command. The following table shows some common commands used to enable Directory Services Changes auditing.

| auditpol Commands | Comments |
|---|---|
| `C:\>auditpol /set / subcategory:"directory service changes" /success:enable` | Enables Directory Services Changes auditing for success events. The audit log includes the previous and new values of attributes for any Active Directory objects that are modified. |
| `C:\>auditpol /set / subcategory:"directory service changes" /failure:enable` | Enables Directory Services Changes auditing for failure events. |
| `C:\>auditpol /set / subcategory:"directory service changes" /success:disable` | Disables Directory Services Changes auditing for success events. |
| `C:\>auditpol /set / subcategory:"directory service changes" /failure:disable` | Disables Directory Services Changes auditing for failure events. |

## Deploying Applications

You can also deploy applications with Group Policy. Advanced tools, such as Microsoft's System Center Configuration Manager (SCCM), give you additional capabilities such as scheduling the deployments. However, you can use Group Policy to deploy applications without buying SCCM.

The following table shows the primary ways that applications are deployed through a GPO.

| Method | Target | Result |
|---|---|---|
| Assign | User | Available on the user's **Start** menu. The application is not installed until the user invokes the application. When the user selects the item on the **Start** menu or double-clicks a file with the matching extension, the application is installed. For example, if Microsoft Excel is assigned to a user, the user can double-click an .xls document and Microsoft Excel will then be installed. |
| Assign | Computer | The application is installed on the next boot of the computer. **TIP** If deploying an application to laptops that might not be connected later, you can assign the application. The next time the laptop is rebooted (while connected to the domain), the application will install. |
| Publish | User | Available through the Control Panel Programs and Features. If users know to look there, they can find the application and install it. The application is installed by double-clicking on a file with the matching extension. For example, if Microsoft Excel is published to a user, the user can double-click an .xls document and it will be installed. |

Figure 15-7 shows the **Group Policy Management Editor** for the **Default Domain Policy**. It has the **Microsoft Shared Fax Client** assigned. The foreground dialog box is from the wizard assigning another application. Notice that **Published** is dimmed. Because you cannot publish to a computer, you cannot select the **Published** option.

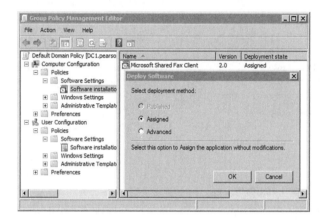

**Figure 15-7** Assigning an application through a GPO

In large enterprises with multiple sites, it's common to deploy applications from a server in the same site. Consider Figure 15-8. If you deployed the application from a single server in the Virginia Beach site, the application would have to be deployed over the slow WAN link to the computers in the Washington DC site.

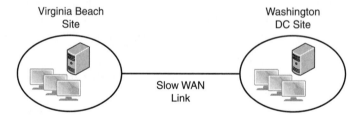

**Figure 15-8** Multiple-site enterprise

In this situation, you create two GPOs. One GPO deploys the application from a server in the Virginia Beach site to computers in Virginia Beach. The second GPO deploys the application from a server in the Washington DC site to computers in Virginia Beach.

The following table shows the overall steps for deploying applications to computers in the site.

| Steps | Comments |
|-------|----------|
| 1. | Create a share on a computer in the site. |
| 2. | Copy the application package to the share. |

| Steps | Comments |
|-------|----------|
| 3. | Create a GPO to deploy the application package. |
| 4. | Link the GPO to the site. |

## Configuring Automatic Updates

A common use of Group Policy is to configure computers to use Automatic Updates. There are several Group Policy settings located in the **Computer Configuration, Policies, Administrative Templates, System, Windows Update** node.

Some of the settings are listed in the following table.

| Setting | Description |
|---------|-------------|
| Configure Automatic Updates | When enabled, computers automatically receive updates without requiring any user intervention. |
| Specify intranet Microsoft update service location | You can use this when you set up your own Windows Server Update Services (WSUS) server to synchronize, approve, and deploy updates. Figure 15-9 shows this setting configured so that clients retrieve updates from a server named wsus1 in the internal network. |
| Enable client-side targeting | Specifies the target group name used to receive updates from a WSUS server. The WSUS server uses this name to determine which updates to deploy. This is valid only when the WSUS server is configured for client-side targeting. |

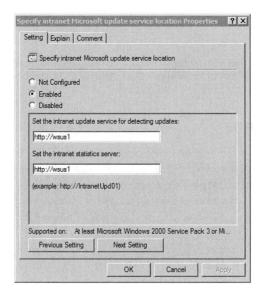

**Figure 15-9** Configuring clients to check with a WSUS server for updates

## Blocking Inheritance

By default, GPO settings from GPOs at higher levels are automatically inherited at lower levels. For example, each OU automatically inherits all GPO settings set at the domain level. In this context, each OU is a child of the domain. Similarly, children OUs automatically inherit GPO settings from parent OUs; however, you can block this behavior.

Figure 15-10 shows how to enable **Block Inheritance** for a child OU. The **West** OU is a child OU of the **Sales** OU. The exclamation icon next to the OU and the checkmark next to **Block Inheritance** show that **Block Inheritance** is enabled.

**NOTE**   You can set **Block Inheritance** on an OU but not on a GPO.

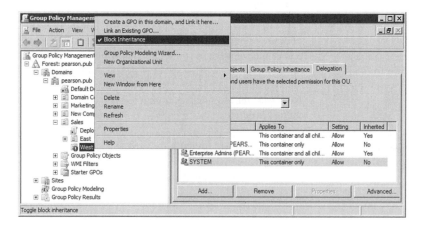

**Figure 15-10**   Configuring Block Inheritance on an OU

**TIP**   When **Block Inheritance** is selected, it blocks all GPOs with one exception. If a GPO from any parent is set to **Enforced**, the Enforced GPO is not blocked.

## Enforcing GPOs

There are times when you want to ensure that settings from a GPO take precedence no matter when they are applied. For example, you might want to ensure that Group Policy settings set at the domain level are not overwritten by settings at an OU level. Similarly, you might want to ensure that GPOs are not blocked even if an OU has **Block Inheritance** configured. You can do so by configuring **Enforced** on the GPO.

Figure 15-11 shows the setting as enforced for the **Default Domain Policy**. Notice that the GPO has a lock icon indicating that it is enforced. Of course, you can right-click it to see the checkmark next to **Enforced**.

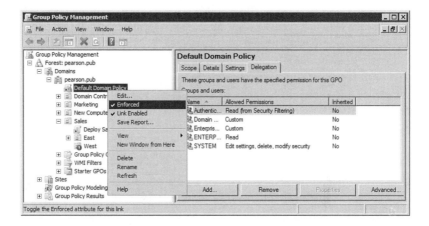

**Figure 15-11**   Configuring Enforced for a GPO

# Using Loopback Processing

Group Policy settings applied to users normally take precedence over Group Policy settings that apply to computers. As a reminder, the last Group Policy that is applied is the one that takes precedence. Because a computer boots up before a user can log on, the Group Policy settings for the computer is applied first, and the Group Policy settings for the user are applied last.

> **NOTE** A simple way of understanding loopback processing is that it ensures that the policies applying to the computer take precedence over the policies applying to the user. For example, if you want to enable folder redirection for users ONLY when they log on to terminal servers, you can enable loopback processing in a GPO that applies to users only when they log on to computers in the terminal server OU.

However, there are times when you want this reversed. In other words, you want the Group Policy settings for the computer to take precedence over the Group Policy settings for the user. You can do so by enabling **Loopback Processing**. Figure 15-12 shows the location of this setting.

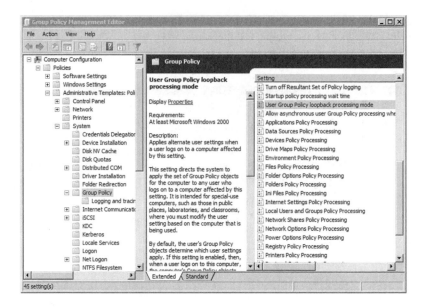

**Figure 15-12**    Enabling Loopback Processing

# Running Scripts with Group Policy

You can write scripts and have them automatically run through Group Policy. The great strength of this is that you write and configure the script once, and it runs on all the computers in your domain or all the computers in a specific OU, depending on where you link the GPO holding the script.

Figure 15-13 shows the locations of these GPO settings and the following table explains them.

| Group Policy Script Events | Comments |
| --- | --- |
| Computer Startup | The script runs when the computer starts. |
| | The Group Policy setting for a domain GPO is in the **Computer Configuration**, **Policies**, **Windows Settings**, **Scripts** node. |
| Computer Shutdown | The script runs when the computer shuts down. |
| | The Group Policy setting for a domain GPO is in the **Computer Configuration**, **Policies**, **Windows Settings**, **Scripts** node. |
| User logon | The script runs when the user logs on. |
| | The Group Policy setting for a domain GPO is in the **User Configuration**, **Policies**, **Windows Settings**, **Scripts** node. |
| User logoff | The script runs when the user logs off. |
| | The Group Policy setting for a domain GPO is in the **User Configuration**, **Policies**, **Windows Settings**, **Scripts** node. |

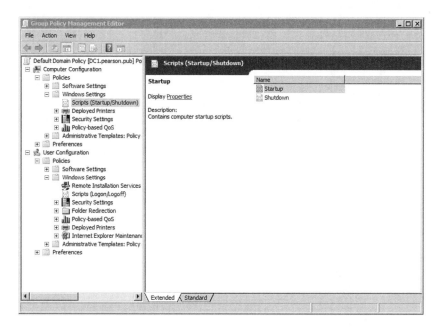

**Figure 15-13**   Group Policy settings for scripts

Scripts can run either synchronously or asynchronously.

| Script Behavior Types | Comments |
|---|---|
| Synchronous | Scripts run one after the other. Users cannot interact with the system until all scripts have completed. |
| Asynchronous | Multiple scripts run at the same time. User can interact with system before the scripts have completed. |

All scripts run asynchronously by default on Windows Server 2008 and Windows Server 2008 R2. This includes both computer startup and user logon scripts.

**TIP**   The default behavior for computer startup and user logon scripts before Windows Server 2008 was synchronous. Users could not interact with the system until all scripts completed. However, computers boot quicker with this set to asynchronous and the behavior is changed in Windows Server 2008, Server 2008 R2, Windows Vista, and Windows 7. You can modify the new default behavior if needed.

CHAPTER 16

# Group Policy Command-Line Tools

This chapter provides information and commands concerning the following topics:

- Viewing Group Policy settings with **gpresult**
- Refreshing Group Policy settings with **gpupdate**

**TIP** You should be familiar with **gpresult** and **gpupdate** commands when preparing for the 70-640 exam.

## Viewing Group Policy Settings with gpresult

You can view current Group Policy settings with the **gpresult** command. The syntax is

`gpresult [switches]`

Common switches are shown in the following table.

| gpresult Switches | Comments |
|---|---|
| Get help.<br><br>`gpresult [/?]`<br>`C:\>gpresult` | Shows the help file if no switches are included or the **/?** switch is used. |
| Display summary data.<br><br>`/r`<br>`C:\>gpresult /r` | Displays Resultant Set of Policy (RSoP) summary data.<br><br>The summary data doesn't include any settings. |
| Send results to an XML file.<br><br>`/x file.xml`<br>`C:\>gpresult /x gpresultsx.xml` | Saves the report in XML format. You can then open the file in Internet Explorer by just entering the filename at the command prompt or double-clicking it in Windows Explorer. |
| Send to an HTML file.<br><br>`/h file.html`<br>`C:\>gpresult /h gpresultsh.html` | Saves the report in HTML format. You can then open the file in Internet Explorer by just entering the filename at the command prompt or double-clicking it in Windows Explorer.<br><br>Figure 16-1 shows what this file looks like in Internet Explorer. |

| gpresult Switches | Comments |
|---|---|
| Overwrite existing file.<br><br>`/f`<br>`C:\>gpresult /x gpresultsx.xml /f`<br>`C:\>gpresult /h gpresultsh.html /f` | Forces **gpresult** to overwrite an existing file. This is used with the **/x** or **/h** command depending on whether you want an XML or HTML format. |
| Verbose mode.<br><br>`/v`<br>`C:\>gpresult /v` | Returns results on the local computer in verbose mode.<br><br>This provides additional details on Group Policy settings. |
| Super verbose mode.<br><br>`/z`<br>`C:\>gpresult /z` | Specifies that the super-verbose mode is used.<br><br>This provides significantly more details on Group Policy settings than the verbose mode.<br><br>**TIP** This output can provide insight into the settings that are applied. |
| Retrieve GPO settings from another computer.<br><br>`/s computername`<br>`C:\>gpresult /z /s dc1` | Specifies a remote system to connect to for Group Policy details.<br><br>**NOTE** The **/s** option can be used only when also using one of the following switches: **/x**, **/h**, **/r**, **/v**, or **/z**. |
| Run the command with a different user.<br><br>`/u user \| domain\user`<br>`C:\>gpresult /s dc1 /z /u`<br>`pearson\administrator` | Runs **gpresult** with a different user account. You are prompted to provide the password.<br><br>**NOTE** The **u** option can only be used when also using the **s** switch, which also requires one of the following switches: **/x**, **/h**, **/r**, **/v**, or **/z**. |
| Run the command with a different user without prompting for a password.<br><br>`/u user \| domain\user   /p password`<br>`C:\>gpresult /s dc1 /z /u`<br>`pearson\administrator /p P@ssw0rd` | Runs **gpresult** with a different user account without prompting for a password. |
| Specify only user or computer settings.<br><br>`/scope user \| computer`<br>`C:\>gpresult /z /scope user`<br>`C:\>gpresult /z /scope compute` | You can retrieve only the user or only the computer settings with the **/scope** switch. |

**TIP** You can output the settings to a text file with the redirect command. For example, **gpresult /z > gpr.txt** sends the output to a text file named gpr.txt.

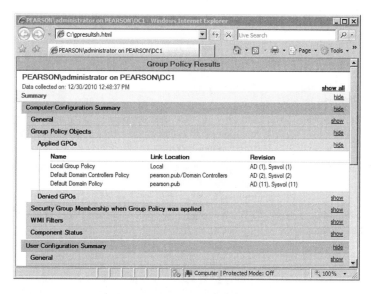

**Figure 16-1**   Group Policy Results in Internet Explorer

The Group Policy Management Console (GPMC) enables you to view these settings in a GUI. Figure 16-2 shows the GPMC with a Group Policy Results report.

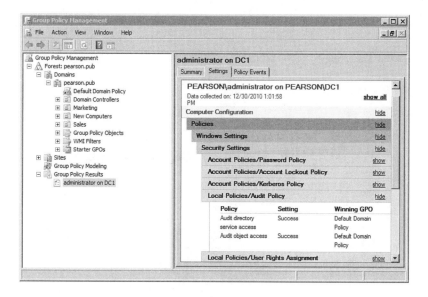

**Figure 16-2**   Group Policy Results in the GPMC

## Refreshing Group Policy Settings with gpupdate

Group Policy settings are applied at different times for computers within a domain, as shown in the following table.

| Automatic Group Policy Update Intervals | Comments |
| --- | --- |
| When the computer starts. | Group Policy settings for computers are applied when the computer starts. The logon screen appears after the settings are applied. |
| When the user logs on. | Group Policy settings for users are applied when the user logs on. The desktop appears after the settings are applied. |
| At a random time every 90 to 120 minutes. | After being initially applied, Group Policy settings are queried from Active Directory every 90 minutes with a random offset of 30 minutes. If there are any changes, the changes are applied.<br><br>**NOTE**  These are default times for all computers except domain controllers. Settings are reapplied to domain controllers every five minutes by default. |
| Every 16 hours for security settings | Computers query Active Directory every 16 hours to retrieve security settings. These are reapplied whether they have been changed or not. |

You can reapply Group Policy settings to a computer using the **gpupdate** command. The syntax is

```
gpupdate [switches]
```

Figure 16-3 and the following command show the common usage of **gpupdate**:

```
gpupdate /force
```

**Figure 16-3**   Executing the **gpupdate /force** command

| gpupdate Switches | Comments |
| --- | --- |
| gpupdate<br><br>`C:\>`**gpupdate** | This queries Active Directory for any changes in Group Policy settings and reapplies any changed settings.<br><br>**NOTE**   Although documentation indicates this is the way it works, it is inconsistent. To ensure changes are applied, you should use the **gpupdate /force** command. |
| gpupdate /force<br><br>`C:\>`**gpupdate /force** | This queries Active Directory and reapplies all policy settings, even settings that haven't changed. |
| gpupdate /force /target<br>*computer │ user*<br><br>`C:\>`**gpupdate /force**<br>**/target computer**<br>`C:\>`**gpupdate /force**<br>**/target user** | You can specify either computer or user Group Policy settings with the **/target** switch.<br><br>With the **/target computer** switch, only computer Group Policy settings are reapplied. With the **/target user** switch, only user Group Policy settings are reapplied. |
| gpupdate /force /target<br>*computer │ user*<br><br>`C:\>`**gpupdate /force**<br>**/logoff** | Some Group Policy settings, such as software installations, are not applied unless the user logs off and back on.<br><br>The **/logoff** switch forces a logoff if it is necessary to apply the settings. |
| gpupdate /force /target<br>*computer │ user*<br><br>`C:\>`**gpupdate /force**<br>**/boot** | Some Group Policy settings are not applied unless the computer shuts down and restarts.<br><br>The **/boot** switch forces a reboot if a reboot is necessary to apply the settings. |

# CHAPTER 17

# Security Configuration Wizard

This chapter provides information and commands concerning the following topics:

- Understanding the Security Configuration Wizard
- Using **scwcmd**

**TIP** You should be familiar with the Security Configuration Wizard when preparing for the 70-642 exam.

## Understanding the Security Configuration Wizard

The Security Configuration Wizard (SCW) can help you increase security on a system (or multiple systems). The wizard leads you through the process of identifying several things you can do to increase the security. Elements the SCW examine include

- Services that are needed (and services that aren't needed)
- Firewall rules to implement
- Registry settings to change
- Audit settings to enable

**TIP** Combined, these settings harden the server by reducing the attack surface.

You can launch the SCW from the **Administrative Tools** menu. It analyzes the current operations of the system and makes recommendations for changes to make the system more secure. You can create a security policy, edit a security policy, apply a security policy, or roll back the last security policy with the SCW.

The following steps show how to create a security policy with the SCW.

| Step | Action |
|------|--------|
| 1. | Launch the **Security Configuration Wizard** from the **Administrative Tools** menu. |
| 2. | Click **Next** on the **Welcome** page. |
| 3. | Select **Create A New Security Policy** and click **Next**. |
| 4. | Type the name of the server you want to analyze and click **Next**. |
| 5. | After the **Security Configuration Database** has been analyzed, click **Next**. |
| 6. | Click **Next** on the **Role-Based Configuration** page. |

| Step | Action |
|------|--------|
| 7. | Review the server roles. These are the roles that are currently installed, and the SCW uses them to determine which services should be running and which ports should be open. Make any changes desired, and then click **Next**. |
| 8. | Review the client features. These are the features that are currently installed and used to enable services or support different client features. Make any changes desired and click **Next**. |
| 9. | Review the options page. These are the administration and other options used to enable services or open ports. Make any changes desired, and then click **Next**. |
| 10. | If the **Additional Services** page appears, review them, make any desired changes, and click **Next**. |
| 11. | On the **Handling Unspecified Services** page, select the desired action. The default is to not change the startup mode, but it is more secure to select **Disable the Service** if it is not needed.<br><br>**NOTE**   Selecting **Disable the Service** is more secure; however, you run the risk of disabling a service that the SCW was unaware was needed and affecting the reliability of your system.<br><br>Choose how to handle unspecified services and click **Next**. |
| 12. | View the changes that the SCW recommends. Your display should look similar to Figure 17-1. When you're satisfied with these changes, click **Next**. |
| 13. | On the **Network Security** section, select **Skip This Section** and click **Next**.<br><br>**NOTE**   The Network Security section enables you to view and manipulate firewall rules for the local firewall. You can click through these settings to identify what the wizard recommends. |
| 14. | On the **Registry Settings** section, select **Skip This Section** and click **Next**.<br><br>**NOTE**   The **Registry Settings** section enables you to view and manipulate different security settings related to SMB security signatures, LDAP signing, and LAN Manager Authentication. You can click through these settings to identify what the wizard recommends. |
| 15. | On the **Audit Policy** section, click **Next**. |
| 16. | Ensure that **Audit Successful Activities** is selected and click **Next**. Review the **Audit Policy Summary** page and click **Next**. |
| 17. | On the **Save Security Policy** page, click **Next**. |
| 18. | Notice that the file is saved in c:\windows\security\msscw\policies\ by default. Add a name such as **scwtest** at the end of the path. Click **Next**.<br><br>**NOTE**   The file is automatically saved as an .xml file with the .xml extension. |
| 19. | Ensure **Apply Later** is selected and click **Next**. Click **Finish**. |

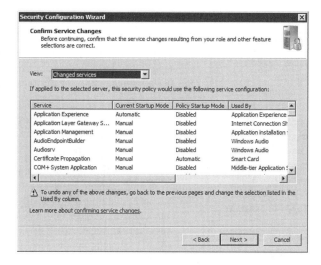

**Figure 17-1** Confirming service changes by the SCW

At this point, you have a policy created and you can use the **scwcmd** tool to manipulate it.

## Using scwcmd

The **scwcmd** tool is used to manipulate policies created by the SCW. The following table shows some common uses.

| scwcmd Command | Comments |
| --- | --- |
| Create a GPO from a SCW policy.<br><br>`scwcmd transform /p:policy-file.xml /g:gpo-name`<br>`C:\>scwcmd transform /p:c:\`<br>`windows\security\msscw\`<br>`policies\scwtest.xml`<br>`/g:SCWTest` | Transforms a security policy file generated by using SCW into a new Group Policy object (GPO) in Active Directory Domain Services (AD DS).<br><br>The **/p** switch needs to include the path to the SCW policy file, and the **/g** switch names the GPO.<br><br>Figure 17-2 shows the GPO named SCWTest created in the Group Policy Management Console (GPMC) from this command.<br><br>**TIP** The case you use for the GPO is used when the GPO is created. For example, if you use **/g:scwtest**, the GPO is named scwtest, but if you use **/g:SCWTest**, the GPO uses the same case named SCWTest.<br><br>**NOTE** Although the GPO is created and accessible in the GPMC, it is not linked anywhere by default. You must take the extra step in the GPMC to link it. |

| scwcmd Command | Comments |
|---|---|
| Analyze a computer against a policy.<br><br>`scwcmd analyze /m:computer-`<br>`name | /ou:ou-DN`<br>`/p:policy-file.xml`<br>`C:\>scwcmd analyze /p:c:\`<br>`windows\security\msscw\`<br>`policies\scwtest.xml`<br>`C:\>scwcmd analyze /m:dc1`<br>`/p:c:\windows\security\msscw\`<br>`policies\scwtest.xml`<br>`C:\>scwcmd analyze`<br>`/ou:"ou=sales, dc=pearson,`<br>`dc=pub"`<br>`/p:c:\windows\security\msscw\`<br>`policies\scwtest.xml` | Determines whether a computer is in compliance with a policy. It compares the policy against the computer (or computers) and creates a file indicating any discrepancies.<br><br>You can run the command against the local computer without the **/m** or **/ou** switch, a remote computer with the **/m** switch, or an OU with the **/ou** switch.<br><br>The first example analyzes the local system, the second example analyzes a server named dc1, and the third example analyzes all the computers in the Sales OU. You can then view the xml file identified by the **/p** switch, which documents any discrepancies. |
| Configure systems with the policy.<br><br>`scwcmd configure /m:computer-`<br>`name | /ou:ou-DN  /p:policy-`<br>`file.xml`<br>`C:\>scwcmd configure /p:c:\`<br>`windows\security\msscw\`<br>`policies\scwtest.xml`<br>`C:\>scwcmd configure /m:dc1`<br>`/p:c:\windows\security\msscw\`<br>`policies\scwtest.xml`<br>`C:\>scwcmd configure`<br>`/ou:"ou=sales, dc=pearson,`<br>`dc=pub"`<br>`/p:c:\windows\security\msscw\`<br>`policies\scwtest.xml` | The **configure** command applies a SCW-generated security policy to one or more computers.<br><br>This syntax is similar to the **analyze** command. You can apply it to the local computer, a remote computer with the **/m** switch, or all computers in an OU with the **/ou** switch. |
| Roll back a policy.<br><br>`scwcmd rollback /m:computer-`<br>`name`<br>`C:\>scwcmd configure /m:dc1` | Applies the most recent rollback policy available, and then deletes that rollback policy. You can roll back a policy on only one computer at a time.<br><br>**NOTE**  Rollback policies are created and stored in the c:\windows\security\msscw\ rollbackfiles folder by default. |
| View a policy.<br><br>`scwcmd view /x:policy-file.xml`<br>`C:\>scwcmd view /x:c:\windows\`<br>`security\msscw\policies\`<br>`scwtest.xml` | Displays an xml file in an interactive page.<br><br>Figure 17-3 shows the result of this command. |

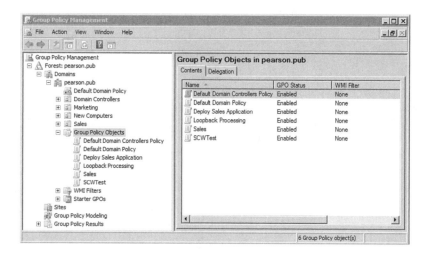

**Figure 17-2** Transforming an SCW policy to a GPO

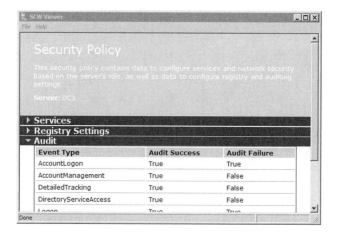

**Figure 17-3** Viewing an SCW policy from **scwcmd**

**TIP** There are more options you can use with the **scwcmd** command. This section scratched the surface. If you want to do more with it, check out the TechNet Web page: http://technet.microsoft.com/library/ff807358.aspx.

# CHAPTER 18

# Configuring Server Core after Installation

This chapter provides information and commands concerning the following topics:

- Installing Server Core
- Restoring the command prompt
- Renaming the computer
- Logging off, shutting down, and rebooting
- Configuring TCP/IP
- Setting the time, date, and time zone
- Joining a domain

> **TIP** You should be familiar with Server Core when preparing for the 70-642 and 70-643 exams.

> **TIP** If you're running Windows Server 2008 R2, it's much easier to complete most of the configuration with sconfig.cmd. It is not available by default on Windows Server 2008, and you're unlikely to see any test questions on it; however, it's a good menu-driven method of setting up a Server Core installation.

## Installing Server Core

Windows Server 2008 Server Core is a streamlined version of Windows Server 2008. Server Core is a limited installation of Windows that only includes the command prompt—no graphical user interface (GUI).

> **NOTE** Server Core is a more secure implementation of Windows because it has a limited attack surface. It includes only the services and protocols that are absolutely necessary.

The following steps show the process of installing Windows Server 2008 Server Core.

| Step | Action |
|------|--------|
| 1. | Boot the system to the installation DVD. |
| 2. | Select the language, time and currency, and keyboard. Click **Next**. |
| 3. | Click **Install Now**. |

| Step | Action |
|------|--------|
| 4. | Select the **Server Core Installation** (instead of the Full Installation) for the version you want. Figure 18-1 shows the selection for **Windows Server 2008 Enterprise Server Core Installation**. Click **Next**. |
| 5. | Review the license terms, select **I Accept the License Terms**, and then click **Next**. |
| 6. | Select **Custom (Advanced)**. |
| 7. | Select the disk where you want to install the Server Core installation and click **Next**. <br><br> NOTE   The installation takes some time but is quicker than a full installation. After the installation completes, it reboots automatically. |
| 8. | Press **Ctrl+Alt+Delete** to log on. Click **Other User**. Type **Administrator** in the **User Name** text box, and press **Enter**. <br><br> TIP   Because this is the first boot, the Administrator password is blank. |
| 9. | Click **OK** to change the password. Leave the **Password** text box blank. Enter a new password in the **New Password** and **Confirm Password** text boxes, and then press **Enter**. A message displays indicating the password has been changed. Click **OK**. <br><br> The system boots into the desktop, which is only a command prompt. |

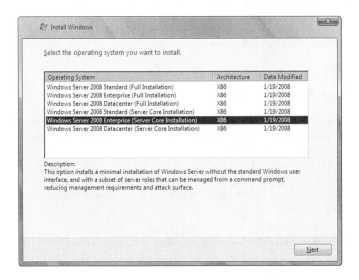

**Figure 18-1**   Selecting Windows Server 2008 Enterprise (Server Core Installation)

## Restoring the Command Prompt

The primary interface you have in Server Core is the command prompt. If you accidentally close it, you can restore it with the following steps.

| Step | Action |
|------|--------|
| 1. | Launch **Task Manager** by pressing **Ctrl+Shift+Esc**. |
| 2. | Click **New Task**. |
| 3. | Type **cmd** in the **Create New Task** box, as shown in Figure 18-2. Click **OK**. |
| 4. | Close **Task Manager**. |

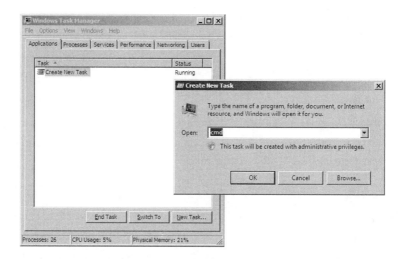

**Figure 18-2**   Restoring the command prompt in Server Core

# Renaming the Computer

Normally, you rename the computer through the **Advanced System Settings** of the **Computer Properties** page. However, these pages aren't available in a Server Core installation. Instead, you need to rename it with the **wmic** command. The basic syntax is

```
wmic computersystem where name="%computername%" rename name = newname
```

For example, if you want to name the computer SC1, you can use the following command:

```
wmic computersystem where name="%computername%" rename name = sc1
```

The output indicates "Method execution successful."

> **TIP**   You can use the actual name of the computer in place of %computername%; however, the name of the computer starts with a long set of random letters and numbers after "WIN-". For example, the computer name might be WIN-JMGZRUP4XHF. You can view the computer name with the command **hostname**.

You must reboot the system after renaming it. The next section shows you how.

**NOTE** Chapter 21, "Manipulating Services," also covers the **wmic** command and how it can be used to manipulate services on local and remote systems.

# Logging Off, Shutting Down, and Rebooting

The primary tool you use to log off, shut down, and reboot a Server Core system is the **shutdown** command. The following table shows some common usage.

| shutdown Commands | Comments |
|---|---|
| Log off.<br><br>`C:\>shutdown /l` | The **/l** ("el", not one) switch is used to log off. The default delay is 30 seconds. |
| Shutdown.<br><br>`C:\>shutdown /s` | The **/s** switch is used to shut down the computer. The default delay is 30 seconds. |
| Reboot system.<br><br>`C:\>shutdown /r` | The **/r** switch is used to shut down and reboot the computer. The default delay is 30 seconds. |
| Hibernate the computer.<br><br>`/h`<br>`C:\>shutdown /h` | Forces the computer into hibernation. |
| Abort a shutdown.<br><br>`C:\>shutdown /a` | The **/a** switch aborts a shutdown, but you have to run it before the time-out period expires. |
| Modify the time-out delay.<br><br>`/t number-seconds`<br>`C:\>shutdown /r /t 60` | You can modify the time-out delay used with the **/l**, **/s**, or **/r** commands. |
| Display Shutdown GUI.<br><br>`C:\>shutdown /i` | Figure 18-3 shows the **Shutdown** GUI. You can use this to easily enter information for the event tracker, such as why the system was rebooted and comments. Even though this GUI is called Remote Shutdown Dialog, it can be used to shut down the local computer by using the local computer name.<br><br>**TIP** Although this section is focused on using **shutdown** to log off and reboot Server Core, you can also use it to shut down remote computers.<br><br>**NOTE** You can also enter event track information from the command line. Use **shutdown /?** to view the syntax. |

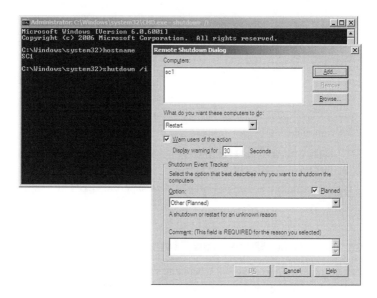

**Figure 18-3**   Launching the Shutdown GUI

## Configuring TCP/IP

If your network doesn't include a DHCP server, or you want to manually assign TCP/IP configuration information, you can do so with the **netsh** command. The following table shows steps you can use to configure TCP/IP.

| Step | Action |
|------|--------|
| 1. | Type **ipconfig /all** and press **Enter** to view the current TCP/IP configuration. |
| 2. | Type **netsh interface ipv4 show interfaces** and press **Enter** to view the name of the network interface cards (NICs) on your system.<br><br>**NOTE**   The default name of the first NIC is **Local Area Connection**, but your system might have more than one NIC. You need to use the name of the NIC that you want to manipulate when using the **netsh** command. |
| 3. | Use the following command to assign an IP address, subnet mask, and default gateway:<br><br>**netsh interface ipv4 set address name=**"*NIC-name*" **static** *IP-address subnet-mask default-gateway*<br><br>For example, to assign an IP address of 192.168.1.100, a subnet mask of 255.255.255.0, and a default gateway of 192.168.1.1 for the NIC named Local Area Connection, use this command:<br><br>C:\>**netsh interface ipv4 set address name="local area connection" static 192.168.1.100 255.255.255.0 192.168.1.1** |

| Step | Action |
|------|--------|
| 4. | Use the following command to assign the IP address of a DNS server in your network:<br><br>**netsh interface ipv4 set dnsserver** *"NIC-name"* **static** *IP-address-of-DNS-server*<br><br>For example, to assign an IP address of 192.168.1.5 for the DNS server, use this command:<br><br>**C:\>netsh interface ipv4 set dnsserver "local area connection" static 192.168.1.5** |
| 5. | Type **ipconfig /all** and press **Enter** to view the updated TCP/IP configuration. |

## Setting the Time, Date, and Time Zone

You can set the time with the **time** command, and you can set the date with the **date** command. However, neither of these tools enables you to set the time zone. You can launch the Control Panel Date and Time GUI with the following command:

```
control timedate.cpl
```

Figure 18-4 shows the Date and Time GUI that launches from this command. Click the **Change Time Zone** button to change the time zone. Click **OK** to dismiss the GUI.

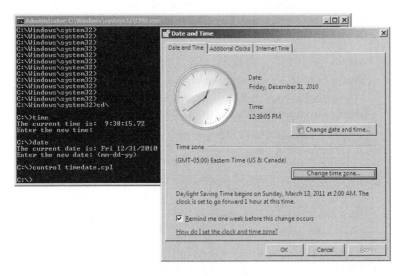

**Figure 18-4**   Launching the Date and Time GUI

## Joining a Domain

After you rename the system, configure TCP/IP, and set the correct time zone, you might want to join the computer to a domain. You can use the **netdom** command to do so.

> **TIP**  Chapter 13, "Using **netdom**," covers **netdom**, including the command used to join a domain. **netdom** works the same way on a Server Core system as it does on a regular system.

The **netdom** command to join a domain has the following syntax:

```
Netdom join %computername% /domain:domain-name
/userd:domain-account /passwordd:password
```

> **NOTE**  The domain account must have permissions to join a computer to a domain. Regular users in a domain have rights to join up to ten computers to a domain.

For example, if you want to join a domain named pearson.pub, using the administrator account that has a password of P@ssw0rd, use the following command:

```
netdom join %computername% /domain:pearson.pub
/userd:administrator /passwordd:P@ssw0rd
```

If successful, you receive a message indicating that the computer needs to be restarted to complete the operation. Restart the system with the following command:

```
shutdown /r
```

> **TIP**  If the command is not successful, check your syntax first. If the syntax is correct, verify that the TCP/IP configuration is correct and that you have the correct IP address for the DNS server.

> **NOTE**  Chapter 24, "Licensing and Activation," includes commands that you can use to activate Server Core from the command prompt.

# CHAPTER 19

# Adding Roles to Server Core

This chapter provides information and commands concerning the following topics:

- Understanding the supported roles
- Using **ocsetup** to add roles to Windows Server 2008
- Using **dism** to add roles to Windows Server 2008 R2
- Adding the Active Directory Domain Services (AD DS) role

**TIP** You should be familiar with Server Core commands when preparing for the 70-642 and 70-643 exams.

## Understanding the Supported Roles

Server Core has a limited number of services that it can support. Because of this, it has a limited number of roles that you can add. The following table shows the supported roles in Windows Server 2008 and Windows Server 2008 R2.

**NOTE** Some adventurous administrators have configured Server Core installations to support more roles than the ones listed; however, these installations are not fully tested by Microsoft and are not supported.

| Role | Server 2008 | Server 2008 R2 |
|---|---|---|
| Active Directory Doman Services (AD DS) | X | X |
| Active Directory Lightweight Directory Services (AD LDS) | X | X |
| Active Directory Certificate Services (AD CS) | | X |
| DHCP Server | X | X |
| DNS Server | X | X |
| File Services | X | X (including File Server Resource Manager) |
| Print Services | X | |
| Print and Document Services | | X |
| Web Server (IIS) | X | X (including a subset of ASP.NET) |
| Streaming Media Services | X | X |
| Hyper-V | X | X |

The following table shows some differences in features that are available in Windows Server 2008 and Windows Server 2008 R2. Most of the changes show additional features supported in the R2 version. The only feature no longer available in Windows Server 2008 R2 is the Removable Storage feature.

| Feature | Server 2008 | Server 2008 R2 |
|---|---|---|
| .NET Framework | | X |
| PowerShell | | X |
| ASP.NET in Web Server role | | X |
| File Server Resource Manager component of File Services | | X |
| Print and Document Services | | X |
| Removable Storage feature | X | |

## Using ocsetup to Add Roles to Windows Server 2008

On a regular installation of Windows Server 2008, you use the Server Manager to install additional roles; however, the Server Manager is not available in Server Core. Instead, use **ocsetup** to add additional roles. The basic syntax is

```
start [/w] ocsetup role-name
```

> **TIP**    The role-name must be entered using the exact case. This is one of the few times when upper- and lowercase matters with the command prompt. Figure 19-1 shows the error message you see if the case is not entered exactly.

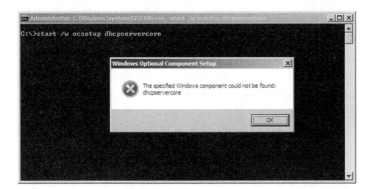

**Figure 19-1    ocsetup** error when incorrect case used

> **TIP**    The **/w** switch prevents the command prompt from returning until the installation of the role completes. This is useful to provide feedback indicating that the role was successfully installed when the command prompt returns.

Some roles require additional steps to configure. The following sections show how to add and configure various roles.

> **NOTE**   The following section shows the basics to add roles with **ocsetup**. For a full listing of command options you can use with the **ocsetup** command, check out this TechNet page: http://technet.microsoft.com/library/dd799247.aspx.

## Adding the DHCP Server Role with ocsetup

The following table shows the syntax to add DHCP. Figure 19-2 shows these commands in the Server Core prompt.

| Commands for DHCP | Comments |
|---|---|
| `C:\>start /w ocsetup DHCPServerCore` | Add DHCP role. |
| `C:\>sc config dhcpserver start= auto` | Configure the DHCP Server service to start automatically. <br><br> **TIP**   There must be a space after the equal sign (=), but there cannot be a space before it in this command. In other words, it's **start=**, a space, and then **auto**. |
| `C:\>net start dhcpserver` | Start the DHCP Server service. <br><br> **TIP**   After the DHCP Server role is added and the DHCP Server service is started, you can configure DHCP remotely using a DHCP console on a different system. Chapter 20, "Configuring Server Core for Remote Administration" shows how to configure Server Core to support remote administration, and how to connect to a Server Core remotely using a Microsoft Management Console (MMC). |
| `C:\>start /w ocsetup DNS-Server-Core-Role /uninstall` | Remove DHCP role. |

**Figure 19-2**   Adding and configuring the DHCP Server role on Windows Server 2008 Server Core

## Adding the DNS Server Role with ocsetup

The following table shows the syntax to add DNS.

| Commands for DNS | Comments |
|---|---|
| `C:\>start /w ocsetup`<br>`DNS-Server-Core-Role` | Add DNS role.<br><br>TIP   After the DNS Server role is added, you can configure it remotely using a DNS console on a different system. |
| `C:\>start /w ocsetup`<br>`DNS-Server-Core-Role /uninstall` | Remove DNS role. |

## Adding File Services with ocsetup

The following table shows the syntax to add the various file services.

NOTE   When you add the file services, the server is configured as a File Server.

| Commands for File Services | Comments |
|---|---|
| `C:\> start /w ocsetup`<br>`FRS-Infrastructure` | Add the File Replication service. |
| `C:\> start /w ocsetup DFSN-Server` | Add the Distributed File System service. |
| `C:\> start /w ocsetup`<br>`DFSR-Infrastructure-ServerEdition` | Add the Distributed File System Replication service. |
| `C:\> start /w ocsetup`<br>`ServerForNFS-Base` | Add Base Services for Network File System (NFS). |
| `C:\> start /w ocsetup`<br>`ClientForNFS-Client` | Add Client Services for NFS. |

## Adding the Print Services Role with ocsetup

The following table shows the syntax to add the Print Services role.

| Commands for Print Services | Comments |
|---|---|
| `C:\> start /w ocsetup`<br>`Printing-ServerCore-Role` | Add the Print Services role. |
| `C:\> start /w ocsetup`<br>`Printing-LPDPrintService` | Add the Line Printer Daemon (LPD) service. |
| `C:\>start /w ocsetup`<br>`Printing-ServerCore-Role`<br>`/uninstall` | Remove the Print Services role. |

## Adding the Web Server (IIS) Role with pkgmgr

The following table shows the syntax to add the Web Server (IIS) role.

**NOTE** Internet Information Services (IIS) is installed when the Web Server (IIS) role is added.

| Commands for Web Server | Comments |
|---|---|
| `C:\>start /w pkgmgr /iu:IIS-WebServerRole;WAS-WindowsActivationService;WAS-ProcessModel` | Adds the Web Server role with a default installation. |
| `C:\>start /w pkgmgr /iu:IIS-WebServerRole;IIS-WebServer;IIS-CommonHttpFeatures;IIS-StaticContent;IIS-DefaultDocument;IIS-DirectoryBrowsing;IIS-HttpErrors;IIS-HttpRedirect;IIS-ApplicationDevelopment;IIS-ASP;IIS-CGI;IIS-ISAPIExtensions;IIS-ISAPIFilter;IIS-ServerSideIncludes;IIS-HealthAndDiagnostics;IIS-HttpLogging;IIS-LoggingLibraries;IIS-RequestMonitor;IIS-HttpTracing;IIS-CustomLogging;IIS-ODBCLogging;IIS-Security;IIS-BasicAuthentication;IIS-WindowsAuthentication;IIS-DigestAuthentication;IIS-ClientCertificateMappingAuthentication;IIS-IISCertificateMappingAuthentication;IIS-URLAuthorization;IIS-RequestFiltering;IIS-IPSecurity;IIS-Performance;IIS-HttpCompressionStatic;IIS-HttpCompressionDynamic;IIS-WebServerManagementTools;IIS-ManagementScriptingTools;IIS-IIS6ManagementCompatibility;IIS-Metabase;IIS-WMICompatibility;IIS-LegacyScripts;IIS-FTPPublishingService;IIS-FTPServer;WAS-WindowsActivationService;WAS-ProcessModel` | Adds the Web Server role with all options. Works for both Windows Server 2008 and Windows Server 2008 R2. |
| `C:\> start /w pkgmgr /uu:IIS-WebServerRole;WAS-WindowsActivationService;WAS-ProcessModel` | Removes the Web Server role. |

## Using dism to Add Roles to Windows Server 2008 R2

Windows Server 2008 R2 uses **dism** instead of **ocsetup** to add additional roles. The basic syntax is

```
dism /online /enable-feature /featurename:feature-name
```

For a full list of roles and features you can add, use the following command:

```
dism /online /get-features /format:table
```

**NOTE**    **dism** is not available on the Windows Server 2008 Server Core installation. However, it is available by default on Windows Server 2008 R2 and Windows Server 2008 R2 Server Core installations.

**TIP**    The *feature-name* must be entered using the exact case as shown in the **get-features** output. This is one of the few times when upper- and lowercase matters with the command prompt (just as it matters with the **ocsetup** command used with Windows Server 2008 Server Core).

Some roles require additional steps to configure. The following sections show how to add and configure various roles.

## Adding the DHCP Server Role with dism

The following table shows the syntax to add the DHCP role.

| Commands for DHCP | Comments |
|---|---|
| `C:\>dism /online /enable-feature /featurename: DHCPServerCore` | Adds the DHCP role. |
| `C:\>sc config dhcpserver start= auto` | Configures the DHCP Server service to start automatically. |
| `C:\>net start dhcpserver` | Starts the DHCP Server service.<br><br>**TIP**    After the DHCP Server role is added and the DHCP Server service is started, you can configure DHCP remotely using a DHCP console on a different system. Chapter 20 shows how to configure Server Core to support remote administration, and how to connect to a Server Core remotely using a Microsoft Management Console (MMC). |
| `C:\>dism /online /disable-feature /featurename: DHCPServerCore` | Removes the DHCP role. |

## Adding the DNS Server Role with dism

The following table shows the syntax to add the DNS role.

| Commands for DNS | Comments |
|---|---|
| `C:\>dism /online /enable-feature /featurename: DNS-Server-Core-Role` | Adds the DNS role.<br><br>**TIP**    After the DNS Server role is added, you can configure it remotely using a DNS console on a different system. |
| `C:\>dism /online /disable-feature /featurename: DNS-Server-Core-Role` | Removes the DNS role. |

## Adding File Services with dism

The following table shows the syntax to add the various file services.

**NOTE**   When you add any of the file services, the server is configured as a File Server.

| Commands for File Services | Comments |
|---|---|
| C:\>dism /online /enable-feature /featurename:FRS-infrastructure | Adds the File Replication service. |
| C:\>dism /online /enable-feature /featurename:DFSN-Server | Adds the Distributed File System service. |
| C:\> dism /online /enable-feature /featurename:ClientForNFS-Base | Adds the Distributed File System Replication service. |
| C:\>dism /online /enable-feature /featurename:ServerForNFS-Base | Adds Base Services for NFS. |
| C:\>dism /online /enable-feature /featurename:ClientForNFS-Client | Adds Client Services for NFS. |

## Adding the Print and Document Services Role with dism

The following table shows the syntax to add the Print and Document Services role.

| Commands for Print Services | Comments |
|---|---|
| C:\>dism /online /enable-feature /featurename:Printing-ServerCore-Role | Adds the Print Services role. |
| C:\>dism /online /enable-feature /featurename:Printing-ServerCore-Role-WOW64 | Adds 32-bit Print Server support. |
| C:\>dism /online /enable-feature /featurename:Printing-LPDPrint-Service | Adds the LPD service. |

## Adding the AD CS Role with dism

The following table shows the syntax to add and remove the AD CS role.

| Commands to Add PowerShell | Comments |
|---|---|
| C:\>dism /online /enable-feature /featurename:Certificate Services | Installs the AD CS role. |
| C:\>dism /online /disable-feature /featurename:Certificate Services | Removes the AD CS role. |

## Adding the AD LDS Role with dism

The following table shows the syntax to add and remove the AD LDS role.

| Commands to Add PowerShell | Comments |
|---|---|
| `C:\>dism /online /enable-feature /featurename: DirectoryServices-ADAM-ServerCore` | Installs the AD LDS role. |
| `C:\>dism /online /disable-feature /featurename: DirectoryServices-ADAM-ServerCore` | Removes the AD LDS role. |

### Adding PowerShell with dism

The following table shows the syntax to add PowerShell.

**NOTE**   PowerShell is not supported in Windows Server 2008 Server Core, but it is supported in Windows Server 2008 R2 Server Core.

| Commands to Add PowerShell | Comments |
|---|---|
| `C:\>dism /online /enable-feature /featurename:MicrosoftWindowsPowerShell` | Installs Windows PowerShell. |
| `C:\>\windows\system32\ WindowsPowerShell\v1.0\powershell.exe` | Starts PowerShell. |

## Adding the AD DS Role

You use the **dcpromo** tool with an unattend file to install AD DS on a Windows Server 2008 or Windows Server 2008 R2 Server Core server. The basic syntax is

`dcpromo /unattend:unattend-file`

**NOTE**   Chapter 9, "Promoting and Demoting a Domain Controller (DC)," shows how to create an unattend file and how to use it with **dcpromo**. You can't run the **dcpromo** GUI on a Server Core installation, but you can run it with the unattend file.

# CHAPTER 20

# Configuring Server Core for Remote Administration

This chapter provides information and commands concerning the following topics:

- Using the Server Core Registry Editor
- Enabling access with remote Microsoft Management Consoles (MMCs)
- Configuring the firewall to reply to ping

> **TIP** You should be familiar with Server Core commands when preparing for the 70-642 and 70-643 exams.

> **TIP** If you're running Windows Server 2008 R2, you can run sconfig.cmd to configure some of the remote administration settings. It is not available by default on Windows Server 2008, and you're unlikely to see any test questions on it; however, it's a good menu-driven method of setting up a Server Core installation.

## Using the Server Core Registry Editor

The Server Core Registry Editor (scregedit.wsf) is a script used to modify the registry on Server Core installations. The script is only available on Server Core installations, not full installations of Windows Server 2008 or Windows Server 2008 R2. The basic syntax of the command is

```
cscript %windir%\system32\scregedit.wsf /property value
```

> **TIP** **cscript** is the command-based script host used to execute the script file and must be entered first.

> **TIP** Because the path (%windir%\system32\, normally C:\windows\system32\) is not known to the system, it must be included in the command.

For example, if you want to enable remote desktop connections from other systems to the Server Core installation, you can use the following command:

```
cscript %windir%\system32\scregedit.wsf /ar 0
```

The **/ar** switch enables or disables remote connections. A value of 0 enables remote desktop connections and a value of 1 disables remote desktop connections. The following table shows the common properties and values used with scrededit.wsf.

| scregedit.wsf Command | Comments |
|---|---|
| Allow Remote Desktop connections.<br><br>`/ar 0 | 1`<br>`C:\>cscript %windir%\system32\`<br>`scregedit.wsf /ar 0`<br>`C:\>cscript %windir%\system32\`<br>`scregedit.wsf /ar 1` | You can enable Remote Desktop with a 0 and disable it with a 1. You can view the current setting with the **/v** switch like the following:<br><br>**C:\>cscript %windir%\system32\ scregedit.wsf /ar /v** |
| Require CredSSP.<br><br>`/ar 0 | 1`<br>`C:\>cscript %windir%\system32\`<br>`scregedit.wsf /cs 0`<br>`C:\>cscript %windir%\system32\`<br>`scregedit.wsf /cs 1` | You can allow connections from earlier versions of Windows that don't support Credential Security Support Provider (CredSSP) with a value of 0, or require CredSSP with a value of 1. If the value is 1, the system blocks connections from computers that don't support CredSSP (pre-Windows Vista computers).<br><br>Figure 20-1 shows this setting in the GUI of a full installation of Windows Server 2008 server (not a Server Core server). Notice that it shows that connections are only allowed **From Computers running Desktop with Network Level Authentication (More Secure)**. This is the same setting as **/cs** with a value of 1 to require CredSSP.<br><br>You can view the current setting with the **/v** switch, such as the following:<br><br>**C:\>cscript %windir%\system32\ scregedit.wsf /cs /v**<br><br>**NOTE** CredSSP is an authentication enhancement used with Remote Desktop Protocol 6.1. It provides an extra layer of security by preventing a client from establishing a session without first authenticating. |
| Configure automatic updates.<br><br>`/au 4 | 1`<br>`C:\>cscript %windir%\system32\`<br>`scregedit.wsf /au 4`<br>`C:\>cscript %windir%\system32\`<br>`scregedit.wsf /au 1` | You can enable automatic updates with a 4 and disable it with a 1. You can view the current setting with the **/v** switch, such as the following:<br><br>**C:\>cscript %windir%\system32\ scregedit.wsf /au /v** |

| scregedit.wsf Command | Comments |
|---|---|
| Allow IPsec Monitor remote management.<br><br>/im 0 \| 1<br>C:\>cscript %windir%\system32\<br>scregedit.wsf /im 0<br>C:\>cscript %windir%\system32\<br>scregedit.wsf /im 1 | You can enable remote management using the IPsec Monitor with a value of 1 and disable it with a 0. You can view the current setting with the /v switch, such as the following:<br><br>**C:\>cscript %windir%\system32\ scregedit.wsf /im /v** |

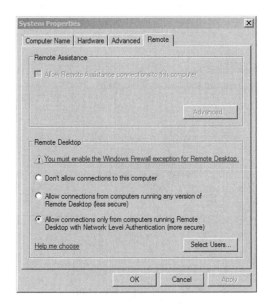

**Figure 20-1**   Enabling Remote Desktop and requiring CredSSP

# Enabling Access with Remote Microsoft Management Consoles (MMCs)

After you add the roles using **ocsetup** or **dism** (as shown in Chapter 19, "Adding Roles to Server Core"), it's often easier to configure the role with the Microsoft Management Console (MMC) from a remote computer. For example, if you enable the DHCP server role on a Server Core computer named SC1, you can then use another computer with a full installation (not Server Core) to remotely connect to SC1 and configure the DHCP server role. First, enter the following line at the Server Core prompt to modify the firewall to enable remote administration of the DHCP server:

```
netsh advfirewall firewall set rule group="dhcp server"
new enable=yes
```

You can then use the DHCP console from another server with the following steps.

| Step | Action |
|------|--------|
| 1. | Launch the DHCP Server console. |
| 2. | Right-click **DHCP** and select **Add Server**. Type the name of the Server Core server hosting DHCP. <br><br> Your display should look similar to Figure 20-2. <br><br> **NOTE**  In the display, the sc1.pearson.pub has already been added to the DHCP console and shows in the background. This enables you to see what it looks like when it's been added. Notice that the dc1.pearson.pub DHCP server has up arrows on the IPv4 and IPv6 nodes indicating that the server has been authorized and scopes have been configured and activated. However, the Server Core DHCP server has not been authorized yet. |
| 3. | Click **OK** to add the server. |
| 4. | After the server has been added, you can right-click the server and select **Authorize**. You can then configure the DHCP server from the console. |

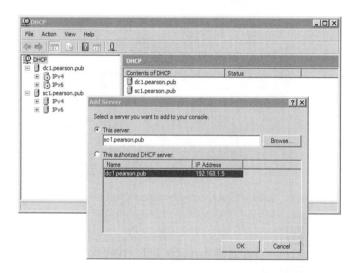

**Figure 20-2**  Adding a Server Core DHCP server to the DHCP console

You can enable remote administration using any MMC with the following command:

```
netsh advfirewall firewall set rule group="remote administration"
new enable=yes
```

You can disable remote administration using any MMC with the following command. Note that you only change **enable=yes** to **enable=no**.

```
netsh advfirewall firewall set rule group="remote administration"
new enable=no
```

You can also enable remote administration of specific consoles (such as just the DHCP server console as shown earlier). Use the following syntax to enable specific consoles:

```
netsh advfirewall firewall set rule group="rule-group-name"
new enable=yes
```

The following table shows the rule group name that you substitute in the command.

| Rule Group Name | Enables You to Use This MMC Snap-In |
| --- | --- |
| DHCP Server | DHCP |
| Remote Event Log Management | Event Viewer |
| Remote Services Management | Services |
| File and Printer Sharing | Shared Folders |
| Remote Scheduled Tasks Management | Task Scheduler |
| Performance Logs and Alerts and File and Printer Sharing | Reliability and Performance |
| Remote Volume Management | Disk Management |
| Windows Firewall Remote Management | Windows Firewall with Advanced Security |
| Remote Administration | All MMC snap-ins |

The preceding table is not all inclusive. To view a list of all rule groups, use the following command:

```
netsh advfirewall firewall show rule name=all | more
```

> **TIP**   The **| more** at the end of the command enables you to view the rules one screen at a time. Use **Enter** to show the rules one line at a time, or the spacebar to show the rules one page at a time. If you press Ctrl+C, it stops the display.

# Configuring the Firewall to Reply to Ping

By default, the firewall on the Server Core installation blocks all ping requests. Pings from other servers time out because the echo requests are not answered with echo replies. If you want to enable the server to reply to pings, use the following command:

```
netsh firewall set icmpsetting 8
```

To disable pings, use the following command:

```
netsh firewall set icmpsetting 8 disable
```

# CHAPTER 21

# Manipulating Services

This chapter provides information and commands concerning the following topics:

- Stopping and starting services with the **net** command
- Manipulating services with **sc**
- Manipulating services with **wmic**

> **TIP** You should be familiar with the **sc**, **net start**, and **wmic** commands when preparing for the 70-640 and 70-643 exams.

## Stopping and Starting Services with the net Command

A basic way to start and stop a service from the command prompt is with the **net** command. The basic syntax to start a service is

```
net start service-name
```

Similarly, the basic syntax to stop a service is

```
net stop service-name
```

For example, if SRV records aren't registered in DNS, you can stop and restart the netlogon service with the following commands:

```
net stop netlogon
net start netlogon
```

> **TIP** The netlogon service registers SRV records on a DNS server. The SRV records are needed to locate servers (such as domain controllers). If the SRV records aren't created, you can force their creation by stopping and restarting the netlogon service.

Similarly, if a network is using a Key Management Server (KMS) but the KMS SRV records aren't registered in DNS, you can run the following commands.

| Command | Operating System |
|---------|------------------|
| net stop slsvc<br>net start slsvc | Use on Windows Server 2008 server hosting KMS. |
| net stop sppsvc<br>net start sppsvc | Use on Windows Server 2008 R2 server hosing KMS. |

The hardest part about running the **net stop** and **net start** commands is identifying the service name. One way is from the **Services** console. You can launch the **Services** console from the **Administrative Tools** menu, browse to any service, and double-click it to see the properties. Figure 21-1 shows the netlogon service open. Notice that the **Service Name** is **Netlogon**.

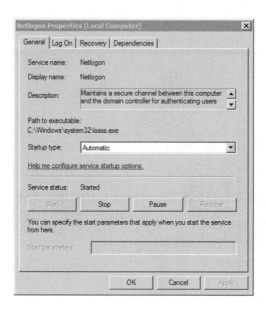

**Figure 21-1** Viewing properties of a service

**TIP** Some services (such as the netlogon service) have the same name used for both the **Service Name** and the **Display Name**; however, many services use different names. You must use the **Service Name** in the **net stop** and **net start** commands.

## Manipulating Services with sc

You can also use the service controller (**sc**) command to start, stop, and manipulate services from the command line. This enables you to perform many of the same functions from the command line as you can do through the **Services** console.

Some of the common functions are shown in the following table.

| Command | Description |
|---|---|
| `C:\>sc query`<br><br>`SERVICE_NAME: Netlogon`<br>`DISPLAY_NAME: Netlogon`<br>`    TYPE              : 20  WIN32_`<br>`SHARE_PROCESS`<br>`    STATE             : 4   RUNNING`<br>`                        (STOPPABLE,`<br>`PAUSABLE, IGNORES_SHUTDOWN)`<br>`        WIN32_EXIT_CODE   : 0  (0x0)`<br>`        SERVICE_EXIT_CODE : 0  (0x0)`<br>`        CHECKPOINT        : 0x0`<br>`        WAIT_HINT         : 0x0` | Lists all *running* services and drivers. The result on the left shows the results for a single service (the net-logon service), but the actual output shows details on all running services and drivers. The output can be quite extensive.<br><br>Of course, you can capture the entire output with the redirect (>) symbol as **sc query > services.txt**<br><br>**TIP** The service name shows the name of the service that you can use in other commands. |
| `sc query state= all │ inactive`<br>`C:\>sc query state= all`<br>`C:\>sc query state= inactive` | Lists all services including services stopped, running, or paused.<br><br>**NOTE** There is no space between **state** and = (**state=**), and there is a space between = and **all** (**= all**).<br><br>You can use **state= inactive** to list only services that are stopped or **state= all** to list all services, including those that are running and those that are stopped. |
| `sc query type= service │ driver │ all`<br>`C:\>sc query type= service`<br>`C:\>sc query type= driver`<br>`C:\>sc query type= all` | Lists all running services or drivers. Notice that there is no space between **type** and = (**type=**), and there is a space between = and **service** (**= service**).<br><br>You can also use **type= driver** to list drivers instead of services, or **type= all** to list both. |

| Command | Description |
|---|---|
| Sc query *service-name*<br>C:\>sc query netlogon<br>SERVICE_NAME: Netlogon<br>DISPLAY_NAME: Netlogon<br>    TYPE          : 20  WIN32_<br>SHARE_PROCESS<br>    STATE         : 4   RUNNING<br>                   (STOPPABLE,<br>PAUSABLE, IGNORES_SHUTDOWN)<br>    WIN32_EXIT_CODE  : 0  (0x0)<br>    SERVICE_EXIT_CODE : 0  (0x0)<br>    CHECKPOINT      : 0x0<br>    WAIT_HINT       : 0x0 | Lists the details on a specific service. The example shows the details on the netlogon service, but you can use the same command for any specific service by specifying the name.<br><br>As a reminder, the *service-name* is the same name you can see in the SERVICE_NAME output from the **sc query** command. |
| sc stop *service-name*<br>C:\>sc stop netlogon | Stop a service. The example stops the netlogon service. You can substitute the service name for any service to stop it. |
| sc start *service-name*<br>C:\>sc start netlogon | You can start the service with the **sc start** command.<br><br>This example starts the netlogon service, but you can substitute the service name for any service to start it. |
| sc pause *service-name*<br>C:\>sc pause netlogon | Pauses the service.<br><br>**NOTE** Not all services can be paused. If the service is listed as PAUSABLE (in the **State** property), it can be paused. If the service is listed as NOT_PAUSABLE, it cannot be paused. |
| sc continue *service-name*<br>C:\>sc continue netlogon | You can restart a paused service with the **continue** command. |

**NOTE** One drawback from stopping and starting services with the **sc** command is that it doesn't let you know when the service stopped or started, like **net stop** and **net start** commands do. However, you can use the **sc query** *service-name* command to identify the current state of the service.

# Manipulating Services with wmic

You can also manipulate services with the Windows Management Instrumentation command-line (**wmic**) tool.

> **NOTE**  WMI is used to query and configure local and remote systems for a wide variety of purposes. **wmic** is the command-line tool used to execute many WMI commands. This section covers only the use of WMIC for services, but **wmic** can be used for much more.

**wmic** is a shell command. You can type **wmic** from the command prompt and press **Enter** to enter the **wmic** shell. The **wmic** shell prompt starts in the root\cli name space, and you can then enter commands from there. For example, to get a listing of all services on a local computer, you can use the **service** command after entering the shell like the following:

```
C:\>wmic
wmic:root\cli>service
```

You can also enter the full **wmic** command from the command prompt by preceding it with **wmic**. For example, the following command provides the same output as the previous command:

```
C:\>wmic service
```

If you want to get information on a remote system, add the **/node:**computer-*name* switch to the **wmic** command like the following:

```
C:\>wmic /node:dc1 service
```

If the remote system's firewall doesn't allow WMI commands, the command will fail. You need to configure the firewall to allow **wmic** commands first, as shown in the following section.

## Configuring the Firewall to Allow wmic

If you want to run **wmic** commands on remote computers, you need to ensure the firewall is configured to allow the remote connections. The primary error you see that indicates that WMI commands are prevented by the firewall is "The RPC server is unavailable."

> **TIP**  You see the error "The RPC server is unavailable" if the remote system is unreachable. You can try the **ping** command to determine whether the remote system is operational and verify you're using the correct host name. If **ping** works but **wmic** is not working, check the firewall.

You can configure the firewall to allow **wmic** commands by allowing the Windows Management Instrumentation (WMI) program through the firewall. Figure 21-2 shows the Windows Firewall Settings screen on a Windows Server 2008 system. You can get to this screen by starting the **Control Panel**, entering **Firewall** in the **Search Control**

**Panel** text box, and selecting **Allow a Program through Windows Firewall**. Ensure that the checkbox for **Windows Management Instrumentation (WMI)** is checked.

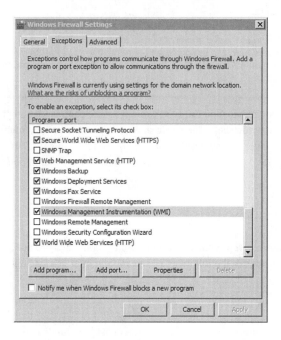

**Figure 21-2**   Enabling WMI in the firewall

## Using the wmic service list Command

**wmic** includes the service command, which you can use to query and manipulate services. The most basic **wmic** service command is

```
wmic service list
```

The following table shows some switches you can use with the **wmic service list** command. Each of these commands can be entered on the local computer by omitting the **/node:**computer-*name* switch, or on a remote computer by using the **/node:***computer-name* switch.

| wmic service list Options | Comments |
|---|---|
| Full in table format:<br><br>C:\>**wmic service list**<br>C:\>**wmic /node:dc1 service list** | Includes all the properties in a table format.<br><br>The examples execute the command on the local computer and on a remote computer named DC1. |

| wmic service list Options | Comments |
|---|---|
| Full in list format:<br><br>`C:\>wmic service list full`<br>`C:\>wmic /node:dc1 service list full` | Includes all the properties in a list format. |
| Brief listing:<br><br>`C:\>wmic service list brief`<br>`C:\>wmic /node:dc1 service list brief` | Includes only the following properties: **ExitCode**, **Name**, **ProcessId**, **StartMode**, **State**, and **Status**. |
| Control:<br><br>`C:\>wmic service list control`<br>`C:\>wmic /node:dc1 service list control` | Includes only the following properties: **AcceptPause**, **AcceptStop**, **ErrorControl**, **Name**, **StartMode**, and **StartName**. |
| Instance:<br><br>`C:\>wmic service list instance`<br>`C:\>wmic /node:dc1 service list instance` | Includes only the **Name** property. |
| Status:<br><br>`C:\>wmic service list status`<br>`C:\>wmic/node:dc1 service list status` | Includes the **Name**, **Status**, and **ExitCode** properties. |

## Using the wmic service call Command

The other valuable command you can use with **wmic service** is the **call** command, which enables you to manipulate services. The **wmic service call** commands use a **where** clause to identify the service that will be manipulated by the **call** command. The **where** clause has the following format:

`where caption="`*display-name*`"`

More specifically, if you want to stop a service, use the following format:

`wmic service where caption="`*display-name*`" call stopservice`

For example, if you want to stop the FTP Publishing Service, you can use the following command:

`wmic service where caption="ftp publishing service" call stopservice`

Note that the **net** and **sc** commands use the service name, while the **where** clause of the **wmic service call** command uses the display-name. You can compare these names in Figure 21-3, which shows both the **Service Name** and the **Display Name** for the **FTP Publishing Service**.

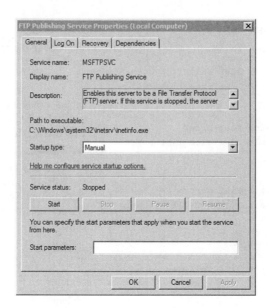

**Figure 21-3**    The FTP Publishing Service properties from the Services console

If you want to stop the FTP Publishing Service, use any of the following commands.

| Stopping the FTP Publishing Service | Comments |
|---|---|
| `C:\>net stop msftpsvc` | Stops the service with the **net** command. |
| `C:\>sc stop msftpsvc` | Stops the service with the **sc** command. |
| `C:\>wmic service where caption="ftp publishing service" call stopservice` | Stops the service with **wmic**. |

The following table shows other uses of the **call** command with **wmic service**.

| wmic service call Command | Comments |
|---|---|
| Modify the start mode of the service.<br><br>`wmic service where caption="`*display-name*`" call changestartmode disabled \| manual \| automatic`<br>`C:\>wmic service where caption="ftp publishing service" call changestartmode disabled` | You can set a service to start automatically, manually, or as disabled by using the **changestartmode** command.<br><br>This refers to the Startup Type of the service. Figure 21-3 shows the Startup Type of the FTP Publishing Service as Manual.<br><br>The example changes the service to disabled. |

| wmic service call Command | Comments |
|---|---|
| Stop or start a service.<br><br>`wmic service where caption="display-name" call stopservice \| startservice`<br>`C:\>wmic service where caption="ftp publishing service" call startservice`<br>`C:\>wmic service where caption="ftp publishing service" call stopservice` | The **call stopservice** and **call startservice** commands stop and start a service, respectively. |
| Pause or resume a service.<br><br>`wmic service where caption="display-name" call pauseservice \| resumeservice`<br>`C:\>wmic service where caption="ftp publishing service" call pauseservice`<br>`C:\>wmic service where caption="ftp publishing service" call resumeservice` | The **call pauseservice** and **call resumeservice** commands pause and resume a service, respectively. |

**TIP**   Any of the commands in the preceding table can be executed on a remote system by adding the **/node:**computer-*name* switch immediately after **wmic**. For example, to change the mode to disabled on a remote computer named dc1, the following command is used:

`wmic /node:dc1 service where caption="ftp publishing service" call changestartmode disabled`

**TIP**   You can also do fuzzy queries with the **like** operator and the percent (%)wildcard if you don't know the exact name. For example: **wmic service where (name like w%)** shows all services that start with "w".

# CHAPTER 22

# Basic Routing on a Server

This chapter provides information and commands concerning the following topics:

- Viewing the routing table with **route print**
- Adding routes to the routing table with **route add**
- Modifying routes in the routing table with **route change**
- Deleting routes from the routing table with **route delete**

> **TIP** You should be familiar with the **route** command when preparing for the 70-642 exam.

## Viewing the Routing Table with route print

The **route** command displays and controls information in the local IP routing table on Windows systems. The **route print -4** command enables you to view the IPv4 routing table.

> **TIP** You can also enter **route print -6** to show only IPv6 information or enter **route print** to show both IPv4 and IPv6 information.

The following text shows a partial output of the **route print** command:

```
C:\>route print
===========================================================================
Interface List
 10 ...00 03 ff 62 13 d7 ...... Intel 21140-Based PCI Fast Ethernet
Adapter
  1 ........................... Software Loopback Interface 1
===========================================================================

IPv4 Route Table
===========================================================================
Active Routes:
Network Destination     Netmask        Gateway      Interface    Metric
        0.0.0.0         0.0.0.0        192.168.1.1  192.168.1.5  276
      127.0.0.0         255.0.0.0      On-link      127.0.0.1    306
      127.0.0.1         255.255.255.255 On-link     127.0.0.1    306
```

```
127.255.255.255     255.255.255.255 On-link       127.0.0.1     306
      192.168.1.0   255.255.255.0   On-link       192.168.1.5   276
      192.168.1.5   255.255.255.255 On-link       192.168.1.5   276
    192.168.1.255   255.255.255.255 On-link       192.168.1.5   276
        224.0.0.0   240.0.0.0       On-link       127.0.0.1     306
        224.0.0.0   240.0.0.0       On-link       192.168.1.5   276
  255.255.255.255   255.255.255.255 On-link       127.0.0.1     306
  255.255.255.255   255.255.255.255 On-link       192.168.1.5   276
===================================================================
Persistent Routes:
  Network Address          Netmask  Gateway Address  Metric
        0.0.0.0            0.0.0.0    192.168.1.1  Default
===================================================================
```

The **route print** command has the following sections.

| route print Section | Comments |
|---|---|
| Interface list | Lists all the physical and virtual network interface cards on the system. |
| IPv4 Route table | Lists the routes known by the system and the path to the default gateway for unknown routes. |
| IPv4 Persistent Routes | Persistent routes are stored in the system and remain even after reboots. The persistent route shown in the output is from the default gateway configured on the NIC. |

The meat of the **route print** output is in the routing table. It has five columns, as explained in the following table.

| Routing Table Column | Comments |
|---|---|
| Network Destination | Identifies the network destination. It is combined with the network mask to identify the network ID of the network. <br><br> **TIP**  The network destination of 0.0.0.0 indicates an unknown network and the default gateway is used. In other words, this path is used for all networks that are not known to the system. |
| Netmask | The netmask, or subnet mask, is matched to the network destination to determine the network ID of the destination network. |
| Gateway | Identifies the IP address of the router that the traffic must pass through to get to other networks. <br><br> **TIP**  On-link indicates that the system is connected to the network. The server used in the **route print** command is connected to the 192.168.1.0/24 network. |

| Routing Table Column | Comments |
|---|---|
| Interface | Shows the IP address of the network interface card used to reach the network. Most systems have a single NIC, and it is used to reach all networks (except for the loopback address). |
| | **NOTE**   The address of 127.0.0.1 is the loopback address used internally by the system. |
| Metric | Identifies the cost. Systems use a least cost path so if there are multiple paths to the same network, the path with the lowest cost, or lowest metric, is used. |

## Adding Routes to the Routing Table with route add

You can add additional routes to a routing table for any system, even if the system is not a router.

Consider Figure 22-1, which shows a network with three subnets separated by two routers. Server2 is in Subnet B and is configured with a default gateway of 192.168.1.1. Because Server2 is in the 192.168.1.0/24 network, the routing table lists all traffic destined for this network with a gateway of On-link, and all unknown traffic uses the gateway of 192.168.1.1.

**NOTE**   The /24 in the address indicates the subnet mask is 255.255.255.0. More specifically, it indicates the first 24 bits of the IP address are a 1 and the last 8 bits are a 0.

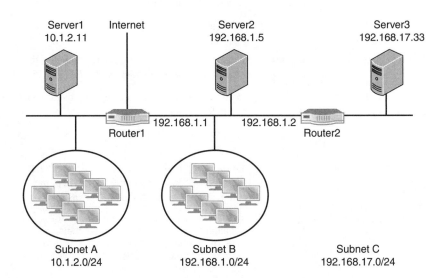

**Figure 22-1**   Network with three subnets

**NOTE**   The output from the **route print** command shown earlier is from Server2.

Server2's default gateway is192.168.1.1 (Router1). Any traffic that is not on the 192.168.1.0/24 subnet is routed to the default gateway. This gives Server2 a path to the 10.1.2.0/24 subnet and the Internet. However, Server2 doesn't have a path to Subnet C unless an additional route is added.

You can add routes to other networks using the **route add** command. The basic syntax is

```
route [-p] add network-destination mask network-mask gateway [metric
metric]
```

The following table shows some common uses of the **route add** command. These examples add two additional routes to the routing table on Server2 (shown in Figure 22-1). One route goes to the 192.168.17.0 subnet, and the second route goes to Server3 (at 192.168.17.33).

| route add Command | Comments |
|---|---|
| Add a route to a network.<br><br>`C:\>route add 192.168.17.0`<br>`mask 255.255.255.0`<br>`192.168.1.2 metric 300`<br>`C:\>route add 192.168.17.0`<br>`mask 255.255.255.0`<br>`192.168.1.2` | The example adds a route to the 192.168.17.0 network with a subnet mask of 255.255.255.0 (192.168.17.0/24) through Router2 (at address 12.168.1.2). It uses a metric, or cost of 300.<br><br>**NOTE**   Because there is only one path to the distant subnet, the metric is meaningless. It can be omitted as shown in the second example.<br><br>If you run **route print** after this command, you see the following line:<br><br>`192.168.17.0    255.255.255.0`<br>`192.168.1.2     192.168.1.5     21` |
| Add a route to a specific computer.<br><br>`C:\>route add 192.168.17.33`<br>`mask 255.255.255.255`<br>`192.168.1.2` | When adding a route to a specific computer, the network mask is always set as 255.255.255.255.<br><br>If you run **route print** after this command, you see the following line:<br><br>`192.168.17.33  255.255.255.255`<br>`192.168.1.2     192.168.1.5     21` |
| Add a persistent route.<br><br>`C:\>route -p add`<br>`192.168.17.0 mask`<br>`255.255.255.0 192.168.1.2` | The **-p** switch makes the route persistent so that it survives reboots. Without the **-p** switch, the route will not appear if the system was rebooted.<br><br>**NOTE**   If you create a route and want to change it to persistent, just repeat the command with the **-p** switch. You don't have to use **route change** or delete the route before re-creating it. |

If you ran the **route print -4** command after adding the persistent route, it should look similar to the following listing:

```
IPv4 Route Table
===========================================================================
Active Routes:
Network Destination     Netmask          Gateway         Interface  Metric
          0.0.0.0             0.0.0.0  192.168.1.1     192.168.1.5    276
        127.0.0.0           255.0.0.0  On-link           127.0.0.1    306
        127.0.0.1     255.255.255.255  On-link           127.0.0.1    306
  127.255.255.255     255.255.255.255  On-link           127.0.0.1    306
      192.168.1.0       255.255.255.0  On-link         192.168.1.5    276
      192.168.1.5     255.255.255.255  On-link         192.168.1.5    276
    192.168.1.255     255.255.255.255  On-link         192.168.1.5    276
     192.168.17.0       255.255.255.0  192.168.1.2     192.168.1.5     21
    192.168.17.33     255.255.255.255  192.168.1.2     192.168.1.5     21
        224.0.0.0           240.0.0.0  On-link           127.0.0.1    306
        224.0.0.0           240.0.0.0  On-link         192.168.1.5    276
  255.255.255.255     255.255.255.255  On-link           127.0.0.1    306
  255.255.255.255     255.255.255.255  On-link         192.168.1.5    276
===========================================================================
Persistent Routes:
  Network Address          Netmask  Gateway Address  Metric
          0.0.0.0          0.0.0.0      192.168.1.1  Default
     192.168.17.0    255.255.255.0      192.168.1.2       1
===========================================================================
```

The routes that were added from the previous examples are bold in this listing. The metric of 21 was assigned automatically when a metric was not provided in the **route add** command, and a metric of 1 was assigned in the persistent route.

## Modifying Routes in the Routing Table with route change

The following syntax changes a route:

```
route change network-destination mask network-mask
gateway [metric metric]
```

For example, imagine that you created a route with the following command:

```
route add 192.168.17.0 mask 255.255.255.0 192.168.1.22
```

You now realize that the gateway should be 192.168.1.2 (not 192.168.1.22). You can just reissue the command using **change** and the correct gateway as follows:

```
route change 192.168.17.0 mask 255.255.255.0 192.168.1.2
```

> **NOTE**  You can also delete the route using the **route delete** command, and then add the route again using the **route add** command.

## Deleting Routes from the Routing Table with route delete

The syntax to delete a route from the routing table is

```
route delete network-destination
```

For example, to delete the two routes added using commands in the previous section, use the following two commands:

```
route delete 192.168.17.0
route delete 192.168.17.33
```

> **NOTE**  You don't have to do anything special to delete a persistent route. Persistent routes are deleted when the route is deleted from the routing table.

# CHAPTER 23

# Working with Printers

This chapter provides information and commands concerning the following topics:

- Publishing printers to Active Directory with **pubprn.vbs**
- Migrating printers with **printbrm**
- Controlling the print queue with **prnqctl.vbs**

> **TIP** You should be familiar with the printer commands when preparing for the 70-642 exam.

## Publishing Printers to Active Directory with pubprn.vbs

You can use the pubprn.vbs script to publish printers to Active Directory. pubprn.vbs is located in the c:\windows\system32\printing_admin_scripts\en-us folder.

> **TIP** For installations outside the U.S., you might not have the en-us folder. However, you can locate the pubprn.vbs file with this command from the root of C: **dir pubprn. vbs /s**.

The basic syntax is

```
[cscript]
c:\windows\system32\printing_admin_scripts\en-us\pubprn.vbs
[server | UNC-printer-path] "LDAP://DN"
```

The following table describes the different elements of the pubprn.vbs script.

| pubprn Syntax Element | Comments |
|---|---|
| cscript | **cscript** is the command-based script host used to execute the pubprn.vbs script file. When used, the output goes to the command prompt. If omitted, the output shows in dialog boxes. <br><br> **TIP** While **cscript** is sometimes optional when running scripts from the command prompt, you should use it to get consistent results with the printer scripts. Some scripts run without it but other scripts do not. |

| pubprn Syntax Element | Comments |
|---|---|
| `c:\windows\system32\` `printing_admin_scripts\` `en-us` | This is the path to the folder holding the pubprn.vbs file.<br><br>**NOTE** Because this path is not known to Windows by default, you either need to include the path in the command or change the directory before executing the command. For example, you can change to the directory with the following command: **cd \windows\system32\ printing_admin_scripts\en-us**. |
| `Server \| UNC-printer-` `path` | This is the name of a print server sharing one or more printers. If you omit the server name, the local computer is used. The Universal Naming Convention (UNC) path can be used to point to a specific printer on a server. If the UNC isn't used, the command uses all shared printers on the target server.<br><br>**NOTE** UNC paths have the format of \\*server-name\share-name*. In this case, the format is \\*server-name\shared-printer-name*. |
| `LDAP://` | **LDAP://** must be entered exactly and with LDAP in uppercase.<br><br>**TIP** This is one of the few times when the case of the command matters. |
| `DN` | This is the distinguished name (dn) of the OU where the printer will be published. For example, if you want to identify an OU named printers in the pearson.pub domain, use the following DN: ou=printers,dc=pearson,dc=pub. The path to the OU must exist or the command will fail.<br><br>**NOTE** Chapter 7, "Using Basic ds Commands," covers distinguished names. |

For example, if you want to publish a single printer shared as Color_Laser on a server named DC2, in an OU named Printers in the pearson.pub domain, you can use the following command:

```
cscript
c:\windows\system32\printing_admin_scripts\en-us\pubprn.vbs
  \\dc2\color_laser "LDAP://ou=printers,dc=pearson,dc=pub"
```

When complete, the command shows the following output:

```
Published printer: LDAP://DC1.pearson.pub/CN=DC2-Color_Laser,
ou=printers,dc=pearson,dc=pub
```

Figure 23-1 shows the printer published into Active Directory Users and Computers from the preceding command.

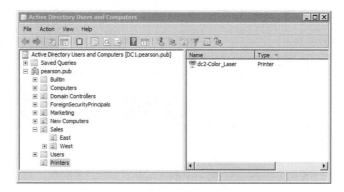

**Figure 23-1**  Printer published from the pubprn.vbs script

**TIP**  The OU must exist in the domain for the command to work. You can add the OU using any method including the **dsadd** command: **dsadd ou** *ou-dn*.

If you want to publish all printers shared on a server named Print1 in an OU named Printers in the pearson.pub domain, you can use the following command:

```
cscript
c:\windows\system32\printing_admin_scripts\en-us\pubprn.vbs dc2
 "LDAP://ou=printers,dc=pearson,dc=pub"
```

You can also publish printers from the printer properties dialog box by selecting **List in the Directory**, as shown in Figure 23-2.

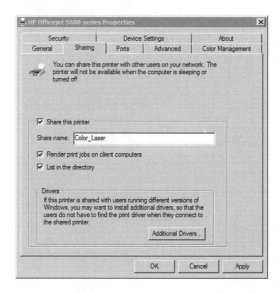

**Figure 23-2**  Publishing a printer by selecting **List in the Directory**

## Migrating Printers with printbrm

You can migrate printers from one print server to another print server with the **printbrm.exe** tool. The tool is located in the c:\windows\system32\spool\tools folder. This tool can be used to back up, restore, and migrate printer information.

> **NOTE**  Because this path is not known to Windows by default, you either need to include the path in the command or change the directory before executing the command. For example, you can change to the directory with the command **cd \windows\system32\spool\tools**.

The switches you use are listed in the following table.

> **NOTE**  Because printbrm.exe is an executable file (not a script like pubprn.vbs), the **cscript** command is not needed.

| printbrm Switches | Comments |
|---|---|
| Target server.<br><br>`-s \\server-name`<br>`-s \\dc1` | The **-s** identifies the server that holds the printer information. |
| File name.<br><br>`-f file-name.printerexport`<br>`-f printers.printerexport` | You can name the file whatever you want, but the extension must be **printerexport**. |
| Backup printer information.<br><br>`-b`<br>`printbrm -s \\source-computername`<br>`-b -f file-name.printerexport`<br>`C:\>c:\windows\system32\spool\`<br>`tools\printbrm -s \\dc2 -b -f`<br>`printers.printerexport` | Backs up the printer information to a file.<br><br>The example command retrieves the printer information from DC2 and stores it in a file named **printers.printerexport**. |
| Query the file.<br><br>`-q`<br>`printbrm -q -f`<br>`filename.printerexport`<br>`C:\>c:\windows\system32\spool\`<br>`tools\printbrm -q -f`<br>`printers.printerexport` | You can query the contents of the file with the **-q** switch. It displays a listing of print queues, printer drivers, printer ports, and print processes contained in the file. |
| Restore printer information.<br><br>`-r`<br>`printbrm -s \\target-computer -r`<br>`-f filename.printerexport`<br>`C:\>c:\windows\system32\spool\`<br>`tools\printbrm -s \\dc1 -r -f`<br>`printers.printerexport` | Restores the configuration information from the file to a server.<br><br>The example reads the data from the file named printers.printerexport and restores it on the server named DC1. |

The following steps show how to migrate printers from one print server (named DC2) to another print server (DC1). You can execute both commands on either DC1 or DC2.

| Step | Action |
|---|---|
| 1. | Back up the printers stored on the source computer (DC2) to a file named **dc2printers.printerexport** with this command:<br><br>`C:\>c:\windows\system32\spool\tools\printbrm -s \\dc2 -b -f`<br>`dc2printers.printerexport` |
| 2. | Migrate the printers to the target computer with the following command:<br><br>`C:\>c:\windows\system32\spool\tools\printbrm -s \\dc1 -r -f`<br>`dc2printers.printerexport` |

## Controlling the Print Queue with prnqctl.vbs

The **prnqctl.vbs** script can be used to control the print queue on local and remote computers. The script is located in the c:\windows\system32\printing_admin_scripts\en-us folder. You can use it to pause printing, resume printing, cancel all printing, and print a test page. The basic syntax is as follows:

```
cscript prnqctl.vbs option -p printer-name
[-s remote-computer] [-u user-name -w password]
```

> **TIP**   The *printer-name* is the actual name of the printer, not the share name.

The following table shows some uses of this script.

> **NOTE**   In the following table, the path was changed to the location of the prnqctl.vbs script with the following command:
>
> `cd \Windows\System32\Printing_Admin_Scripts\en-US.`

| prnqctl Command | Comments |
|---|---|
| Pause printing. | The **-z** switch causes the printer to pause. |
| `-z`<br>`C:\Windows\System32\Printing_`<br>`Admin_Scripts\en-US>cscript`<br>`prnqctl.vbs -z -p "HP Officejet`<br>`5600 series"`<br>`C:\Windows\System32\Printing_`<br>`Admin_Scripts\en-US>cscript`<br>`prnqctl.vbs -z -s dc2 -p "HP`<br>`Officejet 5600 series"` | In the first example, the local printer named HP Officejet 5600 series is paused. Because the printer name has spaces in it, it must be enclosed in quotes. Figure 23-3 shows the result after executing this command. The printer is paused.<br><br>The second example pauses the printer on a server named dc2.<br><br>**NOTE**   When using the **-s** switch to connect to a remote computer, the user's credentials are used. If the user doesn't have permissions, the **-u** and **-w** switches must be used to add a username and password. |

| prnqctl Command | Comments |
|---|---|
| Add a username and password.<br><br>`-u username  -w password`<br>`C:\Windows\System32\Printing_`<br>`Admin_Scripts\en-US>`**`cscript`**<br>**`prnqctl.vbs -z -s dc2 - p "HP`**<br>**`Officejet 5600 series" -u`**<br>**`pearson\administrator -w P@ssw0rd`** | This example pauses the printer on the remote system named dc2 using different credentials. |
| Resume printing.<br><br>`-m`<br>`C:\Windows\System32\Printing_`<br>`Admin_Scripts\en-US>`**`cscript`**<br>**`prnqctl.vbs -m -p "HP Officejet`**<br>**`5600 series"`**<br>`C:\Windows\System32\Printing_`<br>`Admin_Scripts\en-US>`**`cscript`**<br>**`prnqctl.vbs -m -s dc2 -p "HP`**<br>**`Officejet 5600 series"`** | The **-m** switch resumes the printer.<br><br>The first example resumes the local printer. The second example resumes the printer on a remote server named dc2. |
| Cancel all printing.<br><br>`-x`<br>`C:\Windows\System32\Printing_`<br>`Admin_Scripts\en-US>`**`cscript`**<br>**`prnqctl.vbs -x -p "HP Officejet`**<br>**`5600 series"`**<br>`C:\Windows\System32\Printing_`<br>`Admin_Scripts\en-US>`**`cscript`**<br>**`prnqctl.vbs -x -s dc2 -p "HP`**<br>**`Officejet 5600 series"`** | The **-x** switch cancels all print jobs spooled to the printer.<br><br>The first example resumes the local printer. The second example resumes the printer on a remote server named dc2. |
| Print a test page.<br><br>`-e`<br>`C:\Windows\System32\Printing_`<br>`Admin_Scripts\en-US>`**`cscript`**<br>**`prnqctl.vbs -e -p "HP Officejet`**<br>**`5600 series"`**<br>`C:\Windows\System32\Printing_`<br>`Admin_Scripts\en-US>`**`cscript`**<br>**`prnqctl.vbs -e -s dc2 -p "HP`**<br>**`Officejet 5600 series"`** | You can send a test page to the printer with the **-e** switch.<br><br>The first example resumes the local printer. The second example resumes the printer on a remote server named dc2. |

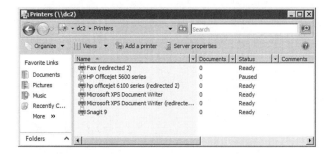

**Figure 23-3**  HP Officejet 5600 series printer paused from **prnqctl.vbs** command

# CHAPTER 24

# Licensing and Activation

This chapter provides information and commands concerning the following topics:

- Managing activation tasks with **slmgr**
- Forcing registration of KMS server SRV records
- Manually creating an SRV record for KMS

> **TIP** You should be familiar with the different licensing and activation steps when preparing for the 70-643 exam.

## Managing Activation Tasks with slmgr

The Software Licensing Management tool (**slmgr.vbs**) is a script you can use to perform several activation tasks. This tool has many capabilities, including simple tasks, such as rearming or activating Windows, to more advanced tasks, such as reviewing the license information or configuring KMS options. The following sections cover the common uses of **slmgr**.

> **NOTE** Although the following sections show the common uses of the **slmgr** tool, they are not all inclusive. The TechNet website has more detailed information: http://technet. microsoft.com/library/ff793433.aspx.

### Managing Basic Tasks with slmgr

The following table shows the syntax of some basic tasks you can perform with **slmgr**.

| slmgr Basic Tasks | Comments |
|---|---|
| Rearm licensing.<br><br>`C:\>slmgr -rearm` | Resets the activation timer or the activation grace period.<br><br>**TIP** Windows Server 2008 can be installed for an evaluation period of up to 60 days without activation. At the end of the activation period, you can rearm it for another 60-day period. You can rearm Windows Server 2008 three times for a possible total of 240 days. |
| Install product key.<br><br>`-ipk product-key`<br>`C:\>slmgr -ipk`<br>`12345-12345-12345-`<br>`12345-12345-12345` | Installs the specified product key. If a key is already installed, the command replaces it. This is needed when you are converting a system to use a different type of activation, such as changing from a retail key to a KMS key.<br><br>**NOTE** The key shown is not a valid key. |

| slmgr Basic Tasks | Comments |
|---|---|
| Activate Windows.<br><br>`C:\>slmgr -ato` | Activates Windows using the installed product key. |
| Clear the product key.<br><br>`C:\>slmgr -cpky` | Removes the product key from the registry to prevent disclosure attacks. |
| Uninstall the product key.<br><br>`C:\>slmgr -upk` | Uninstalls the product key. |

## Viewing License Information with slmgr

There might be times when you just want to view licensing information. You can do so with **slmgr**, as shown in the following table.

| slmgr License Information Switches | Comments |
|---|---|
| Display basic license information.<br><br>`C:\>slmgr -dli` | Displays basic license information similar to Figure 24-1. |
| Display detailed license information.<br><br>`C:\>slmgr -dlv` | Displays more detailed information similar to Figure 24-2. |
| Show expiration date.<br><br>`C:\>slmgr -xpr` | Shows the expiration date of the current license period. If the system is in the grace period, it shows the end of the grace period. If the system is activated by a Key Management Service (KMS) server, it shows the expiration date of the KMS license. Retail licenses and Multiple Access Key (MAK) licenses are permanent and don't have an expiration after they are activated. |

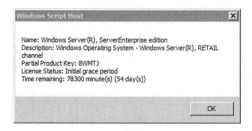

**Figure 24-1**    Basic license information for a server

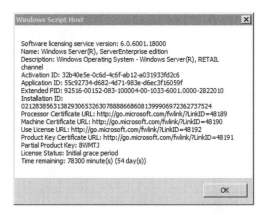

**Figure 24-2**  Detailed license information for a server

**TIP**  If the server is activated, these screens provide different activation information depending on the type of activation.

## Managing KMS Servers with slmgr

If your organization uses a KMS server, you might need to use **slmgr** to manage some of the KMS settings as shown in the following table.

| slmgr Switches for KMS Servers | Comments |
|---|---|
| Set the KMS TCP port.<br><br>**slmgr -sport** *port-number*<br>C:\>**slmgr -sport 1690** | The default port for KMS is 1688, but you can change it with this command. Change it if there is a conflict where another service needs this port. The example changes the port to 1690.<br><br>    **TIP**  If you change the port used on the KMS server, you must also change the port used on the KMS clients. |
| Change the activation interval for KMS clients.<br><br>**slmgr /sai** *interval-in-minutes*<br>C:\>**slmgr -sai 180** | The default activation period for KMS clients is 120 minutes, but you can change it to a number between 15 and 43,200 minutes (30 days). |
| Set the renewal interval.<br><br>**slmgr /sri** *renewal-interval-in-minutes*<br>C:\>**slmgr -sri 10080** | The default renewal period for clients is 10,080 minutes (7 days), but you can change to a time between 15 minutes to 43,200 minutes (30 days). |

| slmgr Switches for KMS Servers | Comments |
|---|---|
| Enable DNS publishing by KMS.<br><br>`C:\>slmgr -sdns` | Ensures that that the KMS server publishes SRV records to the DNS server. This is the default.<br><br>**TIP** If this is enabled and the SRV records are not created on DNS, you might need to restart the service that publishes the records. On Windows Server 2008 the service is slsvc and on Windows Server 2008 R2, it's sppsvc. |
| Disable DNS publishing by KMS.<br><br>`C:\>slmgr -cdns` | Disables publication of the SRV records to the DNS server. |

## Using KMS Activation Keys

If you are converting a system to use KMS activation, you can use the **slmgr** tool. The basic syntax to convert to KMS activation is

```
slmgr -ipk kms-product-key
```

The following table shows the KMS product key for some common Windows products.

**TIP** These keys are the generic product keys and they let clients know that they must activate through a KMS server. The KMS server must have a different key purchased from Microsoft or an authorized reseller.

| Operating System | KMS Product Key |
|---|---|
| Windows 7 Professional | FJ82H-XT6CR-J8D7P-XQJJ2-GPDD4 |
| Windows 7 Enterprise | 33PXH-7Y6KF-2VJC9-XBBR8-HVTHH |
| Windows Web Server 2008 R2 | 6TPJF-RBVHG-WBW2R-86QPH-6RTM4 |
| Windows Server 2008 R2 Standard | YC6KT-GKW9T-YTKYR-T4X34-R7VHC |
| Windows Server 2008 R2 Enterprise | 74YFP-3QFB3-KQT8W-PMXWJ-7M648 |
| Windows Server 2008 R2 Datacenter | 74YFP-3QFB3-KQT8W-PMXWJ-7M648 |
| Windows Server 2008 R2 HPC Edition | FKJQ8-TMCVP-FRMR7-4WR42-3JCD7 |

After installing the key, you can activate the client with the following command:

```
slmgr -ato
```

## Managing KMS Clients with slmgr

If you modify some of the settings on the KMS server, you might also need to modify settings on the KMS clients. The following table shows some common commands.

| slmgr Switches for KMS Clients | Comments |
|---|---|
| Set the name of the KMS server.<br><br>`slmgr -skms KMS-server-name`<br>`C:\>slmgr -skms kms1` | Sets the name of the KMS server for the client. |
| Set the name and port of the KMS server.<br><br>`slmgr -skms KMS-server-`<br>`name:port-number`<br>`C:\>slmgr -skms kms1:1688` | The default port is 1688, so it isn't needed if the port hasn't changed on the KMS server. However, if the port was changed on the KMS server, you can change it on the KMS client with this command. |
| Clear the KMS information.<br><br>`C:\>slmgr -ckms` | Clears the KMS server name and port number on the client. |
| Enable or disable KMS host caching.<br><br>`C:\>slmgr -skhc`<br>`C:\>slmgr -ckhc` | Enables KMS host caching with **-skhc** and disables it with **-ckhc**. |

# Forcing Registration of KMS Server SRV Records

KMS clients locate the KMS server through DNS. More specifically, an SRV record (_vlmcs) in DNS identifies the server running the KMS service. With a typical installation of KMS, a service on the KMS server automatically creates the _vlmcs record on the KMS server.

> **NOTE**   SRV records are easy to identify because they all start with an underscore (such as _vlmcs, _gc, _kerberos, and so on).

This is similar to how the netlogon service automatically creates the SRV records for domain controllers in a domain.

> **TIP**   If the domain SRV records aren't created automatically, you can stop and restart the netlogon service with **net stop netlogon** and **net start netlogon** from the command prompt. Similarly, you can stop and restart either the slsvc or sppsvc service to create the SRV records needed for KMS.

There are a variety of errors that indicate that the SRV Resource Records (RR) are not present in DNS. These include:

- Error 0x8007232B—DNS name does not exist.
- Error 0x800706BA—The RPC server is unavailable.
- Error 0x8007251D—No records found for DNS query.

The solution is to stop and restart the service responsible for creating the _vlmcs record. This service is different on different operating systems that can host the KMS server.

The service, and the steps to restart the service, are shown in the following table.

| Operating System Hosting KMS | Service and Steps |
|---|---|
| Windows Server 2008 (and Windows Vista) | **Slsvc** (Software Licensing Service)<br><br>`C:\>net stop slsvc`<br>`C:\>net start slsvc` |
| Windows Server 2008 R2 (and Windows 7) | **Sppsvc** (Software Protection Service)<br><br>`C:\>net stop sppsvc`<br>`C:\>net start sppsvc` |

# Manually Creating an SRV Record for KMS

You can also manually create the _vlmcs SRV record in DNS. The following steps show you how to create it and verify that it's created correctly.

| Step | Action |
|---|---|
| 1. | Launch the **DNS** console through the **Administrative Tools** menu. |
| 2. | Expand the DNS server, **Forward Lookup Zones**, your domain, and select **_tcp**.<br><br>**NOTE** If _tcp is not present, it indicates that none of the SRV records are created. These are required in a domain and are automatically created by the netlogon service. You can run **net stop netlogon** and then **net start net-logon** to force their creation. |
| 3. | Right-click **_tcp** and select **Other New Records**. |
| 4. | Select **Service Location (SRV)** and click **Create Record**. |
| 5. | Type the following information:<br><br>In the **Service** text box, type **_vlmcs.**<br><br>In the **Protocol** text box, type **_tcp.**<br><br>In the **Port Number** text box, type **1688.**<br><br>In the **Host Offering This Service** text box, type the FQDN of your server.<br><br>**NOTE** The default values of the **Priority** and **Weight** are **0**, and they can remain as 0.<br><br>Your display should look similar to Figure 24-3. Click **OK**.<br><br>Figure 24-4 shows what the record looks like in the DNS console. |

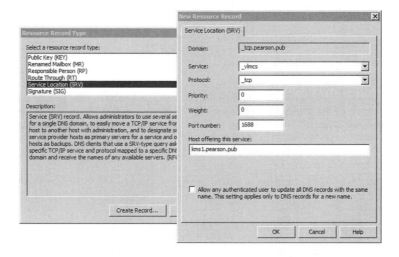

**Figure 24-3**  Creating a _vlmcs SRV record in DNS

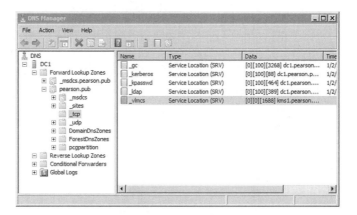

**Figure 24-4**  Viewing the _vlmcs SRV record in DNS

You can verify that the record was created correctly and users can reach it with the **nslookup** command, as shown in the following text:

```
C:\>nslookup -type=srv _vlmcs._tcp
Server:  dc1.pearson.pub
Address:  192.168.1.5


_vlmcs._tcp.pearson.pub SRV service location:
        priority     = 0
```

```
        weight        = 0
        port          = 1688
        svr hostname  = kms1.pearson.pub
dc1.pearson.pub internet address = 192.168.1.7
```

**TIP**   The first two lines of the **nslookup** response require a reverse lookup zone and a PTR record on the DNS server. However, even if a reverse lookup zone or a PTR record is not present, you still should be able to view the last six lines of the **nslookup** output that show the _vlmcs record (as long as the _vlmcs record is created correctly).

# CHAPTER 25

# Using netsh

This chapter provides information and commands concerning the following topics:

- Understanding **netsh**
- Understanding **netsh** contexts
- Configuring IPv4 with **netsh**
- Configuring an IPv6 address with **netsh**
- Disabling IPv6 in Windows Server 2008

**TIP** You should be familiar with the **netsh** command when preparing for the 70-640, 70-642, and 70-646 exams.

## Understanding netsh

The Net Shell (**netsh**) command is a rich command-line scripting tool that enables you to display and modify the network configuration of local and remote computers. You can run **netsh** commands from the **netsh** prompt, from the command prompt, or from a batch file.

For example, the following table shows different ways you can create a rule to open port 6789 on the firewall, and how to delete the rule.

| Methods of Using netsh | Comments |
|---|---|
| `C:\>netsh`<br>`netsh>advfirewall`<br>`netsh advfirewall>firewall`<br>`netsh advfirewall firewall>add rule name`<br>`= "open port 6789" dir = in action =`<br>`allow protocol = tcp localport = 6789`<br>`Ok.`<br>`netsh advfirewall firewall>delete rule`<br>`name = "open port 6789"`<br>`Deleted 1 rule(s).`<br>`Ok.` | You can enter the **netsh** shell and enter the commands. The benefit of doing it this way is that after you enter context, you can type **help** or **?** to get a list of possible commands and contexts.<br><br>First, type **netsh** to access the shell. Next, enter **advfirewall** to enter the advfirewall context. You can then create the rule with the **add rule** statement.<br><br>You can delete rules using the **delete rule** statement and the name of the rule. |

| Methods of Using netsh | Comments |
|---|---|
| `C:\>netsh advfirewall firewall add rule`<br>`name = "Open6789" dir = in action = allow`<br>`protocol = tcp localport = 6789`<br>`Ok.`<br>`C:\>netsh advfirewall firewall delete`<br>`rule name = "Open6789"`<br>`Deleted 1 rule(s).`<br>`Ok.` | You can enter the entire line from the command line (or put it into a batch file). You are entering the same data but instead of entering it one command at a time to reach the **netsh advfirewall** firewall context, you enter all the data at the same time.<br><br>Similarly, you can delete the rule with a single-line entry. |

Figure 25-1 shows how these commands look when entered at the command prompt. When using the **netsh** command, you can see how the context changes as commands are entered.

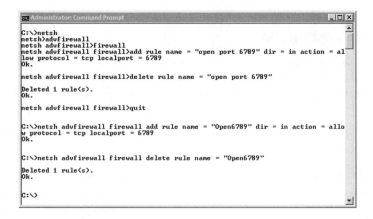

**Figure 25-1**   Using **netsh** commands

## Understanding netsh Contexts

The **netsh** command has multiple command contexts. Each time you enter a context, you have a different set of commands you can use. For example, if you are in the **netsh interface** context, the following commands are available to you.

| Context | Description |
|---|---|
| `netsh interface>? or help` | Displays a list of commands. |
| `netsh interface>6to4` | Changes to the 'netsh interface 6to4' context. |
| `netsh interface>ipv4` | Changes to the 'netsh interface ipv4' context. |

| Context | Description |
|---|---|
| netsh interface>ipv6 | Changes to the 'netsh interface ipv6' context. |
| netsh interface>tcp | Changes to the 'netsh interface tcp' context. |
| netsh interface>teredo | Changes to the 'netsh interface teredo' context. |
| netsh interface>httpstunnel | Changes to the 'netsh interface httpstunnel' context. |
| netsh interface>portproxy | Changes to the 'netsh interface portproxy' context. |
| netsh interface>set | Sets configuration information. |
| netsh interface>show | Displays information. |
| netsh interface>dump | Displays a configuration script. |

If you instead enter the **advfirewall** command, you have access to a different set of commands associated with the advfirewall context. You can view the available commands by entering **help** or **?** at any context command.

Some of the contexts you might use with Windows Server 2008 are listed in the following table.

| Context | Description |
|---|---|
| Interface (IPv4 and IPv6)<br><br>netsh>interface ipv4<br>netsh interface ipv4><br>netsh>interface ipv6<br>netsh interface ipv6> | You can display and configure IPv4 and IPv6 information for network interfaces from the ipv4 and ipv6 shell contexts. Previous examples in this book (and at the end of this chapter) show how you can configure the IPv4 configuration for a system. There are also many additional commands you can use to view information. |
| Windows firewall with advanced security<br><br>netsh>advfirewall<br>netsh advfirewall>show allprofiles | You can use **netsh advfirewall** commands to work with the Windows Firewall with Advanced Security. These commands help with the creation, administration, and monitoring of Windows Firewall and IPsec and can be useful when configuring Windows Firewall with Advanced Security settings to a large number of computers. You can embed the commands in a batch file to automate the configuration of the systems. |
| Windows firewall<br><br>netsh>firewall | This command displays and configures firewall settings.<br><br>**NOTE** This context has been deprecated in favor of the advfirewall firewall context. It modifies only firewall rules for the domain and private profiles. |

| Context | Description |
|---|---|
| Wired local area network (**lan**)<br><br>`netsh>lan`<br>`netsh lan>show profiles` | You can use the **netsh** local area network (**lan**) context to configure and manage 802.3 wired Ethernet connectivity. If you have computers that connect IEEE 802.1x servers for authentication, you can configure the security settings here. You can also display information about network adapter drivers, network profiles, and more. As an example, the **show profiles** command shows any existing wired profiles on the system.<br><br>**NOTE**   This context needs the Wired AutoConfig Service (dot3svc) to be running. |
| Wireless Local Area Network (**wlan**)<br><br>`netsh>wlan`<br>`netsh wlan>show profiles`<br>`netsh wlan>show alltt` | You can use the **netsh** wireless local area network (**wlan**) context to configure and manage 802.11 wireless connectivity and security settings. Additionally, the **netsh wlan** commands can display information about 802.11 wireless adapter drivers, wireless network profiles, and more.<br><br>As an example, the **show profiles** command shows a list of any existing profiles, wireless adapters, and networks.<br><br>**NOTE**   This context needs the Wireless AutoConfig Service (wlansvc) to be running. |
| Windows Hypertext Transfer Protocol (**winhttp**)<br><br>`netsh>winhttp`<br>`netsh winhttp>show proxy` | You can use the **winhttp** context to configure proxy and tracing settings for Windows HTTP. For example, if you want to view current proxy settings, you can use **show proxy**.<br><br>**TIP**   A result of "Direct access (no proxy server)" indicates a proxy server hasn't been configured. |

No matter which context you enter, you have several core commands available to you. Some of these commands are shown in the following table.

| Command | Description |
|---|---|
| `..`<br>`netsh winhttp>..`<br>`netsh>` | Moves the context up one level. |
| `alias`<br>`netsh>alias nic "local area connection"`<br><br>`netsh>alias`<br>`nic      local area con-`<br>`nection` | Creates an alias that can be used within the **netsh** session. An alias is one string of characters that can take the place of another string of characters.<br><br>The example shows how to create an alias named **nic** to represent "local area connection".<br><br>When entered by itself, it lists all known aliases just like **show alias**. |

| Command | Description |
|---------|-------------|
| unalias *alias-name*<br>netsh>**unalias nic** | You can delete an existing alias with the **unalias** command. The alias is also deleted if you exit **netsh**.<br><br>**TIP**  The existing alias name must be entered with the exact case (uppercase and lowercase). In other words, **unalias NIC** does not work in this example. |
| bye, exit, or quit<br>netsh>**bye**<br>C:\> | Exits **netsh**. |
| dump<br>netsh>**dump**<br>netsh>**dump > c:\data\**<br>**config.txt** | Displays all of the current **netsh** context configuration data. You can execute this from the command prompt to redirect the output to a text file. The text file can then be used to reconfigure the system with the **exec** command. |
| exec *scriptfile*<br>netsh>**exec c:\data\**<br>**config.txt** | Executes a script file. This can be used to reconfigure a computer using the settings in the script file. You can create the script file with the **dump** command. |
| help or ?<br>netsh>**help** | Displays help. Help information includes commands that can be listed in any context and the current context. |
| set file [open \| append<br>\| close] *file*<br>netsh>**set file open**<br>**c:\data\netsh.txt**<br>netsh>**set file append**<br>**c:\data\netsh.txt**<br>netsh>**set file close** | Copies all data from the **netsh** session to a file. You can use the **set file** command to capture all the activity in your session. The **open** command creates a new file. **append** appends the data to an existing file.<br><br>The **close** command stops sending the data to the file. Note that you don't enter the name of the file in the **close** command. |
| set machine<br>set machine [name<br>=] *computer* [user =<br>*DomainName\UserName*]<br>[pwd = ] [*Password* \| *]<br>netsh>**set machine name**<br>**= dc1 user = pearson\**<br>**administrator pwd =**<br>**P@ssw0rd**<br>[dc1] netsh> | You can use the **set machine** command to connect to a remote system and perform the tasks on it. The default is the local system. For example, if you want to use **netsh** to administer a server named DC1 in the Pearson domain, you can use the Pearson\Administrator account with the administrator's password (P@ssw0rd in the example). The prompt changes to include the remote computer's name. |

| Command | Description |
|---|---|
| `set mode [ online \| offline ]`<br>`netsh>set mode online`<br>`netsh>set mode offline` | You can set the mode to online or offline. In online mode, **netsh** commands are run immediately after you type them and press **Enter**. In offline mode, **netsh** commands are saved and can be run with the **commit** command or aborted with the **abort** command. |
| `abort`<br>`netsh>abort` | The **abort** command discards any changes made in offline mode. It does not have any effect if executed in online mode. |
| `commit`<br>`netsh>commit` | The **commit** command commits any changes made in the offline mode. It does not have any effect in online mode. |
| `show`<br>`netsh>show alias`<br>`netsh>show helper`<br>`netsh>show mode` | You can view alias, helper, and mode information with the **show** command. Aliases aren't created by default but many default helper DLLs are available by default to provide help in different contexts. |

## Configuring IPv4 with netsh

The **netsh** command is presented briefly in Chapters 2, 4, and 18. These chapters show how to set the IP address, subnet mask, and default gateway of a network interface card (NIC). The basic syntax is

```
netsh interface ipv4 set address name = ""
static IP-address subnet-mask default-gateway
```

For example, you can use the following command to configure the NIC named "Local Area Connection" with an IP address of 192.168.1.15, a subnet mask of 255.255.255.0, and a default gateway of 192.168.1.1.

```
netsh interface ipv4 set address name = "local area connection"
static 192.168.1.15 255.255.255.0 192.168.1.1
```

> **NOTE** The default name of the first NIC is **Local Area Connection** on Windows systems. Because the NIC's name (Local Area Connection) has spaces within it, it must be enclosed in quotes.

Some other commands you can use to configure the NIC are shown in the following table.

| Command | Description |
|---|---|
| Get TCP/IP information from DHCP.<br><br>`netsh interface ipv4`<br>`set address [name=]`<br>`"NIC-name" [source=]`<br>`dhcp`<br>`C:\>netsh interface`<br>`ipv4 set address name =`<br>`"local area connection"`<br>`source = dhcp` | Changes the NIC so that it gets TCP/IP configuration automatically from DHCP. |
| Get DNS from DHCP.<br><br>`netsh interface ipv4`<br>`set dnsserver [name=]`<br>`"NIC-name " [source=]`<br>`dhcp`<br>`C:\> netsh interface`<br>`ipv4 set dnsserver`<br>`"local area connection"`<br>`dhcp` | Changes the NIC to get the DNS address automatically from DHCP. |
| Set IP address of preferred DNS server with **set.**<br><br>`netsh interface ipv4 set`<br>`dnsserver [name=]"NIC-`<br>`name" [source=]static`<br>`[address=]Preferred-`<br>`DNS-IP-Address`<br>`C:\>netsh interface`<br>`ipv4 set dnsserver`<br>`name="local area`<br>`connection"`<br>`source=static`<br>`192.168.1.5` | Sets the IP address of the preferred DNS server.<br><br>**NOTE**  This command removes all other DNS Server IP addresses, if any are configured. |

| Command | Description |
|---------|-------------|
| Set IP address of preferred DNS server with **add**.<br><br>`netsh interface`<br>`ipv4 add dnsserv-`<br>`er [name=] "NIC-name"`<br>`[address=] Preferred-`<br>`DNS-IP-Address index=1`<br>`C:\>netsh interface`<br>`ipv4 add dnsserver`<br>`name="local area`<br>`connection" 192.168.1.6`<br>`index=1` | **NOTE**   The **add** command has slightly different syntax than the **set** command. For example, you cannot use the **index** clause with the **set** command.<br><br>This command adds the address of a DNS server and sets it as the preferred DNS server (with an index of 1). If other DNS servers are in the list, they are moved down the list.<br><br>**NOTE**   You cannot use this command to modify the order of existing DNS server addresses. If you use an IP address of a DNS server already in the list, the command fails. However, you can use the **set** command to set one DNS server address, and then use the **add** command to add additional DNS server addresses with the **index** clause to specify the order.<br><br>Figure 25-2 shows the result of this command in combination with the previous **add** command. The **set** command is configured 192.168.1.5 as the preferred DNS server. The **add** command with an index of 1 is set 192.168.1.6 as the preferred DNS server, and bumped 19.168.1.6 to the alternate. |
| Set alternate DNS server.<br><br>`netsh interface`<br>`ipv4 add dnsserv-`<br>`er [name=] "NIC-name"`<br>`[address=] Preferred-`<br>`DNS-IP-Address index=2`<br>`C:\>netsh interface`<br>`ipv4 add dnsserver`<br>`name="local area`<br>`connection" 192.168.1.7`<br>`index=2` | This command adds 192.168.1.7 as the alternate. If another server was designated as the alternate, it will be moved down one in the list.<br><br>**TIP**   You can add DNS servers with different indexes. |

**TIP**   If you want to identify the names of the IPv4 interfaces on the system, you can use the following command:

```
netsh interface ipv4 show interfaces
```

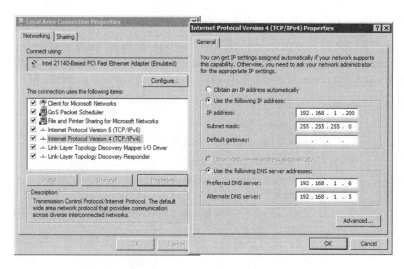

**Figure 25-2**   Configuring DNS server addresses

## Configuring an IPv6 Address with netsh

You can also configure IPv6 addresses with **netsh** though the syntax is a little different. The basic syntax is

```
netsh interface ipv6 set address [[interface=]
] [address=]
[[type=] unicast | anycast]
```

> **TIP**   If you want to identify the names of the IPv6 interfaces on the system, you can use the following command:
>
> ```
> netsh interface ipv6 show interfaces
> ```

For example, if you want to set the unicast IPv6 address of a NIC named Local Area Connection to fe80::4, you can use the following command:

```
netsh interface ipv6 set address interface =
"local area connection" address = fe80::4 type = unicast
```

The **ipv6 set** command defaults to **unicast**, so you can also use the following command with **type** omitted:

```
netsh interface ipv6 set address "local area connection" fe80::4
```

> **TIP**   There is much more to **netsh**. If you want to dig into it a little deeper, check out the TechNet site: http://technet.microsoft.com/library/cc770948.aspx.

# Disabling IPv6 in Windows Server 2008

In previous versions of Windows, you can remove IPv6 using the **netsh** command; however, you are unable to remove it from Windows Server 2008 or Windows Server 2008 R2. The best you can do is disable it. The following steps show how to disable IPv6.

| Step | Action |
|------|--------|
| 1. | Click **Start**, **Control Panel**. |
| 2. | Type **Network** in the **Control Panel Search** box. |
| 3. | Click **View Network Connections**. |
| 4. | Right-click over the network connection you want to disable IPv6 on and select **Properties**. |
| 5. | Deselect the checkbox next to **Internet Protocol Version 6 (TCP/IPv6)** as shown in Figure 25-3. |
| 6. | Click **OK** and close all Windows. |

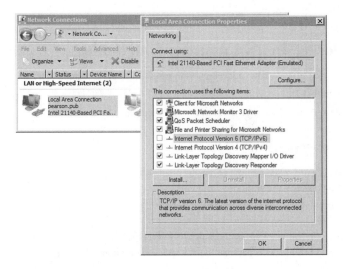

**Figure 25-3** Disabling IPv6 in Windows Server 2008

# CHAPTER 26

# Working with Event Subscriptions

This chapter provides information and commands concerning the following topics:

- Enabling the source computer with **winrm**
- Enabling the collector computer with **wecutil**
- Adding an account to the Event Log Readers group
- Enabling and testing event subscriptions
- Managing subscriptions with **wecutil**
- Logging events with **eventcreate**

**TIP** You should be familiar with event subscriptions and their associated commands when preparing for the 70-640 and 70-642 exams.

## Enabling the Source Computer with winrm

Event subscriptions are configured so that they travel from a source computer to a collector computer, as shown in Figure 26-1. The events are generated on the source computer(s) and can be viewed on the collector computer.

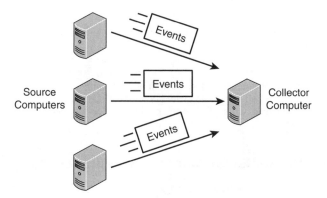

**Figure 26-1** Event subscriptions from source computers to a collector computer

**TIP** The source computer is also called the forwarding computer. An event subscription can have a single source computer or multiple source computers.

You enable the source computers with the following command:

```
winrm quickconfig
```

After entering the command, you are prompted to make changes to the firewall. If you confirm the changes, it creates a WinRM listener on HTTP://* so that it can accept Web Services Management (WS-MAN) requests, and it enables the WinRM firewall exception.

The following listing shows exactly what you see. You first enter **winrm quickconfig,** and then press **y** to confirm the changes.

```
C:\>winrm quickconfig
WinRM is not set up to allow remote access to this machine
for management.
The following changes must be made:

Create a WinRM listener on HTTP://* to accept WS-Man requests to
any IP on this machine.
Enable the WinRM firewall exception.

Make these changes [y/n]? y

WinRM has been updated for remote management.

Created a WinRM listener on HTTP://* to accept WS-Man requests to
any IP on this machine.
WinRM firewall exception enabled.
```

**NOTE**  This must be entered on each computer that provides source events for the event subscription.

**TIP**  Although a WinRM listener is not required on both computers for an event subscription, it is required when using **winrs** commands. Chapter 32, "Remote Administration," includes more information on **winrm** and **winrs** commands.

## Enabling the Collector Computer with wecutil

You can use the **wecutil** command to configure the collector computer. First enter **wecutil qc** and then, when you are prompted to change the startup mode of the service, click **y** for yes. The following listing shows the output.

```
C:\>wecutil qc
The service startup mode will be changed to Delay-Start.
Would you like to proceed ( Y- yes or N- no)?y
Windows Event Collector service was configured successfully.
```

**NOTE** Services configured with a startup mode of Delay-Start starts when the system boots, but only after all the services set to Automatic start. This is slightly different from the startup mode of Automatic because users can interact with the system before Delay-Start services start. In contrast, users cannot interact with the system until all services set to Automatic start.

# Adding an Account to the Event Log Readers Group

Those who aren't administrators are not allowed to read event logs by default. However, you can add an account to the Event Log Readers group to grant permission to read the event logs.

When creating event subscriptions, you must use an account that has access to the event logs on all your source computers, and it's best not to use the administrator account. Instead, you can use the machine account of the collector computer or create an account specifically for this purpose. You then add the account to the Event Log Readers group.

You can create a user with the **net user** command like the following:

```
net user event_sub P@ssw0rd /add
```

Alternatively, you can use the **dsadd** command to create the same account. The format is as follows:

```
dsadd user dn -pwd password
```

**TIP** Chapter 7, "Using Basic ds Commands," covers the uses of the **dsadd** command in much more depth, including how to format a distinguished name (DN).

The following command adds the user to the Users container in the pearson.pub domain with a password of P@ssw0rd:

```
dsadd user "cn=event_sub, cn=users, dc=pearson, dc=pub"
-pwd P@ssw0rd
```

**TIP** This account is a service account (used only as a service, not a user) and you need to manage the password. If the password expires, the event subscriptions will no longer work.

The following table shows how to add a machine account and a user account to the Event Log Readers group.

| Add Account to Event Log Readers Group | Comments |
|---|---|
| Add a machine account.<br><br>`net localgroup "event log readers"` *machine-name$*`[`*@domain-name*`]`<br>`/add`<br>`C:\>net localgroup "event log readers" dc1$ /add`<br>`C:\>net localgroup "event log readers" dc1$@pearson.pub /add` | When adding a machine name, you can use just the computer name followed by a dollar sign ($) or use the universal principal name (UPN), with the dollar sign after the machine name.<br><br>The examples add the computer named dc1 in the pearson.pub domain to the group.<br><br>**TIP**  You use **localgroup** instead of **group** even when you're adding the account to the Event Log Readers group on a domain controller. |
| Add a user account.<br><br>`net localgroup "event log readers"` *user-name*<br>`/add`<br>`C:\>net localgroup "event log readers" event_sub /add` | If you use a service account, you can add the service account to the group using the same format but enter the user name instead.<br><br>This example adds the user account (named event_sub created previously) to the Event Log Readers group. |

Figure 26-2 shows the properties of the Event Log Readers group with both the DC1 server and the event_sub user added as members.

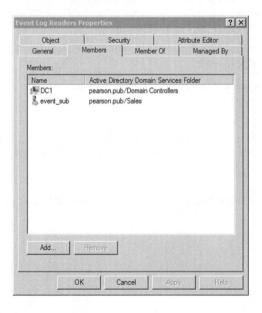

**Figure 26-2**  Membership of Event Log Readers group

## Enabling and Testing Event Subscriptions

The following table shows the steps to enable and test event subscriptions. These steps are performed on two domain controllers (DC1 and DC2). DC2 (as the source computer) forwards Active Directory Replication and other events to DC1 (as the collector).

| Step | Action |
|---|---|
| 1. | Configure each of the source (or forwarder) computers for event subscriptions. At a command prompt with administrative permissions, execute the following command:<br><br>C:\>**winrm quickconfig**<br><br>When prompted, press **Y** to confirm the changes. |
| 2. | Add the collector computer account to the Event Log Readers group on each source computer. In this example, the collector computer's name is DC1.<br><br>C:\>**net localgroup "event log readers" dc1$ /add** |
| 3. | Configure the collector computer for event subscriptions with the following command:<br><br>C:\>**wecutil qc**<br><br>When prompted, press **Y** to confirm the changes. |
| 4. | On the collector computer, launch **Event Viewer** from the **Administrative Tools** menu. |
| 5. | Right-click **Subscriptions** and select **Create Subscription**. |
| 6. | On the **Subscription Properties** page, enter **AD Replication** for the subscription name. Ensure that **Forwarded Events** is selected as the **Destination Log**. |
| 7. | Ensure that **Collector Initiated** is selected and click the **Select Computers** button. |
| 8. | Click **Add Domain Computers**. Type the name of a computer that will be a source computer. Click **Check Names** to verify that the computer is in the domain and click **OK**.<br><br>**NOTE**   You can add multiple computers here as long as they are configured with the **winrm quickconfig** command. |
| 9. | Click **Test** to ensure that you can connect with the source computer. Your display should look similar to Figure 26-3. In the figure, DC2 is added as a source computer. |
| 10. | Click **OK** to dismiss the test dialog box. Click **OK** to dismiss the **Computers** dialog box. |
| 11. | On the **Subscription Properties** page, click **Select Events**. |
| 12. | Select the checkbox next to each of the event levels: **Critical Warning, Verbose, Error**, and **Information**. |

| Step | Action |
|------|--------|
| 13. | On the **Query Filter** page, click the drop-down box next to **Event Logs**. Select the checkbox next to **Windows Logs.** This selects all of the **Windows Logs** (**Application**, **Security**, **Setup**, **System**, and **Forwarded Events**). <br><br> **NOTE** You can select or deselect any logs that you want to forward here. |
| 14. | Click the plus sign (**+**) to expand the **Applications and Services Logs**. Select the **DFS Replication** log. This logs replication events if the source computer is a domain controller. Your display should look similar to Figure 26-4. |
| 15. | Click **OK** to accept the query filter. |
| 16. | Click **Advanced**. You can change the **User Account** to use a **Specific User** account, or leave it as the **Machine Account**. Because the previous step added the DC2 machine account to the **Event Log Readers** group on each source computer, leave the **Machine Account** selected. Click **Cancel**. |
| 17. | Your display should look similar to Figure 26-5. Click **OK**. |

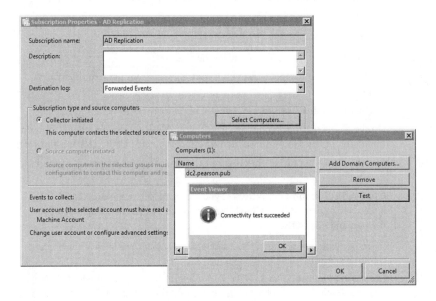

**Figure 26-3** Adding and testing source computers for an event subscription

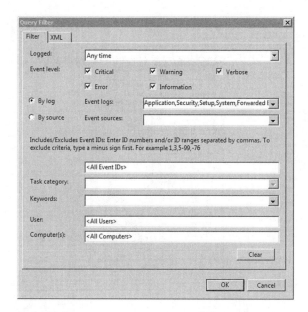

**Figure 26-4**  Selecting event levels and event logs for the event subscription

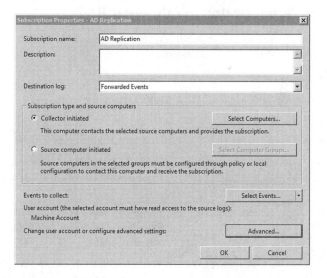

**Figure 26-5**  A completed event subscription

After the event subscription is created, you can view the events in the **Forwarded Events** log on the collector computer, as shown in Figure 26-6.

**NOTE**  You might need to wait as long as 15 minutes before an event is forwarded.

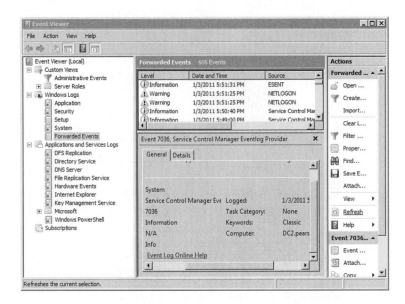

**Figure 26-6**   Viewing Forwarded Events

# Managing Subscriptions with wecutil

The basic command you use with **wecutil** is **qc** (as **wecutil qc**) to configure the collector computer. However, there are more commands.

| wecutil Command | Comments |
|---|---|
| Enumerate subscriptions.<br><br>`C:\>wecutil es` | Lists existent subscriptions. |
| Get runtime status of subscription.<br><br>`wecutil gr subscription-name`<br>`C:\>wecutil gr "ad replication"` | Gets subscription runtime status.<br><br>The example retrieves the status of the subscription created earlier in this chapter. |
| Export a subscription to an XML file.<br><br>`wecutil gs "subscription-name"`<br>`/f:xml > filename`<br>`C:\>wecutil gs "ad replication"`<br>`/f:xml > adrep.xml` | The **gs** command gets subscription configuration. The **/f:xml** switch formats the output as XML.<br><br>You can redirect this to an XML file with the > symbol to a file. |

| wecutil Command | Comments |
|---|---|
| Create subscription from XML file.<br><br>`wecutil cs `*`xml-file`*<br>`C:\>wecutil cs adrep.xml` | Creates a new subscription.<br><br>If you have an XML file, you can create (or re-create) the subscription using the **cs** command. |
| Delete the subscription.<br><br>`wecutil ds "`*`subscription-name`*`"`<br>`C:\>wecutil ds "ad replication"` | The **ds** command deletes the subscription. |
| Set event delivery optimization.<br><br>`wecutil ss "`*`subscription-name`*`"`<br>`/cm:normal \| minlatency \|`<br>`minbandwidth \| custom`<br>`C:\>wecutil ss "ad replication"`<br>`/cm:normal`<br>`C:\>wecutil ss "ad replication"`<br>`/cm:minlatency`<br>`C:\>wecutil ss "ad replication"`<br>`/cm:minbandwith` | You can modify a subscription with the **ss** (set subscription) command.<br><br>The **/cm** switch enables you to change the **Event Delivery Optimization** settings (shown as the **Advanced Subscription Settings** in Figure 26-7 after clicking the **Advanced** button).<br><br>You can use the **/cm:custom** switch to configure more advanced settings, such as changing the latency. This requires an additional switch as shown in the next example. |
| Set latency to 15 seconds.<br><br>`wecutil ss "subscription-name"`<br>`/cm:custom /dmlt:`*`number-of-`*<br>*`milliseconds`*<br>`C:\>wecutil ss "ad replication"`<br>`/cm:custom /dmlt:15000` | You can use the **/dmlt** switch to specify the time between updates (delivery maximum latency time). It is set in milliseconds. You can change this only when you change the configuration mode to custom with **/cm:custom**.<br><br>The example changes the latency to 15,000 so that updates are sent every 15 seconds.<br><br>Figure 26-7 shows the result of this command. Notice that it is set to custom, and custom is dimmed. You can change this back by changing the configuration mode using **/cm:normal**, **/cm:minlatency**, or **/cm:bandwidth**. |

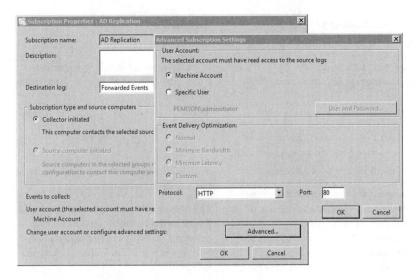

**Figure 26-7**   Changing the latency to a custom configuration

**TIP**   There are many more settings you can configure with **wecutil** commands. If you want to dig deeper, check out the TechNet website: http://technet.microsoft.com/library/cc753183.aspx.

## Logging Events with eventcreate

In the context of event logs, there might be times when you want to log specific information into either the Windows Server 2008 Application or System logs. You can do this from the command line or from a batch file using the **eventcreate** command. The syntax is

```
eventcreate  [/l application | system ] /t error | warning |
information  /id eventid /d description
```

For example, if you want to log an error in the Application log to indicate an application failure, you can use either of the following commands. Because it defaults to the Application log, you don't have to include the **/l** switch.

```
eventcreate /l application /t error /id 999
/d "Application Failure"
eventcreate /t error /id 998 /d "Application Failure"
```

Figure 26-8 shows the event logged in the Application log from these commands.

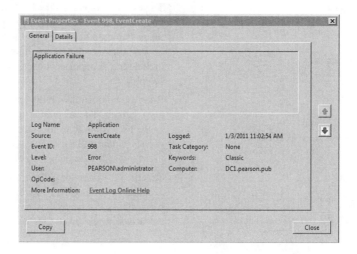

**Figure 26-8**  An event created from the **eventcreate** command

The following table identifies the different elements within an **eventcreate** command.

| eventcreate Switches | Comments |
|---|---|
| Target log.<br><br>`/l application \| system`<br>`/l system` | The **/l** (the lowercase letter l, not the number 1) switch specifies the log where you want the event recorded.<br><br>You can specify either the **application** or **system** log. If you don't specify a log, it defaults to the **application** log. |
| Identify type of log entry.<br><br>`/t error \| warning \| information`<br>`/t error` | The **/t** switch is used to specify the type of entry.<br><br>You must specify **error**, **warning**, or **information** as the type. |
| ID number.<br><br>`/id number`<br>`/id 999` | The **/id** identifies the number for the event.<br><br>You can use any number between 1 and 1,000. |
| Description of event.<br><br>`/d "description"`<br>`/d "Application failed"` | Add a free text description with the **/d** switch.<br><br>The description is logged with the event and must be enclosed in quotes if it has spaces. |

| eventcreate Switches | Comments |
|---|---|
| Remote system.<br><br>**/s** *remotecomputername* \| *IP-address*<br>**/s** `dc2`<br>**/s** `192.168.1.6` | The event is logged on the local computer by default. However, you can use the **/s** switch to have the event logged on a remote computer. You must include the **/u** and **/p** switches with this switch. |
| Username.<br><br>**/u** *domain\user*<br>**/u** `pearson\administrator` | Runs the command with the specified user account. The account is specified as the user name for a local account, or the domain and user name (domain\username) for a domain account. |
| Password.<br><br>**/p** *password*<br>**/p** `P@ssw0rd` | Specifies the password of the user account. If you put the password in a batch file, it can be read by anyone that has access to the batch file. |

**TIP**   A new feature available with Windows 2008 is the capability to attach tasks to events. These tasks can run files or scripts, display a dialog box, or send an email. In other words, if you created an event with event ID of 999, you can then attach a task to that event.

# CHAPTER 27

# Using wbadmin

This chapter provides information and commands concerning the following topics:

- Adding **wbadmin** to a server
- Backing up system state data with **wbadmin**
- Restoring system state data with **wbadmin**
- Restoring system state data on a domain controller with **wbadmin**
- Backing up volumes with **wbadmin**
- Restoring volumes with **wbadmin**

**TIP**  You should be familiar with the **wbadmin** command when preparing for the 70-640 and 70-642 exams.

## Adding wbadmin to a Server

**wbadmin** is the command-line tool you can use to access Windows Server backup capabilities. The **wbadmin** tool is not available on Windows Server 2008 by default. You must add it as a feature by performing the following steps.

| Step | Action |
|------|--------|
| 1. | Start **Server Manager** from the **Administrative Tools** menu. |
| 2. | Select **Features**. Select **Add Features**. |
| 3. | Scroll down and expand **Windows Server Backup Features**. Select **Windows Server Backup**. Your display should look similar to Figure 27-1. <br><br>**TIP**  It's not necessary to select the checkbox for **Command-Line Tools**. **wbadmin** is installed as part of Windows Server Backup. The command-line tools provide additional functionality with PowerShell. |
| 4. | Click **Next**. Click **Install**. |
| 5. | When the installation completes, click **Close**. |

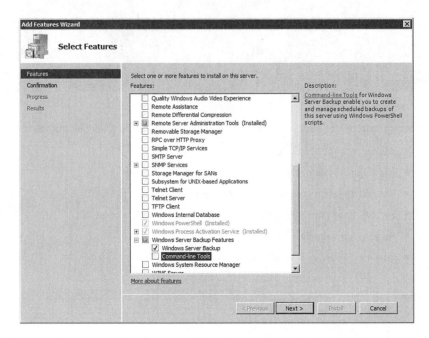

**Figure 27-1**    Adding Windows Server Backup features

**TIP**    The Windows Server Backup tools replaced the **ntbackup** utility used in previous versions of Windows. You cannot restore backups created with **ntbackup** using the **wbadmin** tool. If you have legacy backups that need to be restored, you can download a compatible **ntbackup** version at http://go.microsoft.com/fwlink/?LinkId=82917.

# Backing Up System State Data with wbadmin

System state data includes the following components on a Windows Server 2008 system.

| System State Data | Comments |
|---|---|
| Active Directory Domain Services (AD DS) database | If the server is a domain controller |
| SYSVOL folder | If the server is a domain controller |
| Certificate Services database | If the server is running Certificate Services |
| Internet Information Services (IIS) meta-directory | If the server is hosting the Web Server (IIS) role |
| Cluster Service information | If the server is a member of a cluster |
| Boot files, including system files | All servers |
| System files under Windows File Protection (WFP) | All servers |
| COM+ Class registration database | All servers |

You can back up system state data on a server with the commands shown in the following table.

| Backup System State Data Commands | Comments |
| --- | --- |
| Back up system state data.<br><br>`wbadmin start systemstatebackup`<br>`-backuptarget:`*volume-name* `[-quiet]`<br>`C:\>wbadmin start systemstatebackup`<br>`-backuptarget:e:` | The **start systemstatebackup** command backs up system state to the volume you specify (drive **e:** in this example).<br><br>By default, this queries you to confirm the backup before it starts, but you can suppress the confirmation with the **-quiet** switch. |
| Back up critical volumes.<br><br>`wbadmin start backup -backuptarget:`<br>*volume-name*`: -allcritical`<br>`C:\>wbadmin start backup`<br>`-backuptarget:e: -allcritical` | The **-allcritical** switch used with the **start backup** command includes all volumes that include system state data. |

> **TIP**  You cannot back up to a critical volume. A critical volume is any drive that includes the system partition and the boot partition, and holds the paging file and any Active Directory database files.

# Restoring System State Data with wbadmin

After you back up system state data, you can restore it. However, you need to have version information for the commands. You can get version information for backups stored on the system with the following command:

`wbadmin get versions [-backupTarget:` *VolumeName*
`| NetworkSharePath]`

For example, if you back up data to the E: drive, you can use the following command:

`wbadmin get versions -backuptarget:e:`

The following listing shows the output of this command, including the key piece of information you need: The version is **01/03/2011-20:51**.

```
C:\>wbadmin get versions -backuptarget:e:
wbadmin 1.0 - Backup command-line tool
(C) Copyright 2004 Microsoft Corp.

Backup time: 1/3/2011 3:51 PM
Backup target: Fixed Disk labeled E:
Version identifier: 01/03/2011-20:51
Can Recover: Application(s), System State
```

The command you use to restore system state data is as follows:

```
wbadmin start systemstaterecovery
-showsummary | -version:version-identifier
[-backuptarget:volume-name | network-share-path]
[-machine:backup-machine-name]
[-recoverytarget:target-path-for-recovery] [-authsysvol] [-quiet]
```

The following table describes these switches.

| Start systemstaterecovery Switches | Comments |
| --- | --- |
| -showsummary<br>C:\>wbadmin start<br>systemstaterecovery -showsummary | Reports the summary of the last system state recovery. It shows the status of the system after the recovery and after it reboots.<br><br>**NOTE**   This option cannot be accompanied by any other options. |
| -version:version-identifier<br>-version: 01/03/2011-20:51 | Version identifier of the backup is in the format of *mm/dd/yyyy-hh:mm*:<br><br>**TIP**   You can get the information with the **wbadmin get versions** command. |
| -backuptarget: [*volume-name* \|<br>*network-share-path*]<br>-backuptarget:e: | Specifies the storage location that contains the backup. |
| -machine:*backup-machine-name*<br>-machine:dc1 | Specifies the name of the computer for which you want to do the recovery. This is useful when multiple computers are backed up to the same location. The default is the local computer. |
| -recoverytarget:*target-path-for-recovery*<br>-recoverytarget:d: | Identifies the existing directory where you want to restore the data. You can use this to restore the data to an alternative location. |
| -authsysvol | Performs an authoritative restore of the SYSVOL folder. |
| -quiet | Runs the command without prompting the user for input. |

For example, you can issue the following command to restore system state data on a server:

```
wbadmin start systemstaterecovery -version:01/03/2011-20:51
```

The following listing shows what you see when the restore has completed.

```
Summary of recovery:
--------------------


Restore of system state completed successfully [1/3/2011 7:31 PM]

Log of files successfully restored
'C:\Windows\Logs\WindowsServerBackup\SystemStateRestore
03-01-2011 18-33-20.log'



Please restart the machine to complete the operation.
NOTE: When you restart your server, System State Recovery will
attempt to recover many system files which may take several
minutes to complete depending on the number of files that are
getting replaced. The machine might reboot multiple times in the pro-
cess. Please be patient and do not interrupt the reboot process.
```

**TIP**   If the server is a domain controller, you need to restore system state data while in directory services mode.

## Restoring System State Data on a Domain Controller with wbadmin

If the server is a domain controller, you need to take a couple of extra steps to restore system state. You are not able to restore Active Directory while Active Directory is running, so you need to enter Active Directory Restore Mode and then restore it. The following table shows the steps in this process.

**TIP**   This is also called performing a critical volume restore.

| Step | Action |
|------|--------|
| 1. | Reboot the system and press **F8** to access the **Advanced Boot Options** page. |
| 2. | Select **Directory Services Restore Mode** and press **Enter**. When prompted, log on with the user name of **.\administrator** and the DSRM password. |
| 3. | Launch a command prompt. |
| 4. | Type the following command to identify the version information for the system state backup:<br><br>**wbadmin get versions** |

| Step | Action |
|------|--------|
| 4. | Type the **wbadmin** command to restore system state data using the version information retrieved with the previous step. The command has the following format:<br><br>**wbadmin start systemstaterecovery -version:***mm/dd/yyyy-hh:mm***wbadmin start systemstaterecovery -version:01/03/2011-20:51** |
| 5. | When prompted to continue with the restore, press **y**.<br><br>When this is complete, the non-authoritative restore of Active Directory is complete. If you want to do an authoritative restore of an object or an OU, you can use the **ntdsutil** command at this time.<br><br>    **TIP**   Chapter 12, "Using **ntdsutil**," shows the process for an authoritative restore. The basic command to restore an OU is<br><br>**restore subtree** *dn-of-the-ou*<br><br>The basic command to restore an object (such as a user) is<br><br>**restore object** *dn-of-the-object* |
| 6. | After the restore has completed, reboot the domain controller. |

## Backing Up Volumes with wbadmin

You can use the **start backup** command to back up entire volumes. The basic syntax is

```
wbadmin start backup -backuptarget:volume-where-backup-stored
-include:volumes-to-back-up
```

For example, the following command backs up the E: volume to F:

```
wbadmin start backup -backuptarget:f: -include:e:
```

The following listing shows the output:

```
C:\>wbadmin start backup -backuptarget:f: -include:e:
wbadmin 1.0 - Backup command-line tool
(C) Copyright 2004 Microsoft Corp.


Retrieving volume information...


This would backup volume Data(E:) to f:.


Do you want to start the backup operation?
[Y] Yes [N] No y


Backup to F: is starting.
```

```
Creating the shadow copy of volumes requested for backup.
Running backup of volume Data(E:), copied (0%).
Running backup of volume Data(E:), copied (84%).
Backup of volume Data(E:) completed successfully.
Backup completed successfully.


Summary of backup:
-----------------


Backup of volume Data(E:) completed successfully.
```

The following table shows switches you can use with the **wbadmin start backup** command.

| wbadmin Start Backup Switches | Comments |
| --- | --- |
| `-backuptarget:` *volume-name* \| *network-share-path*<br>`-backuptarget: e:` | Specifies the storage location for this backup.<br><br>This requires either a drive letter or a Universal Naming Convention (UNC) path to a remote shared network folder in the format of \\\\*servername*\\*share-name*\.<br><br>**NOTE**   If a remote shared folder is specified, this backup overwrites any existing backups of this server in that location. |
| `-include:` *volumes-to-back-up*<br>`-include: c:,d:` | Identifies a comma-delimited list of volume drive letters, volume mount points, or GUID-based volume names to include in the backup. |
| `-allcritical` | Automatically includes all critical volumes (volumes that contain operating system components) in the backup. This can be used with the **-include** parameter.<br><br>**TIP**   This command is useful if you are creating a backup for full system or system state recovery. |
| `-noverify` | If specified, backups written to removable media (such as a DVD) are not verified for errors. If you do not use this parameter, backups written to removable media are verified. |
| `-user:`*username*<br>`-user:sally` | Specifies the user name with write access to the target location. |
| `-password:`*password*<br>`-password:P@ssw0rd` | Specifies the password for the user name that is specified with the **-user** switch. |

| wbadmin Start Backup Switches | Comments |
|---|---|
| -vssfull | If specified, it performs a full backup using the Volume Shadow Copy Service (VSS). Each file's history is updated to reflect that it was backed up. |
| | If this parameter is not specified, start backup makes a copy backup, but the history of files being backed up is not updated. |
| | **TIP**  Do not use this parameter if you are using a product other than Windows Server Backup to back up applications that are on the volumes included in the current backup. Doing so can potentially break the incremental, differential, or other type of backups the other backup product is taking. |
| -quiet | Runs the command with no prompts to the user. |

## Restoring Volumes with wbadmin

You can also restore entire volumes with the **wbadmin** tool. This is useful if one or more drives on your system ever suffers a catastrophic failure. The basic syntax to recover a volume is

```
wbadmin start recovery -version:mm/dd/yyyy-hh:mm -itemtype:volume
-items:volume-to-recover -recoverytarget:volume-to-recover-to
```

For example, the following command restores the volume E: contained in the backup to the g: volume:

```
C:\>wbadmin start recovery -version:01/04/2011-11:15
-itemtype:volume -items:e: -recoverytarget:g:
```

The following listing shows the output you see from this command:

```
G:\>wbadmin start recovery -version:01/04/2011-11:15
-itemtype:volume -items:e: -recoverytarget:g:
wbadmin 1.0 - Backup command-line tool
(C) Copyright 2004 Microsoft Corp.

Retrieving volume information...

You have chosen to recover volume(s) e: from the backup taken on
1/4/2011 6:15 AM to a different location, g:.
```

WARNING:

You have chosen to recover a full volume. This will DELETE any
existing data on the volume you recover to, even if the operation
is canceled or fails. Before you continue, make sure that this
volume does not contain any data that you might want in the future.

Note: If the recovered volume contains applications, you will need
to recover those applications after you recover the volume.

Do you want to continue?
[Y] Yes [N] No **y**

Running recovery for volume Data(E:), copied (0%).
Running recovery for volume Data(E:), copied (90%).
Recovery for volume Data(E:) completed successfully.

Recovery operation completed.

Summary of recovery:
--------------------

Recovery for volume Data(E:) completed successfully.

The following table shows some switches you can use with **wbadmin start recovery**.

| wbadmin start recovery Switches | Comments |
|---|---|
| `-version:`*version-identifier*<br>`-version: 01/03/2011-20:51` | Version identifier of the backup is in the format of *mm/dd/yyyy-hh:mm*:<br><br>**TIP** You can get the information with the **wbadmin get versions** command. |
| `-itemtype: volume | file | app`<br>`-itemtype:volume` | Specifies the type of items to recover. Must be **volume, file**, or **app**.<br><br>**TIP** Applications you can restore include Active Directory and Windows SharePoint Services (WSS) or SharePoint Portal applications.<br><br>**TIP** When restoring SharePoint applications to a different target system, you must first install WSS on the target system. |

| wbadmin start recovery Switches | Comments |
|---|---|
| `-items:`*volumes-to-recover* &#124; *files-folders-to-recover* &#124; *apps-to-recover*<br>`-items:c:,d:`<br>`-items:d:\scripts`<br>`-items:adifm` | Identifies a comma-delimited list of volumes, files, or applications to recover.<br><br>If **-itemtype** is **volume**, it can be only a single volume that is specified by providing the volume drive letter, volume mount point, or GUID-based volume name.<br><br>If **-itemtype** is **file**, it can be files or directories, but it should be part of the same volume and should be under the same parent.<br><br>If **-itemtype** is **app**, it can be only a single application. Applications that have registered with Windows Server Backup can be recovered. You can also use the value **adifm** to recover an installation of Active Directory. |
| `-recursive`<br>`-items:d:\scripts`<br>`-recursive` | Valid only when recovering files. Recovers the files in the folders and all files subordinate to the specified folders. By default, only files that reside directly under the specified folders are recovered. |
| `-recoverytarget:`*volume-to-recover-to*<br>`-recoverytarget:g:` | Specifies the drive letter to restore to.<br><br>This is useful if the drive is different from the one that was previously backed up. You can use this to restore volumes or files. If you are restoring a volume, you can specify the volume drive letter of the alternative volume. If you are restoring a file or application, you can specify an alternative backup path. |
| `-overwrite:overwrite` &#124; `createcopy` &#124; `skip`<br>`-overwrite:overwrite`<br>`-overwrite:createcopy`<br>`-overwrite:skip` | Valid only when recovering files.<br><br>Specifies the action to take when a file that is being recovered already exists in the same location.<br><br>**overwrite** causes the recovery to overwrite the existing file with the file from the backup.<br><br>**createcopy** causes the recovery to create a copy of the existing file so that the existing file will not be modified.<br><br>**skip** causes the recovery to skip the existing file and continue with recovery of the next file. |
| `-quiet` | Runs the command with no prompts to the user. |

# CHAPTER 28

# Troubleshooting Networking Issues

This chapter provides information and commands concerning the following topics:

- Viewing and manipulating TCP/IP configuration with **ipconfig**
- Checking connectivity with **ping**
- Viewing the router path with **tracert**
- Checking for data loss with **pathping**

**TIP** You should be familiar with these commands when preparing for the 70-642 and 70-646 exams.

## Viewing and Manipulating TCP/IP Configuration with ipconfig

The **ipconfig** command is a useful command you can use to view and manipulate TCP/IP configuration information. The most common way to use it is to view the TCP/IP configuration data for a system. You can do so with this command:

```
ipconfig
```

or

```
ipconfig /all
```

The following table shows some of the output you'll see.

| Basic ipconfig Output | Comments |
|---|---|
| `C:\>ipconfig`<br>`Windows IP Configuration` | **ipconfig** without any switches gives basic TCP/IP configuration data for each network interface card (NIC). This example shows two NICs named Local Area Connection and Local Area Connection 2. |

| Basic ipconfig Output | Comments |
|---|---|
| Ethernet adapter Local Area Connection:<br>   Connection-specific DNS Suffix  . :<br>   IPv4 Address. . . . . . . . . . :<br>192.168.1.10<br>   Subnet Mask . . . . . . . . . . :<br>255.255.255.0<br>   Default Gateway . . . . . . . . :<br>192.168.1.1 | This output shows the actual IP address, subnet mask, and default gateway assigned to the NIC. |
| Ethernet adapter Local Area Connection 2:<br>   Media State . . . . . . . . . . :<br>Media disconnected<br>   Connection-specific DNS Suffix  . : | If a NIC is disconnected at the computer or the network device (such as a switch), or the cable is broken anywhere in between, it shows Media Disconnected. |

**ipconfig /all** shows much more detailed information, as shown in the following table.

| Output of ipconfig /all | Comments |
|---|---|
| C:\>ipconfig /all<br>Windows IP Configuration<br><br>   Host Name . . . . . . . . . . .<br>: DC1<br>   Primary Dns Suffix  . . . . . . :<br>Pearson.pub<br>   Node Type . . . . . . . . . . . .<br>: Hybrid<br>   IP Routing Enabled. . . . . . . :<br>No<br>   WINS Proxy Enabled. . . . . . . : No<br>   DNS Suffix Search List. . . . . :<br>Pearson.pub | It starts with global information for the system, which applies to all NICs.<br><br>The Host Name is the name of the computer. If the computer is joined to a domain, it is indicated in the Primary DNS Suffix. This is blank for workgroup computers.<br><br>The Node Type indicates how NetBIOS names are resolved. Hybrid indicates a WINS server is queried first (if configured) and then it broadcasts. It can also be Mixed, indicating it is broadcast first and then queries WINS. Broadcast indicates it broadcasts only, and Peer-to-peer indicates it queries only a WINS server.<br><br>It's not common to enable IP routing or a WINS proxy on a Windows 7 computer, so these are almost always No. If you want host names to search additional suffixes beyond the primary DNS suffix (such as training.pearson. pub), they can be added and will show in the DNS Suffix Search List. |

| Output of ipconfig /all | Comments |
|---|---|
| ```
Ethernet adapter Local Area Connection:
   Connection-specific DNS Suffix  . :
   Description . . . . . . . . . :
Intel 21140-Based PCI Fast Ethernet
Adapter
   Physical Address. . . . . . . :
00-03-FF-9C-02-00
   DHCP Enabled. . . . . . . . . : No
   Autoconfiguration Enabled . . . . :
Yes
   Link-local IPv6 Address . . . . . :
fe80::41f0:f763:5451:198a%10(Preferred)
   IPv4 Address. . . . :
192.168.1.122(Preferred)
   Subnet Mask . . . . . . . . . . :
255.255.255.0
   Default Gateway . . . . . . . . :
192.168.1.1
   DNS Servers . . . . . . . . . . :
192.168.1.10
   NetBIOS over Tcpip. . . . . . . :
Enabled
``` | Each NIC has specific information starting with the name. The default name of the first NIC is Local Area Connection, but you can change the name of the NICs. It lists the brand and model of the NIC as a Description.

Physical Address is the MAC or Ethernet address.

When the IP address is statically assigned, DHCP Enabled is No. Autoconfiguration refers to Automatic Private IP Addressing (APIPA). When Autoconfiguration Enabled is set to Yes, APIPA automatically assigns an IP address in the range of 169.254.y.z to a DHCP client if the DHCP server doesn't respond. It doesn't have any effect for non-DHCP clients or clients with a statically assigned IP address.

If a static IPv6 address isn't assigned, a link-local address (with a prefix of fe80) is automatically assigned.

**NOTE**  IPv6 has been included in Windows systems since Windows XP SP2. It is installed and enabled by default in Windows Server 2008 and Windows Server 2008 R2.

The default gateway must be on the same subnet. If you're having problems with name resolution, you can ping the IP address of the DNS server as a check. |

In addition to the **/all** switch, you can use several additional switches with ipconfig. The following table lists some of the switches commonly used with **ipconfig**.
```

| ipconfig Switches | Comments |
|---|---|
| /release<br>ipconfig /release [adapter]<br>C:\>ipconfig /release<br>C:\>ipconfig /release "local area connection"<br>C:\>ipconfig /release local* | Releases the DHCP lease for the specified adapters that have DHCP leases. If you leave the adapter blank, it attempts to release the DHCP lease for all adapters that have DHCP leases.<br><br>You can use the entire name of the connection or use wildcards. **local\*** represents all connections that start with local. |
| /release6<br>ipconfig /release6 [adapter]<br>C:\>ipconfig /release6<br>C:\>ipconfig /release6 "local area connection"<br>C:\>ipconfig /release6 local* | The **/release6** switch works the same way as **/release**, but only for IPv6 addresses. |
| /renew<br>ipconfig /renew  [adapter]<br>C:\>ipconfig /renew<br>C:\>ipconfig /renew "local area connection"<br>C:\>ipconfig /renew local* | You can renew DHCP leases with the **/renew** switch. It attempts to reach a DHCP server and obtain a new DHCP lease or renew the existing lease. The lease includes an IP address and subnet mask at a minimum but also includes other data, such as the default gateway, the address of DNS, and the domain name. You can identify the adapter the same way you can with the **/release** switch. |
| /renew6<br>ipconfig /renew6  [adapter]<br>C:\>ipconfig /renew6 "local area connection"<br>C:\>ipconfig /renew6 local* | The **/renew6** switch works the same way as **/renew** but for IPv6 addresses. |
| /displaydns<br>C:\>ipconfig /displaydns | The DNS cache, or host cache, shows names that have been resolved by DNS and items that are in the Hosts file. You can view the cache with the **/displaydns** switch.<br><br>Items in the cache stay in it until the Time To Live (TTL) times out. The TTL value is shown in seconds and is provided by DNS when the name is resolved to an IP address.<br><br>**NOTE**  Items in the Hosts file (%windir%\System32\Drivers\etc\hosts) are automatically placed in the cache. |

| ipconfig Switches | Comments |
|---|---|
| Using /displaydns<br><br>`C:\>`**`ping dc1`**<br><br>pinging dc1.pearson.pub<br>[192.168.1.10] with 32 bytes of<br>data:<br>Reply from 192.168.1.10:<br>bytes=32 time<1ms TTL=128<br>Reply from 192.168.1.10:<br>bytes=32 time<1ms TTL=128<br>Reply from 192.168.1.10:<br>bytes=32 time<1ms TTL=128<br>Reply from 192.168.1.10:<br>bytes=32 time<1ms TTL=128<br>ping statistics for<br>192.168.1.10:<br>    Packets: Sent = 4, Received<br>= 4, Lost = 0 (0% loss),<br>Approximate round trip times in<br>milli-seconds:<br>    Minimum = 0ms, Maximum =<br>0ms, Average = 0ms<br>`C:\>ping dc77`<br>Ping request could not find<br>host dc77. Please check the<br>name and try again.<br>`C:\>`**`ipconfig /displaydns`**<br>    dc1.pearson.pub<br>    - - - - - - - - - - - - - - - - - - - - - - - - - - -<br>- - - - - - - - - - - -<br>    Record Name . . . . . : dc1.<br>pearson.pub<br>    Record Type . . . . . : 1<br>    Time To Live  . . . . : 3581<br>    Data Length . . . . . : 4<br>    Section . . . . . . . :<br>Answer<br>    A (Host) Record . . . :<br>192.168.1.10<br><br>    Dc77<br>    - - - - - - - - - - - - - - - - - - - - - - - - - - -<br>- - - - - - - - - - - - -<br>    Name does not exist. | In this example, DC1 is pinged in the pearson.pub domain.<br><br>The first line shows that it was successfully resolved to 192.168.1.10 (underlined for emphasis), and then ping sends four echo requests and receives four Echo replies.<br><br>**NOTE**  The next section covers ping in more detail if you need some reminders of what it does.<br><br>DC77 is also pinged, but the DNS server doesn't have a record of DC77 and responds with a negative response (underlined).<br><br>With some data in the DNS resolver cache, you can now view the cache. Notice that both DC1 and DC99 are in cache, but DC1 has an IP address and DC99 simply states that the name doesn't exist. Both entries came from DNS.<br><br>A TTL of 3581 is close to 60 minutes (3581 seconds divided by 60 = 59.6 minutes). This TTL continuously counts down until it reaches zero, and then it is automatically dropped from cache.<br><br>If the data is in cache, DNS is not queried again. In other words, if DC1 and DC99 are pinged again, the ping uses the data from cache.<br><br>Negative responses stay in cache for 15 minutes unless flushed out of cache using the **ipconfig /flushdns** command. |

| ipconfig Switches | Comments |
|---|---|
| `/flushdns`<br>`C:\>ipconfig /flushdns` | There are times when you will want to remove data from cache without waiting for the TTL to expire. For example, if there is a negative cache entry in cache because DNS doesn't have a record for the client, you can purge the DNS cache with the **/flushdns** switch. This also purges any entries that haven't timed out.<br><br>**NOTE**  Items in the Hosts file (%windir%\system32\drivers\etc\hosts) are not purged when you use the **/flushdns** switch. The only way to remove these items from cache is to remove them from the Hosts file. |
| `/registerdns`<br>`C:\>ipconfig /registerdns` | The **/registerdns** switch initiates manual dynamic registration for the DNS names and IP addresses that are configured at a computer. Dynamic DNS (DDNS) is used in Microsoft domains to dynamically create and update records on DNS servers, and it normally occurs when a computer boots. You can use this switch to troubleshoot a failed DNS name registration or resolve a dynamic update problem between a client and the DNS server without rebooting the client computer. |

If you want to see the effect of adding entries in the hosts file, you can do so with the following steps.

| Steps to Modify Hosts File | Comments |
|---|---|
| 1. Launch Notepad with elevated permissions. | Click **Start**, type **Notepad** in the **Start Search** text box, right-click **Notepad**, and select **Run As Administrator**. If prompted by UAC to continue, click **Yes**. |
| 2. Browse to the Hosts file and open it. | Click **File, Open**. Browse to the %windir%\system32\drivers\etc\ folder. Change Text Documents (*.txt) to **All Files** in the Open dialog box. Select the hosts file and click **Open**. |
| 3. Add a bogus record after the last line in the Hosts file. | Scroll to the bottom of the file and enter the following line:<br>**192.168.1.2      DC77** |
| 4. Save the Hosts file. | Select **File, Save** to save the file.<br><br>**NOTE**  If you didn't launch Notepad with administrative permissions, you cannot save the file. |

| Steps to Modify Hosts File | Comments |
|---|---|
| 5. View the cache entry with **ipconfig /displaydns**. | Launch a command prompt and enter **ipconfig /displaydns** to view the entry. |
| 6. Try to purge the hosts file entry. | Enter **ipconfig /flushdns** to purge all entries. Type **ipconfig /displaydns** to verify the Hosts entry remains. |
| 7. Ping DC77 to show that it can be resolved. | Type **ping dc77** and press **Enter**. In the first line, you'll see that the ping successfully resolves it to 192.168.1.2. The echoes fail because creating a record in the hosts file doesn't actually create a server, but this does verify that the hosts file provides name resolution. |
| 8. Return the Hosts file to normal. | Return to Notepad. Delete the line you added (192.168.1.2 DC77). Select **File**, **Save** to save the file. Close Notepad. |

# Checking Connectivity with ping

One of the most valuable troubleshooting tools to check connectivity is **ping**. It can quickly tell you whether systems are up and operational and if you are able to resolve names to IP addresses. The basic syntax is

```
ping hostname
```

or

```
ping IP-address
```

> **TIP**  If the pinged system responds, you know the system is operational. However, if the pinged system doesn't respond, it doesn't necessarily mean that it is not operational. The remote system's firewall, or a firewall between your system and the remote system, can block ICMP requests.

If you ping the hostname, the first thing that **ping** does is resolve the name to an IP address. This can be valuable to determine whether name resolution works. As an example, consider the following **ping** command and its output:

```
C:\>ping dc1
pinging DC1.Pearson.pub [192.168.1.10] with 32 bytes of data:
Reply from 192.168.1.10: bytes=32 time=1ms TTL=128
Reply from 192.168.1.10: bytes=32 time<1ms TTL=128
Reply from 192.168.1.10: bytes=32 time<1ms TTL=128
Reply from 192.168.1.10: bytes=32 time<1ms TTL=128
ping statistics for 192.168.1.10:
    Packets: Sent = 4, Received = 4, Lost = 0 (0% loss),
Approximate round trip times in milli-seconds:
    Minimum = 0ms, Maximum = 1ms, Average = 0ms
```

**NOTE**   Because the system is a member of the pearson.pub domain, the pearson.pub suffix is appended to the hostname of dc1, giving a fully qualified domain name (FQDN) of dc1.pearson.pub.

Notice that the first line shows that DC1.Pearson.pub has been resolved to 192.168.1.10. In this domain, it is resolved by DNS, but it can also be resolved from the hosts file, the lmhosts file, WINS, or a broadcast.

You can get a few different errors from ping, as shown in the following table.

| Error | Example | Remarks |
|-------|---------|---------|
| Could not find host. | `C:\>ping dc99`<br>Ping request could not find host dc99. Please check the name and try again. | Name resolution methods cannot resolve the name to an IP address. This commonly means that the name is not known by the DNS server. |
| Request timed out. | `C:\>ping 192.168.1.1`<br>pinging 192.168.1.1 with 32 bytes of data:<br>Request timed out.<br>Request timed out.<br>Request timed out.<br>Request timed out.<br>ping statistics for 192.168.1.1:<br>    Packets: Sent = 4, Received = 0, Lost = 4 (100% loss), | This indicates that the system is not responding. It can be because the system is not operational; however, the ping could also be blocked by a firewall. |
| Destination host unreachable. | `C:\>ping 192.168.3.10`<br>pinging 192.168.3.10 with 32 bytes of data:<br>Reply from 192.168.1.11:<br>Destination host unreachable.<br>Reply from 192.168.1.11:<br>Destination host unreachable.<br>Reply from 192.168.1.11:<br>Destination host unreachable.<br>Reply from 192.168.1.11:<br>Destination host unreachable.<br>ping statistics for 192.168.3.10:<br>    Packets: Sent = 4, Received = 4, Lost = 0 (0% loss), | This often indicates that the default gateway on the local system or the remote system is not configured correctly. The default gateway should be on the same subnet. |

**NOTE**   You might occasionally see the first reply timeout but other replies succeed. This can be due to delays with routers and the time it takes for ARP to get the MAC address.

Another error you might read about but rarely see is TTL Expired in Transit. The TTL value determines the maximum amount of time an IP packet can live in the network without reaching its destination. If you have networking problems with routers and routes on your network, a ping might get caught in a routing loop and expire on the wire, causing this error.

It's important to reiterate that a Request Timed Out error doesn't necessarily indicate the system is not operational. The firewall setting might be preventing a ping. You can ensure that the firewall is allowing ICMP ping requests with **netsh**, as shown in the following table.

| Enable and Disable ping in the Firewall | Comments |
| --- | --- |
| `C:\>netsh firewall set icmpsetting 8`<br>`IMPORTANT: Command execut-`<br>`ed successfully.`<br>`However, "netsh firewall"`<br>`is deprecated;`<br>`use "netsh advfirewall`<br>`firewall" instead.` | Enables echo requests.<br><br>**NOTE**   The **netsh firewall** commands have been deprecated in Windows Server 2008 R2but not Windows Server 2008. The system complains to you if you use them, but they do work. |
| `C:\>netsh firewall set icmpsetting 8 disable` | Disables echo requests. |
| `C:\>netsh advfirewall firewall add rule name = "allow icmp incoming v4 echo request" protocol = icmpv4:8,any dir = in action = allow`<br>`Ok.` | You can use the **netsh advfirewall firewall** command to create a rule. This rule also enables echo requests.<br><br>**NOTE**   This command works on both Windows Server 2008 and Windows Server 2008 R2. |
| `C:\>netsh advfirewall firewall delete rule name = "allow icmp incoming v4 echo request"`<br>`Deleted 1 rule(s).`<br>`Ok.` | Deletes the **advfirewall** rule. |

**ping** supports several switches, many of which are shown in the following table.

| ping Switches | Comments |
| --- | --- |
| `-t`<br>`C:\>ping dc1 -t` | You can use the **-t** switch to have **ping** continue pinging the specified host until you stop it. You can stop it by pressing Ctrl+C.<br><br>While it's running, you can press the Ctrl+Break keys to view statistics. |

| ping Switches | Comments |
|---|---|
| `-n`<br><br>`ping` *name-or-IP-address* `-n` *number-of-echoes*<br><br>`C:\>ping 192.168.1.10 -n 10` | You can specify the number of echo requests to send with the **-n** switch. By default, four ping echo requests are sent, but you can give a number such as 10 to send 10 instead. |
| `-a`<br><br>`C:\>ping -a 192.168.1.10` | The **-a** switch can be used to resolve addresses to hostnames. This requires a reverse lookup zone and an associated PTR (pointer) record on the DNS server, so it won't always work. |
| `-l`<br><br>`ping` *name-or- IP-address* `-l` *packet-size*<br>`C:\>ping 192.168.1.10 -l 64` | You can change the size of the ping packet with **-l** (a lowercase "el," not the number 1). The size is specified in bytes and the default size is 32 bytes. |
| `-i`<br><br>`ping` *name-or- IP-address* `-i` *new-TTL*<br>`C:\>ping 192.168.1.10 -i 10` | You can modify the TTL with the **-i** switch. The default is 128. |
| `-4`<br><br>`ping` *name* `-4`<br>`C:\>ping dc1 -4` | You can use the **-4** switch to force ping to use IPv4. |
| `-6`<br><br>`ping` *name* `-6`<br>`C:\>ping dc1 -6` | You can use the **-6** switch to force ping to use IPv6. |

You can also ping using the IPv6 address. For example, the following listing shows the output when pinging the IPv6 link-local address of another computer:

`C:\>ping fe80::c065:e623:4104:1469`

```
Pinging fe80::c065:e623:4104:1469 from fe80::84e0:3272:e623:21c6%10 with
32 bytes of data:
Reply from fe80::c065:e623:4104:1469: time=7ms
Reply from fe80::c065:e623:4104:1469: time=2ms
Reply from fe80::c065:e623:4104:1469: time=1ms
Reply from fe80::c065:e623:4104:1469: time=3ms

Ping statistics for fe80::c065:e623:4104:1469:
    Packets: Sent = 4, Received = 4, Lost = 0 (0% loss),
Approximate round trip times in milli-seconds:
    Minimum = 1ms, Maximum = 7ms, Average = 3ms
```

> **TIP** You can verify the operation of IPv6 on a remote computer by pinging its link-local address. You can use **ipconfig /all** on any computer to identify its link-local IPv6 address.

## Viewing the Router Path with tracert

If you have several routers between your system and the destination computer, you can use the **tracert** command to trace the route. It lists each of the routers by IP address, and if the IP address can be resolved to a name, it lists the name. The basic syntax is

```
tracert hostname
```

or

```
tracert IP address
```

The following example shows the output when using **tracert** to trace the route to a specific server in a network.

| tracert Switches | Comments |
|---|---|
| `tracert -d dc1.pearson.pub`<br>`Tracing route to dc1.pearson.pub [10.55.99.211]`<br>`over a maximum of 30 hops:`<br>`1   103 ms    79 ms    79 ms    10.174.112.192`<br>`2   75 ms     89 ms    106 ms   10.174.115.255`<br>`3   173 ms    76 ms    74 ms    10.83.27.193`<br>`4   85 ms     89 ms    89 ms    10.83.26.18`<br>`5   117 ms    126 ms   125 ms   10.55.99.211` | **tracert** first resolves the name to an IP address. It then records the time it takes to get to each router and the IP address of the router.<br><br>Without the **-d** command, it also attempts to resolve the IP address to a name. |

You have some other ways you can use **tracert**, and the following table shows two of those ways.

| `-4`<br>`tracert -4 name-or- IP-address`<br>`C:\>tracert -4 dc1.pearson.pub` | You can force the trace to use IPv4 with the **-4** switch. |
|---|---|
| `-6`<br>`tracert -6 name-or- IP-address`<br>`C:\>tracert -6 dc1.pearson.pub` | You can force the trace to use IPv6 with the **-6** switch. |

## Checking for Data Loss with pathping

Occasionally you might notice that the network response is slow. There are several reasons why the network might be slow, but the **pathping** command can help you narrow down where it's slow.

More specifically, **pathping** traces the route to the destination just like **tracert**, and then sends 100 echo requests to each router in the path to test for data loss. Anything less than 100 echo replies indicates a percentage of data loss. The **pathping** usually takes a little over 5 minutes to complete. It finishes tracing the route rather quickly, but it takes time to send and receive the 100 pings for each router. The basic syntax of **pathping** is

```
pathping hostname
```

or

```
pathping IP address
```

Additionally, you can use a few switches with **pathping**.

| pathping Switches | Comments |
| --- | --- |
| -h<br>`pathping name-or- IP-address -h maximum_hops`<br>`C:\>pathping dc1.pearson.pub -h 15` | The default maximum number of hops, or routers, is 30 but you can modify this number with the **-h** switch. |
| -n<br>`C:\>pathping dc1.pearson.pub -n` | **pathping** normally tries to resolve the IP addresses to hostnames, but this can be suppressed with the **-n** switch. |
| -p<br>`pathping name-or- IP-address -p period`<br>`C:\>pathping dc1.pearson.pub -p 100` | You can cause the system to wait a period of time (specified in milliseconds) between pings with the **-p** switches. |
| -q<br>`pathping name-or- IP-address -q num_queries`<br>`C:\>pathping dc1.pearson.pub -q 10` | The default number of queries per hop is 100, but you can modify this to a different number with the **-q** switch. |
| -4<br>`C:\>pathping dc1.pearson.pub -4` | You can force the trace to use IPv4 with the **-4** switch. |
| -6<br>`C:\>pathping dc1.pearson.pub -6` | You can force the trace to use IPv6 with the **-6** switch. |

# Using the Reliability and Performance Monitor

This chapter provides information and commands concerning the following topics:

- Gathering information from the Reliability Monitor
- Running System Data Collector Sets
- Writing a script to run Data Collector Sets
- Scheduling a script to run Data Collector Sets

**TIP**   You should be familiar with the Reliability and Performance Monitor when preparing for the 70-640, 70-642, and 70-646 exams.

## Gathering Information from the Reliability Monitor

The Reliability Monitor provides a quick snapshot of your system's performance. Figure 29-1 shows the Reliability Monitor on a Windows Server 2008 system. As you can see, this gives you information about the following:

- Software installs and uninstalls
- Application failures
- Hardware failures
- Windows failures
- Miscellaneous failures

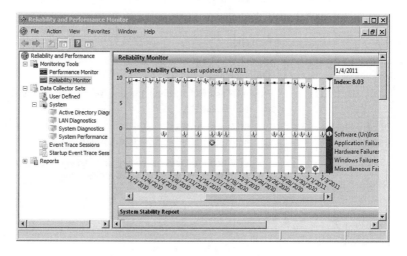

**Figure 29-1**   Windows Reliability Monitor

Although the Reliability Monitor looks the same in both Windows Server 2008 and Windows Server 2008 R2, you access it a little differently in each. The following steps show how to launch the Reliability Monitor in Windows Server 2008.

| Steps | Windows Server 2008 Actions |
|---|---|
| 1. Launch the **Performance and Reliability Monitor.** | Click **Start**, type **perfmon** in the **Start Search** text box, and then press **Enter**. |
| 2. Access the **Reliability Monitor**. | Expand **Monitoring Tools** and select **Reliability Monitor**. |

The following steps show how to launch the Reliability Monitor in Windows Server 2008 R2.

| Steps | Windows Server 2008 Actions |
|---|---|
| 1. Launch the **Performance and Reliability Monitor**. | Click **Start**, type **perfmon** in the **Start Programs and Files** text box, and then press **Enter**. |
| 2. Access the **Reliability Monitor**. | Right-click **Monitoring Tools**, and then select **View System Reliability**. |

Reliability information is gathered from the Reliability Analysis Component agent scheduled task. On Windows Server 2008, this task is called **RACAgent** and is scheduled to run on boot and once an hour. However, on Windows Server 2008 R2, it is called **RACTask** and runs only when Event ID 1007 for the Customer Experience Improvement Program occurs. It includes an hourly trigger, but it's disabled by default.

**TIP** If the task doesn't run, reliability information isn't collected and the display is blank.

You can check to see whether the task is scheduled on Windows Server 2008 and Windows Server 2008 R2 with the following steps.

| Steps | Actions |
|---|---|
| 1. Launch **Task Scheduler**. | Launch the **Task Scheduler** from the **Administrative Tools** menu. |
| 2. Locate the **RAC** task. | Expand **Task Scheduler Library**, **Microsoft**, **Windows**, and then select **RAC**. |
| 3. Display hidden tasks if necessary. | If **RACAgent** or **RACTask** isn't shown, right-click **RAC**, and then select **View**, **Show Hidden Tasks**. |
| | **TIP** When the task is showing, you can view the **Last Run Time** to see whether it has run recently. |

| Steps | Actions |
|---|---|
| 4. Determine whether the hourly trigger is enabled. | Select the **Triggers** tab. Your display should look similar to Figure 29-2. This shows the triggers for the task in Windows Server 2008. In Figure 29-2, you can see that one of the triggers is disabled and never runs.<br><br>**NOTE**   The tasks are slightly different in Windows Server 2008 R2.<br><br>**TIP**   The key task to gather reliability information is disabled by default in Windows Server 2008 R2 but enabled by default in Windows Server 2008. |
| 5. Access the task **Properties** page. | Right-click the task and select **Properties**. |
| 6. Look at the **Triggers**. | Select the **Triggers** tab. |
| 7. Enable or disable the trigger. | Select either of the triggers, and then select **Edit**. You can select the checkbox next to **Enabled** on the **Edit Trigger** page to enable the trigger as shown in Figure 29-3.<br><br>**TIP**   If you enable the trigger, you might want to monitor the performance of your system when the task runs. It has been known to bog down a system. This is probably one of the primary reasons it's disabled by default in Windows Server 2008 R2. |
| 8. Clean up the display. | Close all open windows. |

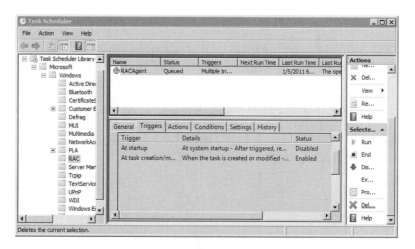

**Figure 29-2**   Viewing the status of the RACAgent task in Task Scheduler (in Windows Server 2008)

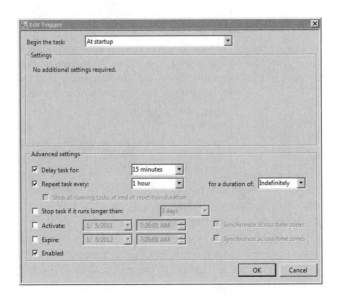

**Figure 29-3** Enabling a trigger in the RACAgent task in Task Scheduler

## Running System Data Collector Sets

Data Collector Sets are a great new feature available in Windows Server 2008 and Windows Server 2008 R2. System Data Collector Sets have preconfigured counters that enable you to easily run a test on your system and check its performance.

> **NOTE** Data Collector Sets are part of the Reliability and Performance Monitor in Windows Server 2008 and part of the Performance Monitor in Windows Server 2008 R2.

Figure 29-4 shows the Performance Monitor in Windows Server 2008 R2. If you compare this to Figure 29-1 (showing the Reliability and Performance Monitor in Windows Server 2008), you can see they are similar. The biggest difference is that the Reliability Monitor is not shown in Windows Server 2008 R2.

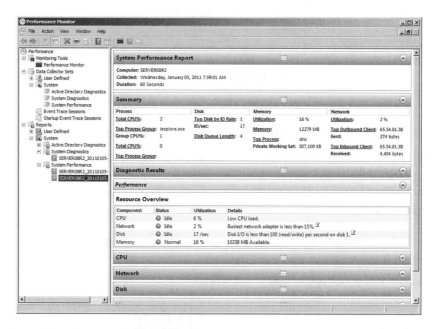

**Figure 29-4**   Performance Monitor in Windows Server 2008 R2

**NOTE**   The display pane in Figure 29-4 shows the contents of a report from a System Performance Data Collector Set.

You can use the following steps to manually run the System Data Collector Sets.

| Steps | Actions |
|---|---|
| 1. Start the **Reliability and Performance Monitor**. | Launch the **Reliability and Performance Monitor** (or the **Performance Monitor** in Windows Server 2008 R2) from the **Administrative Tools** menu. |
| 2. Access the System Data Collector Set. | Expand the **Data Collector Sets** and **System**. |
| 3. Start the **System Performance** Data Collector Set. | Right-click the **System Performance** Data Collector Set and select **Start**. This runs for 1 minute and stops automatically. |
| 4. Start the **System Diagnostics** Data Collector Set. | When the **System Performance** Data Collector Set stops, right-click the **System Diagnostics** Data Collector Set and click **Start**. This runs for 10 minutes and stops automatically.<br><br>**NOTE**   You cannot run two Data Collector Sets at the same time. |
| 5. View the **System Performance** report. | While the **System Performance** Data Collector Set is running, expand **Reports**, **System**, and **System Performance**. Select the report you just ran. The report looks similar to Figure 29-4.<br><br>**NOTE**   The summary shows key information about the usage of the CPU, disk, memory, and NIC. |

| Steps | Actions |
|---|---|
| 6. View the **System Diagnostics** report. | When the **System Diagnostics** Data Collector Set stops, view its report. You can see it in the **Reports**, **System**, **System Diagnostics** node. |

## Writing a Script to Run Data Collector Sets

These Data Collector Sets don't run automatically; however, you can write a script to run them, and then schedule the script. The command you use is **logman** and the basic syntax is

```
logman start "system\data-collector-set-name"
```

For example, if you want to start the System Performance Data Collector Set, you can use the following command:

```
logman start "system\system performance"
```

> **TIP** If you create a User Defined Data Collector Set, you don't need to schedule this from the command line. Instead, you can schedule it using the **Schedule** tab of the Data Collector Set. However, you can't modify any of the predefined System Data Collector Sets.

The following table shows some of the switches you can use with **logman**.

| logman Switches | Comments |
|---|---|
| Start a Data Collector Set.<br><br>`logman start`<br>`"node\data-collector-`<br>`set-name"`<br>`C:\>logman start`<br>`"system\system`<br>`diagnostics"` | The node is **System** for the predefined System Data Collector Sets and **User Defined** for any Data Collector Sets created by you or other administrators. The example starts the System Diagnostics Data Collector Set. |
| Stop a Data Collector Set.<br><br>`logman stop "node\data-`<br>`collector-set-name"`<br>`C:\>logman start`<br>`"system\system`<br>`diagnostics"` | The LAN Diagnostics Data Collector Set included in Windows Server 2008 doesn't have an automatic stop. You can use the **logman stop** command to stop it (or any other Data Collector Set). |
| Start or stop on a remote computer.<br><br>`-s computer-name`<br>`C:\>logman start`<br>`"system\system`<br>`performance"` | You can run the command on remote computers using the **-s** switch. |

| logman Switches | Comments |
|---|---|
| Send commands to Event Trace Sessions.<br><br>`-ets`<br>`logman stop "node\data-`<br>`collector-set-name"`<br>`C:\>logman start`<br>`"system\system`<br>`performance" -ets` | This switch sends commands to Event Trace Sessions directly without saving or scheduling them. |

Use the following steps to create a script to start the System Performance Data Collector Set. The next section shows how to schedule this script with the Task Scheduler.

| Steps | Action |
|---|---|
| 1. Start **Notepad**. | Launch an instance of Notepad by clicking **Start**, typing **Notepad**, and pressing **Enter**. |
| 2. Add script to **Notepad** file. | Type the following line in the Notepad file:<br><br>**logman start "system\system performance" -ets** |
| 3. Save the script. | Press Ctrl+S to save the file. Browse to the root of C:. Create a folder named **Scripts** if you don't have one already. Browse to the **C:\Scripts** folder. In the **File Name** section, type **sysperf.bat**.<br><br>TIP  If you don't include the .bat in the filename, the file will be as a text file with a .txt extension. You can schedule and run a batch file with a .bat extension, but you can't schedule or run a text file. |
| 4. Clean up. | Click **Save**. Close all open windows. |

## Scheduling a Script to Run Data Collector Sets

If you created a script to start a Data Collector Set (as shown in the previous section), you can use the steps in the following table to schedule it to run regularly.

TIP  When the Data Collector Set is scheduled to run regularly, you can view the reports at any time via the Reports node. However, reports are regularly archived and older reports are deleted. If you want to keep these reports, you must copy them.

| Steps | Action |
|---|---|
| 1. Start **Task Scheduler**. | Launch Task Scheduler from the **Administrative Tools** menu. |
| 2. Launch the **Create Basic Task** wizard. | Right-click **Task Scheduler (Local)** and select **Create Basic Task**. |
| 3. Name the task. | Name the task **Run System Performance Data Collector Set,** and then click **Next**. |

| Steps | Action |
|-------|--------|
| 4. Define the type of trigger. | Accept the default trigger of **Daily**, and then click **Next**. |
| 5. Set the time for the trigger. | You can change the start date and time or leave it as is. Click **Next**. |
| 6. Configure task to start a program. | Ensure that **Start a Program** is selected, and then click **Next**. |
| 7. Add the batch file. | Click **Browse**. Browse to the **C:\scripts\sysperf.bat** file (or another executable file if desired). Select the file and click **Open**. Click **Next**. Your display will look similar to Figure 29-5. |
| 8. Finish the task. | Review the information on the summary page. Click **Finish**. |

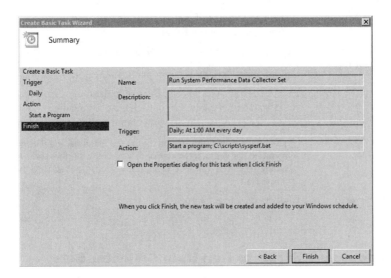

**Figure 29-5** Scheduling a task

# Using Network Monitor and nmcap

This chapter provides information and commands concerning the following topics:

- Installing Network Monitor
- Starting and using Network Monitor
- Using **nmcap** to capture traffic
- Automatically starting, stopping, and terminating **nmcap**
- Adding filters to **nmcap**
- Enabling promiscuous mode in **nmcap**

**TIP**  You should be familiar with Network Monitor and **nmcap** when preparing for the 70-642 exam.

## Installing Network Monitor

Network Monitor is a free protocol analyzer, or network sniffer, available from Microsoft. It is used to capture and analyze network traffic. At the time of writing this, the current version is 3.4. You can download and install it on Windows Server 2008 or Windows Server 2008 R2 with the steps in the following table.

**TIP**  The free version of Network Monitor in previous versions of Windows was limited. It didn't work in promiscuous mode and captured only traffic sent to or from the collecting computer. However, Network Monitor version 3.x does work in promiscuous mode. The last section in this chapter talks about promiscuous mode and how to enable it.

| Step | Action |
|------|--------|
| 1. Access Microsoft's download site. | Go to Microsoft's download site (http://www.microsoft.com/ downloads/) and type **Network Monitor**. |
| 2. Locate Microsoft Network Monitor. | Click the link for the current version of **Microsoft Network Monitor**. |
| 3. Download the version for your system. | Locate the download for your operating system (x86 for 32-bit systems, x64 for 64-bit systems, and ia64 for Itanium based 64-bit systems). Click **Download**. Click **Save**. Browse to a location on your system and click **Save**. |
| 4. Launch the install file. | Launch Windows Explorer and browse to where you saved the download. Double-click it to start it. |

| Step | Action |
|------|--------|
| 5. Start the installation. | A small dialog box appears indicating this will install the **Microsoft Network Monitor** and the **Microsoft Network Monitor Parsers**. Click **Yes**. |
| 6. Review the Welcome page. | Review the information on the Welcome page and click **Next**. |
| 7. Review the license agreement. | Review the **End-User License Agreement**, select **I Accept the Terms in the License Agreement,** and then click **Next**. |
| 8. Decide on automatic updates or not. | Select whether you want to use Microsoft Update and click **Next**. |
| 9. Start a Typical install. | Click **Typical** to install the most common program features. Click **Install**. |
| 10. Complete the installation. | When the **Completing the Setup Wizard** page appears, click **Finish**. The installation of the **Parsers** starts. This runs and completes without any more user interaction needed. |

## Starting and Using Network Monitor

The following steps show how to launch Network Monitor and capture some traffic.

> **NOTE** If you're already familiar with Network Monitor, you can skip this section because it is basic. However, it does provide some context for launching and using Network Monitor from the command prompt with **nmcap**.

| Step | Action |
|------|--------|
| 1. Launch Network Monitor. | Start Network Monitor 3.4 by clicking **Start**, **All Programs**, **Microsoft Network Monitor 3.4**, **Microsoft Network Monitor 3.4**. You might be prompted to use Microsoft Update. Choose **Yes** or **No**. |
| 2. Select the NIC. | In the **Select Networks** section (bottom left) ensure that at least one NIC is checked as shown in Figure 30-1. This is the NIC that data is collected on and if one isn't selected, data won't be captured.<br><br>**TIP** If you want the capture to use promiscuous mode, click the button for **P-Mode** in the **Select Networks** section. |
| 3. Open a capture window. | Click **New Capture** at the upper left. This opens a capture window. |
| 4. Start a capture. | Click the **Start** button to start the capture process. |

| Step | Action |
|---|---|
| 5. Generate ICMP traffic. | Launch a command prompt and ping another computer on the network. This generates some basic ICMP traffic. Click **Stop**.<br><br>**NOTE**   Depending on network activity, you might capture much more traffic than just the ICMP echoes. |
| 6. Filter ICMP traffic. | Type **icmp** in the text box below **Display Filter**. Click **Apply**. Your display should look similar to Figure 30-2.<br><br>Notice how the filter removed all non-ICMP traffic. |
| 7. Save the capture. | Click **Save As**. Type **ping** and click **Save**. This saves the capture as **ping.cap**. |
| 8. Close the capture. | Right-click over the **Capture** tab and select **Close This Tab**. |
| 9. Open a saved capture. | Click **Open Capture**. Select the **ping.cap** capture file you just saved and click **Open**. You can now browse through the saved capture. |
| 10. Clean up. | Close all open windows. |

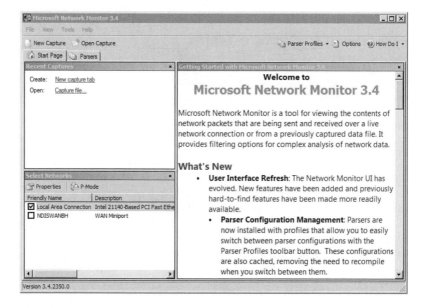

**Figure 30-1**   Selecting Networks in Network Monitor

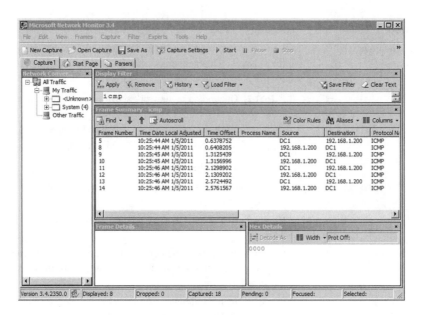

**Figure 30-2**  Capturing and filtering traffic with Network Monitor

# Using nmcap to Capture Traffic

When you install Network Monitor, you also install the command-line tool called **nmcap**. You can use **nmcap** to start and stop captures, and it includes a rich set of switches to control the capture.

> **TIP**  Due to the overhead of the GUI of Network Monitor, Microsoft does not recommend using it on production systems. Instead, Microsoft recommends using **nmcap** to minimize the effect on system resources.

The basic syntax to start a capture is

```
nmcap /network *  |  adapter-name /file filename.cap:size
```

For example, if you want to start a capture on all adapters for a system, save the capture to a file named **dc1cap.cap**, and limit the size to 10 MB, you can use the following command:

```
nmcap /network * /capture /file dc1cap.cap:10mb
```

The following listing shows what you see as the capture runs:

```
c:\>nmcap /network * /capture /file dc1cap.cap:10mb
Network Monitor Command Line Capture (nmcap) 3.4.2350.0
```

```
Saving info to: c:\\dc1cap.cap - using circular buffer of size
10.00 MB.

ATTENTION: Conversations Disabled: Some filters require
conversations and will not work correctly (see Help for details)

ATTENTION: Process Tracking Disabled: Use /CaptureProcesses to
enable (see Help for details)
Note: Process Filtering Disabled.

Exit by Ctrl+C

Capturing | Received: 12 Pending: 0 Saved: 12 Dropped: 0 |
Time: 27 seconds.
```

Files captured this way can be opened by typing in the name of the file (such as **dc1cap. cap**) at the command prompt. Because **.cap** is associated with Network Monitor, this launches Network Monitor and opens the capture within it. You can also open Network Monitor and browse to the capture file as shown previously.

The previous command runs the capture on all available NICs; however, you can choose just a single NIC if desired. First, you can view a list of available network cards with the **/displaynetworks** switch as shown in the following listing.

```
c:\>nmcap /displaynetworks
Network Monitor Command Line Capture (nmcap) 3.4.2350.0
0. Local Area Connection (Intel 21140-Based PCI Fast Ethernet
Adapter)
1. NDISWANBH (WAN Miniport)
```

If you want to run the command on only the NIC named Local Area Connection, use the number 0 with the **/network** switch like the following:

```
nmcap /network 0 /capture /file dc1cap.cap:10mb
```

# Automatically Starting, Stopping, and Terminating nmcap

**nmcap** has some switches to start at a certain time, stop after a period of time, or terminate based on certain conditions. The following table shows some of the uses.

| Start, Stop, and Terminate Commands | Comments |
|---|---|
| Start the capture at a specific time.<br><br>`/startwhen /time hh:mm:ss xm`<br>`mm/dd/yyyy`<br>`c:\>nmcap /network * /capture /file`<br>`dc1cap.cap:10mb /startwhen /time`<br>`11:00:00 am 01/30/2011` | You can specify a time when you want the capture to start by combining the **/startwhen** and **/time** switches. You specify the time of day by including am or pm. The example starts the capture at 11 AM on January 30, 2011.<br><br>**NOTE**   You can also use **/time-after** to start the capture after a certain amount of time, as shown in the following example. |
| Stop the capture after a specific amount of time.<br><br>`/stopwhen /timeafter number-of-min-`<br>`utes min /stopwhen /timeafter num-`<br>`ber-of-minutes min`<br>`c:\> nmcap /network * /capture`<br>`/file dc1cap.cap:10mb /startwhen`<br>`/timeafter 5 min /stopwhen`<br>`/timeafter 30 min` | When you use the **/startwhen** switch, you can also use the **/stopwhen** switch.<br><br>The example causes the capture to start after 5 minutes, and then stop after 30 minutes.<br><br>**NOTE**   The **/stopwhen** switch does not terminate the program if the **/startwhen** switch has not been used. However, you can use the **/terminatewhen** switch by itself.<br><br>**TIP**   You can also use **hours** instead of **mins**. |
| Terminate a capture.<br><br>`/terminatewhen [/keypress key`<br>`/timeafter number-of-minutes min]`<br>`c:\>nmcap /network * /capture /file`<br>`dc1cap.cap:10mb /terminatewhen`<br>`/keypress q`<br>`c:\>nmcap /network * /capture /file`<br>`dc1cap.cap:10mb /terminatewhen`<br>`/timeafter 30 min`<br>`c:\>nmcap /network * /capture /file`<br>`dc1cap.cap:10mb /terminatewhen`<br>`/keypress q /timeafter 30 min`<br>`c:\>nmcap /network * /capture /file`<br>`dc1cap.cap:10mb /terminatewhen q`<br>`/timeafter 30 min /keypress` | You can use the **/terminatewhen** switch to cause the capture to stop after a specific key is pressed, a time has passed, or both.<br><br>When using both the **/timeafter** and **/keypress** switches in the same command, both conditions must occur and in the correct order.<br><br>For example, in the third example (**/keypress q /timeafter 30 min**) the capture stops 30 minutes after the **q** key is pressed.<br><br>In the fourth example (**/timeafter 30 min /keypress q**) the capture stops after 30 minutes have passed and then the user presses the **q** key. |

## Adding Filters to nmcap

You can filter the **nmcap** capture based on protocols, ports, IP addresses, and MAC or
Ethernet addresses. The following table shows some common uses with these filters.

| Filtering Traffic Commands | Comments |
|---|---|
| Capture traffic based on specific protocols.<br><br>`/capture protocol-list`<br>`nmcap /network * \| adapter-name`<br>`filter-protocol /file filename.`<br>`cap:size`<br>`C:\>nmcap /network * /capture icmp`<br>`/file dccap.cap:10mb`<br>`C:\>nmcap /network * /capture ldap`<br>`/file dccap.cap:10mb`<br>`C:\>nmcap /network * /capture !ldap`<br>`/file dccap.cap:10mb`<br>`C:\>nmcap /network * /capture (ldap`<br>`and icmp and dns)  /file dccap.`<br>`cap:10mb` | You can add protocols to filter in the **nmcap** after the **/capture** switch.<br><br>The first example captures only ICMP traffic and ignores all other traffic. The second example captures only LDAP traffic. The third example captures all traffic except for LDAP traffic.<br><br>**TIP** The **!** character is used as a Boolean NOT character. In other words, if you want to capture LDAP traffic, use **ldap** as the filter. If you want to capture everything but LDAP, use **!ldap** (read as NOT ldap).<br><br>The fourth example captures all LDAP, ICMP, and DNS traffic. You can use as many Boolean ANDs in the filter as desired. For example, it can be **ldap and icmp and ftp**, and so on. |
| Capture traffic based on a specific port.<br><br>`/capture tcp\|udp.port==port-number`<br>`C:\>nmcap /network * /capture`<br>`tcp.port==80 /file dccap.cap:10mb`<br>`C:\>nmcap /network * /capture`<br>`udp.port==53 /file dccap.cap:10mb`<br>`C:\>nmcap /network * /capture`<br>`(tcp.port==80 and udp.port==53)`<br>`/file dccap.cap:10mb` | You can specify traffic to capture based on the TCP or UDP port used.<br><br>The first example captures traffic using TCP port 80, the second example captures traffic using UDP port 53, and the third example captures traffic from both TCP port 80 and UDP port 53.<br><br>**NOTE** The == is two equal symbols put together. |
| Capture traffic based on IP addresses.<br><br>`/capture ipv4.address==IP-address`<br>`C:\>nmcap /network * /capture`<br>`ipv4.address==192.168.1.5 /file`<br>`dccap.cap:10mb` | You can add a filter for specific IP addresses. The example captures only traffic to or from the system with the IPv4 address of 192.168.1.15. |

| Filtering Traffic Commands | Comments |
|---|---|
| Capture traffic based on MAC addresses. `/capture ipv4.address==IP-address` `C:\> nmcap /network * /capture ethernet.address==00-03-ff-62-13-d7 /file dccap.cap:10mb` | You can also filter based on Ethernet addresses (also called MAC addresses or physical addresses). The example captures only traffic to and from the system with the specified MAC address. |

## Enabling Promiscuous Mode in nmcap

By default, Network Monitor and **nmcap** capture only traffic sent directly to or coming from the local IP address and broadcast traffic. However, you frequently want to be able to capture all traffic that reaches the NIC. To do so, you need to enable promiscuous mode, or P-Mode, with the **/disablelocalonly** switch.

| Enabling Promiscuous Mode with nmcap | Comments |
|---|---|
| Enable Promiscuous Mode. `/disablelocalonly` `C:\>nmcap /network * /capture /file dc3cap.cap:10mb /disablelocalonly` | Disables local-only capture, which enables promiscuous mode, or P-Mode. All frames that reach the network cards are captured regardless of their source and destination IP addresses. |

# Remote Desktop Services

This chapter provides information and commands concerning the following topics:

- Adding the Remote Desktop Services role
- Viewing and manipulating the install mode with **change user**
- Modifying logon capabilities with **change logon**
- Connecting and disconnecting sessions with **tscon** and **tsdiscon**
- Identifying open sessions with query user or **quser**
- Resetting sessions with **reset session**

**TIP** You should be familiar with the commands used to manage Remote Desktop Services and Terminal Services sessions when preparing for the 70-642 and 70-643 exams.

## Adding the Remote Desktop Services Role

Remote Desktop Services (RDS) in Windows Server 2008 R2 enables users to access remote applications, or even full Windows desktops. A central RD Session Host server hosts the Windows applications, and clients are able to run the applications remotely.

The primary command-line command you need to know when working with RDS is the **change** command. When installing some applications, you must be able to change the mode to **install** mode, and then back to **execute** mode.

**TIP** RDS was previously known as Terminal Services. Microsoft changed the name to Remote Desktop Services in Windows Server 2008 R2.

Before these commands work, the RDS or Terminal Services role must be installed. You can use the steps in the following table to do so.

**NOTE**   These steps are written for both Windows Server 2008 and Windows Server 2008 R2. When there are differences, they are labeled in the steps.

| Steps | Action |
|---|---|
| 1. | Launch Server Manager through the **Administrative Tools** menu. |
| 2. | Select **Roles** and click **Add Roles**. |
| 3. | Click **Next** on the **Before You Begin** page. |
| 4. | Windows Server 2008: Select the checkbox next to **Terminal Services** as shown in Figure 31-1.<br><br>Windows Server 2008 R2: Select the checkbox next to **Remote Desktop Services** as shown in Figure 31-2.<br><br>Click **Next**. |
| 5. | Review the information on the introduction screen and click **Next**. |
| 6. | Windows Server 2008: Select the checkbox next to **Terminal Server**.<br><br>Windows Server 2008 R2: Select the checkbox next to **Remote Desktop Session Host**.<br><br>Click **Next**. |
| 7. | Review the information about **Application Compatibility** and click **Next**. |
| 8. | Select the desired **Authentication Method**. **Network Level Authentication** is the most secure but older clients don't support it. Click **Next**. |
| 9. | On the **Specify Licensing Mode** page, accept the default of **Configure Later**, and click **Next**. |
| 10. | On the **User Groups** page, you can add additional groups if desired. The **Administrators** group is added by default. Click **Next**. |
| 11. | Windows Server 2008 R2 only: Review the choices on the **Configure Client Experience** page. Select any features desired and click **Next**. |
| 12. | On the **Confirmation** page, click **Install**. When the install completes, click **Close**. Click **Yes** to restart the server. |
| 13. | After the system reboots, log on. The install wizard resumes and completes the installation. When it completes, click **Close**. |

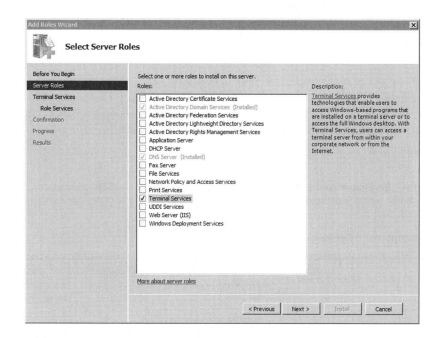

**Figure 31-1**   Adding the Terminal Services Role to Windows Server 2008

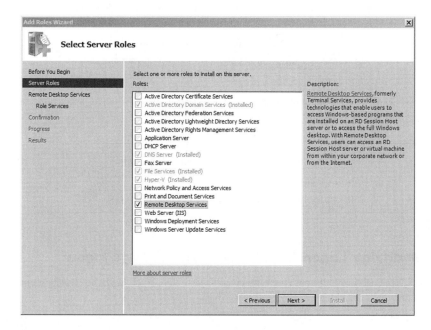

**Figure 31-2**   Adding the Remote Desktop Services Role to Windows Server 2008 R2

## Viewing and Manipulating the Install Mode with change user

The best way to install applications on an RDS Session Host or Terminal Services server is with Microsoft Installer (.msi) files. When you use .msi files, you don't need to take any additional steps. However, if you install an application that doesn't use an .msi file, you need to take additional steps with the **change user** command. The basic syntax is

```
change user /execute | /install | /query
```

> **TIP**  The **chgusr** command is an alias for **change user**. In other words, you can use **chgusr** with any of these switches just as you use **change user** with these switches.

| change user Commands | Comments |
|---|---|
| Prepare to install applications.<br><br>`C:\>change user /install` | Enables install mode. When in install mode, you can then install applications and the RDS Session Host server or Terminal Services server records the process. |
| Return system to execute mode.<br><br>`C:\>change user /execute` | Enables execute mode. After installing the application, this command returns the server to execute mode. |
| Identify current mode.<br><br>`C:\>change user /query` | Displays current settings.<br><br>If the system is in execute mode, it indicates "Application EXECUTE mode is enabled."<br><br>If the system is in install mode, it indicates "Application INSTALL mode is enabled." |

If you need to install an application that isn't using Microsoft Installer, perform the steps in the following order:

| Steps | Action |
|---|---|
| 1. | Run **change user /install** from the command prompt. |
| 2. | Install the application. |
| 3. | Run **change user /execute** from the command prompt. |

## Modifying Logon Capabilities with change logon

You can enable and disable client logons to RDS or TS servers with the **change logon** command.

| change logon Commands | Comments |
|---|---|
| Disable logons.<br><br>`C:\>change logon /disable` | You can use this to prevent new users from logging on without affecting the users who are currently logged on.<br><br>**NOTE**   Logons are automatically reenabled when the system is restarted. |
| Enable logons.<br><br>`C:\>change logon enable` | Reenables user logons after they have been disabled. |
| Identify current mode.<br><br>`C:\>change logon /query` | Displays the current session logon status. |
| `C:\>change logon /drain` | Disables new user logons but allows reconnections to existing sessions. |
| `C:\>change logon /drainuntilrestart` | Disables new user logons until the server is restarted but allows reconnections to existing sessions. |

**TIP**   These settings affect administrator sessions also. In other words, if you disable logons and then log off, you will not be able to log on to the administrator session until logons are reenabled.

# Connecting and Disconnecting Sessions with tscon and tsdiscon

You can use the **tscon** and **tsdiscon** commands to connect and disconnect RDS and TS sessions. The **tscon** command connects a user to a session running on an RDS or TS server. The **tsdiscon** disconnects a user from a session.

The basic syntax of **tsdiscon** is

`tsdiscon` *sessionid | sessionname*

For example, consider Figure 31-3 showing Terminal Services Manager on a Windows Server 2008 server. It shows a single session open with a session ID of 2 and a session name of RDP-Tcp#0.

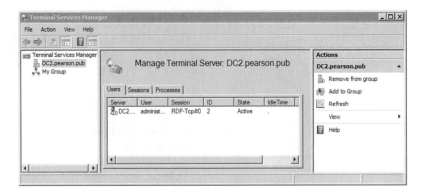

**Figure 31-3**   Terminal Services Manager with a single session open

You can disconnect this session with either of the following commands:

```
tsdiscon 2
tsdiscon rdp-tcp#0
```

Similarly, if the session is disconnected, you can connect it with the **tscon** command. The basic syntax of **tscon** is

```
tsdiscon sessionid | sessionname
```

You can connect the session with either of the following commands:

```
tscon 2
tscon rdp-tcp#0
```

## Identifying Open Sessions with query user or quser

You can use the **query user** (or its alias, **quser**) command to identify open sessions. The following listing shows the output of these commands:

```
C:\Users>query user quser

 USERNAME          SESSIONNAME   ID   STATE    IDLE TIME   LOGON TIME
>administrator     rdp-tcp#0      2   Active        .  1/5/2011 2:00 PM


C:\Users>quser

 USERNAME          SESSIONNAME   ID   STATE    IDLE TIME   LOGON TIME
>administrator     rdp-tcp#0      2   Active        .  1/5/2011 2:00 PM
```

This is similar information that was shown in Figure 31-3 through the Terminal Services Manager. Notice that you can view the session name, ID, and idle time with this output.

> **TIP**  If sessions are idle for too long, it might indicate that the user disconnected from the session instead of logging off. The session continues to consume system resources until it is reset or terminated.

# Resetting Sessions with reset session

You can reset (terminate) sessions with the **reset session** command. The **rwinsta** command is an alias for **reset session** and works the same. The basic syntax is

```
reset session sessionid | sessionname
rwinsta sessionid | sessionname
```

You can reset or terminate the session with any of the following commands:

```
reset session 2
reset session rdp-tcp#0
rwinsta 2
rwinsta rdp-tcp#0
```

# Remote Administration

This chapter provides information and commands concerning the following topics:

- Configuring, verifying, and removing **winrm**
- Using **winrs** to issue commands
- Connecting to remote systems with **mstsc**

> **TIP**  You should be familiar with remote administration methods when preparing for the 70-642, 70-646, and 70-647 exams.

## Configuring, Verifying, and Removing winrm

When using Windows Remote Management (**winrm**) and Windows Remote Shell (**winrs**), both computers must be configured with **winrm**. The basic command to configure the computers is

```
winrm quickconfig
```

> **NOTE**  Chapter 26, "Working with Event Subscriptions," shows how to use **winrm quickconfig** to configure a source computer in an event subscription. You can then use **wecutil qc** to configure the collector computer.

You're prompted to confirm the changes and after you do, **winrm** creates a **winrm** listener and a firewall exception.

You can view the details on the listener with the **winrm enumerate** command, and you can shorten **enumerate** to just **e**. The following listing shows the command and the output:

```
C:\>winrm e winrm/config/listener
Listener
    Address = *
    Transport = HTTP
    Port = 80
    Hostname
    Enabled = true
    URLPrefix = wsman
    CertificateThumbprint
    ListeningOn = 127.0.0.1, 192.168.1.5, ::1,
fe80::5efe:192.168.1.5%12, fe80::c065:e623:4104:1469%10
```

> **TIP**    If the **winrm e winrm/config/listener** command doesn't give any output, it means that the **winrm** listener is not installed. Execute the **winrm quickconfig** command to install it.

The **winrm** HTTP listener on port 80 listens for and acts on **winrs** commands that send their commands through HTTP on port 80.

If you want to delete the **winrm** listener, you can use the following command:

```
winrm invoke restore winrm/config @{}
```

> **NOTE**    There are no spaces before or after the slash (/) in the **winrm/config** clause, but there is a space after **config**.

## Using winrs to Issue Commands

After **winrm** has configured both computers, you can then use **winrs** to issue commands against either computer. The basic syntax is

```
winrs -r:server-name command
```

For example, if you want to enable a remote Server Core computer named SC1 to respond to pings, use this command *locally* on the Server Core computer:

```
netsh firewall set icmpsetting 8
```

However, you can also use this command from a *remote* computer:

```
winrs -r:sc1 netsh firewall set icmpsetting 8
```

The following table shows some commands you can use. Each of these examples is run against a remote Windows Server 2008 Server Core computer named **sc1** (identified in the command as **-r:sc1**).

> **NOTE**    The majority of the commands in the following table are used in other areas of the book. The only difference is that the **winrs** command is executing them on remote computers.

| Example winrs Commands | Comments |
|---|---|
| Retrieve version of remote computer.<br><br>`C:\>winrs -r:sc1 ver` | Shows the version of the computer. Windows Server 2008 is Microsoft Windows [Version 6.0.6001].<br><br>Windows Server 2008 R2 is Microsoft Windows [Version 6.1.7600]. |

| Example winrs Commands | Comments |
|---|---|
| View TCP/IP configuration.<br><br>`C:\>winrs -r:sc1 ipconfig/all` | Views the TCP/IP configuration of the remote system.<br><br>**NOTE**   Chapter 28, "Troubleshooting Network Issues," covers **ipconfig** in more depth. |
| Set address of alternate DNS server.<br><br>`C:\>winrs -r:sc1 netsh`<br>`interface ipv4 add dnsserver`<br>`name="local area connection"`<br>`192.168.1.7 index=2` | You can use the **netsh** command to set the address of the DNS server. The alternate DNS server is configured with the **add** command and using an **index** of 2.<br><br>**NOTE**   Chapter 26 covers **netsh** in more depth. |
| View file listing.<br><br>`C:\>winrs -r:sc1 dir c:\` | Shows the file listing of all the files in the root of C on the remote system. |
| Install an application.<br><br>`C:\>winrs -r:sc1 msiecec.exe`<br>`/i c:\apps\app.msi /quiet` | You can use the **msiexec** command with the **/i** switch to install a file from the command prompt. The example installs an application named app.msi in the c:\apps folder and the **/quiet** switch suppresses confirmation. |
| Restart the **netlogon** service.<br><br>`C:\>winrs -r:sc1 net stop`<br>`netlogon`<br>`C:\>winrs -r:sc1 net start`<br>`netlogon` | These commands stop and restart the netlogon service, which forces the registration of SRV records.<br><br>**NOTE**   Chapter 21, "Manipulating Services," covers different service commands in more depth. |
| List services and their state.<br><br>`C:\>winrs -r:sc1 wmic service`<br>`list brief` | Lists the services on the remote computer.<br><br>**TIP**   You can issue any **wmic** commands against the remote computer.<br><br>**NOTE**   Chapter 21 covers the **wmic** service commands in more depth. |
| Access the command prompt on a remote system.<br><br>`C:\>winrs -r:sc1 cmd.exe` | After executing this command, the command prompt directly interacts with the remote system. You don't need to add **winrs** prefixes but instead just type the commands (such as **ipconfig** or **ping**).<br><br>**NOTE**   The prompt changes but it's not apparent that you are on the remote system. To double-check whether you enter commands against the local system or the remote system, use **hostname**.<br><br>**TIP**   To exit the remote command prompt, type **exit**. |

## Connecting to Remote Systems with mstsc

You can launch the Remote Desktop Connection from the command line with the **mstsc** command, which is short for Microsoft Terminal Services Connection. You can enter it from the command prompt or from the **Start Search** box after clicking **Start**.

> **TIP**  Microsoft renamed Terminal Services to Remote Desktop Services in Windows Server 2008 R2; however, commands such as **mstsc** still work. In other words, the acronym has not been renamed from **mstsc** to **msrdsc**.

Figure 32-1 shows the Remote Desktop Connection tool after clicking **Options**. You can also access this by clicking **Start**, **All Programs**, **Accessories**, **Remote Desktop Connection**.

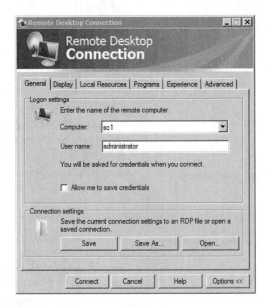

**Figure 32-1**  Remote Desktop Connection

At this point, you can enter the computer name and click **Connect**. You are prompted to enter the credentials of a user that has permission to log on remotely.

> **NOTE**  You can configure the settings you want for the connection in any of the tabs, and then click **Save As** to save the settings as an .rdp configuration file. You can then use this file to connect.

The following table shows some of the switches you can use with **mstsc**.

| mstsc Switch | Description |
|---|---|
| Use a connection file.<br><br>mstsc *file path and name*<br>c:\>**mstsc c:\data\dc1.rdp** | If you have an .rdp file that includes the connection information, you can use it with the **mstsc**. You won't need to reconfigure all the settings each time you connect to a server. |
| **/v**:*server*[:*port*]<br>c:\>**mstsc /v:dc1**<br>c:\>**mstsc /v:dc1:6789** | The **/v** switch enables you to specify which server to connect to and specify the port.<br><br>The default port is 3389 but it can be changed. For example, if the port was changed to 6789 on the server, you can use the example command. |
| /admin<br>c:\>**mstsc /admin /v:dc1** | Connects to one of the two administrator sessions. This is the default as long as the remote server is not running Remote Desktop Services as a Session Host server. In other words, as long as the remote server is not hosting RDS desktops or applications, the **/admin** switch is not needed.<br><br>**NOTE**   Microsoft recommends using this instead of the **/console** switch to connect to Windows Server 2003 servers. |
| /console<br>c:\>**mstsc /console**<br><br>The preferred method is<br><br>c:\>**mstsc /admin /v:dc1** | This was used to connect to the console session for Windows Server 2003 computers. However, it has been deprecated and can cause errors in certain situations, so it should be replaced with the **/admin** switch. It is ignored when connecting to a Windows Server 2008 or Windows Server 2008 R2 server. |
| /f<br>c:\>**mstsc /f /v:dc1** | Connects in full-screen mode. |
| **/w**:*number*<br>mstsc **/w**:*number*<br>c:\>**mstsc /w:800 /v:dc1** | Specifies the width of the screen in pixels. This directly affects the displayed resolution. |
| **/h**:*number*<br>mstsc **/h**: *number*<br>c:\>**mstsc /h:600 /w:800 /v:dc1** | Specifies the height of the screen in pixels. This directly affects the displayed resolution.<br><br>The example specifies a screen size of 800×600. |
| /span<br>c:\>**mstsc /span /v:dc1** | Enables spanning across multiple monitors if the local computer is using multiple monitors.<br><br>Matches the remote desktop width and height with the local virtual desktop, |

| mstsc Switch | Description |
|---|---|
| /multimon<br>c:\>mstsc /multimon /v:dc1 | Configures the remote desktop session monitor layout to be identical to the current client-side configuration. |
| /public<br>c:\>mstsc /public /v:dc1 | Runs RDC without caching the passwords and bitmaps. |
| /edit *file path and name*<br>c:\>mstsc /edit c:\data\dc1.rdp | Opens up the RDC console. You can then edit the settings and save over the original .rdp file by clicking **Save**.<br><br>**TIP**  The .rdp file is a simple text file. It's also possible to view and edit the file in Notepad by entering **notepad** *file path and name*. |

**NOTE**  Windows Server 2008 and Windows Server 2008 R2 servers are limited to only two remote administrator connections at a time. In Windows Server 2003, you can connect to the console remotely giving you access to three sessions. However, the console session is not available for remote connectivity in Windows Server 2008 and Windows Server 2008 R2.

# Using Windows Deployment Services

This chapter provides information and commands concerning the following topics:

- Adding the WDS role
- Configuring the WDS role
- Adding boot images to WDS with **wdsutil**
- Creating image groups using **wdsutil**
- Adding install images using **wdsutil**
- Configuring server properties using **wdsutil**
- Running the **sysprep** GUI
- Running **sysprep** from the command line

**TIP** You should be familiar with remote administration methods when preparing for the 70-643 exam.

## Adding the WDS Role

Windows Deployment Services (WDS) is a built-in role that enables you to capture images on systems, and then multicast them to target computers. Figure 33-1 shows the overall process.

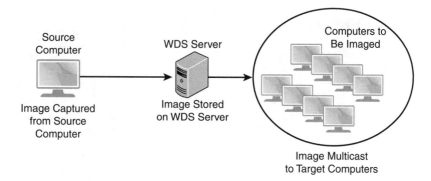

**Figure 33-1** Images captured and multicast from a WDS server

**TIP** You can capture the images directly on the computer using **imagex** or with tools built in to WDS. If you create the images on the computer with **imagex**, you can still copy them to WDS and multicast them to other systems.

To use WDS, you need the following:

- The server must be a member of an Active Directory Domain.
- The network must have a DHCP server.
- The network must have a DNS server.
- The server must have an NTFS partition where the images can be stored.

The primary command-line tool used to manage WDS is **wdsutil**; however, **wdsutil** is not available until you add the WDS role to a server. The following steps show how to add the WDS role.

| Step | Action |
|------|--------|
| 1. | Start Server Manager from the **Administrative Tools** menu. |
| 2. | Select **Features**. Click **Add Roles.** |
| 3. | Click **Next** on the **Before You Begin** page. |
| 4. | Select **Windows Deployments Services** as shown in Figure 33-2. Click **Next**. |
| 5. | Review the information on the **Introduction** page and click **Next**. |
| 6. | On the **Select Role Services** page, ensure that both the **Deployment Server** and the **Transport Server** are selected, and click **Next**.  <br><br>**NOTE**  The **Transport Server** service is optional and provides multicasting support for WDS. |
| 7. | On the **Confirmation** page, click **Install**. When the installation completes, click **Close**. |

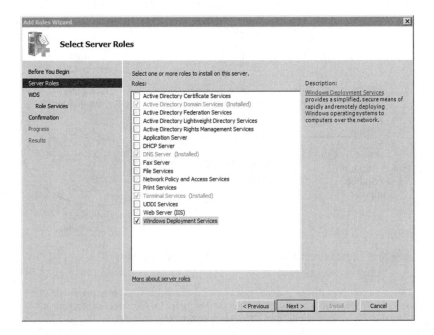

**Figure 33-2**  Adding the WDS role

## Configuring the WDS Role

After installing WDS, you can configure it with the following steps.

| Step | Action |
|------|--------|
| 1. | Start Windows Deployment Services from the **Administrative Tools** menu. |
| 2. | Expand **Servers**. Right-click over your server and select **Configure Server**. |
| 3. | Review the information on the **Welcome** page and click **Next**. |
| 4. | On the **Remote Installation Folder Location**, accept the default of **C:\ RemoteInstall** or select another location. Click **Next**.<br><br>**NOTE**  Microsoft recommends using a different volume than the system volume so if you choose a system volume, you get a warning. However, it still works. If the warning appears, click **Yes** to continue. |
| 5. | Accept the default of **Do Not Respond to Any Client Computer** and click **Finish**. |
| 6. | Deselect the checkbox to **Add Images to the Windows Deployment Server Now**, and click **Finish**. |

## Adding Boot Images to WDS with wdsutil

The following table shows a command you can use to add a boot image to WDS.

**NOTE**  Boot images boot a system into the Windows preinstallation environment (WinPE). The user is then able to connect to a WDS server and pick an installation to install on the computer.

| Adding a Boot Image with wdsutil | Comments |
|----------------------------------|----------|
| Add a boot image.<br><br>`wdsutil /add-image /`<br>`imagefile:image-file-path-and-name`<br>`/imagetype:boot [/name:image-name]`<br>`[/description:image-description]`<br>`C:\>wdsutil /add-image`<br>`/imagefile:d:\sources\boot.wim`<br>`/imagetype:boot /name:"Server 2008`<br>`Boot Image"` | You can add boot images with the **/add-image** switch and the **/imagetype:boot** switch.<br><br>The example adds the image and gives it a name of Server 2008 Boot Image as shown in Figure 33-3. |

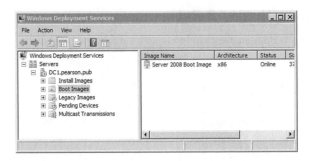

**Figure 33-3** Adding a boot image to WDS

## Creating Image Groups Using wdsutil

You can organize images within image groups on the WDS server. For example, you might have different images created for users in different departments. You can create image groups using the department name, and then add the images to the image group.

| Adding an Image Group with wdsutil | Comments |
|---|---|
| Add an image group.<br><br>`wdsutil /add-imagegroup`<br>`/imagegroup:`*image-group-name*<br>`C:\>wdsutil /add-imagegroup`<br>`/imagegroup:Training` | The **/add-imagegroup** switch adds an image group into the **Install Images** folder. The example adds an image group named **Training**.<br><br>**NOTE** The image group is created using the exact case you use in the command. If you want it displayed with uppercase letters, you must use uppercase letters here. |

## Adding Install Images Using wdsutil

After you create an image group on the WDS server, you can add images to the group. The following table shows how to identify images within an image file and add images to the image group.

| Viewing and Adding Install Images with wdsutil | Comments |
|---|---|
| View images in an image file.<br><br>`wdsutil /get-imagefile`<br>`/imagefile:`*image-file-path-and-*<br>*name*<br>`C:\>wdsutil /get-imagefile`<br>`/imagefile:d:\sources\`<br>`install.wim` | The **/get-imagefile** switch enables you to get a listing of images in an image file. You can use this output to add images to a system.<br><br>In the example, a listing of all the images in the installation DVD install.wim file is retrieved and listed. |

| Viewing and Adding Install Images with wdsutil | Comments |
|---|---|
| Add an install image.<br><br>`wdsutil /add-image /`<br>`imagefile:`*image-file-path-and-*<br>*name* `/imagetype:install`<br>`[/imagegroup:`*image-group-name*`]`<br>`[/singleimage:`*image-name-in-*<br>*image-file*`]` `[/name:`*image-name-*<br>*in-wds*`]`<br>`C:\>wdsutil /add-image`<br>`/imagefile:d:\sources\`<br>`install.wim /imagetype:`<br>`install /imagegroup:training`<br>`C:\>wdsutil /add-image`<br>`/imagefile:d:\sources\`<br>`install.wim /imagetype:install`<br>`/imagegroup:training`<br>`/singleimage:"windows longhorn`<br>`serverstandcore" /name:"Server`<br>`2008 Server Core"` | You can add install images with the **/add-image** switch and the **/imagetype:install** switch.<br><br>The first example installs all the images from the install.wim file into the **Training** image group.<br><br>The second example installs only a single image from the install.wim file (identified with the **/singleimage** switch) and renames it with the **/name** switch. Figure 33-4 shows the WDS console with this image added to the **Training** image group.<br><br>**NOTE** The image name is created using the exact case you use in the command. If you want it displayed with uppercase letters, you must use uppercase letters here. |

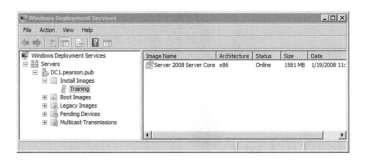

**Figure 33-4**  Adding an install image to an install group on WDS

**TIP**  This section covers some basics with **wdsutil** and the **/add-image** switch. To dig deeper, check out the **/add-image** page on TechNet: http://technet.microsoft.com/library/cc742159.aspx.

## Configuring Server Properties Using wdsutil

| Set | |
|---|---|
| Configure DHCP option for PXE support.<br><br>`wdsutil /set-server`<br>`/dhcpoption60:yes \| no`<br>`C:\>wdsutil /dhcpoption60:yes` | Specifies whether DHCP option 60 should be configured for preboot execution enabled (PXE) support.<br><br>The example sets the option to yes.<br><br>**TIP** If DHCP and Windows Deployment Services are running on the same server, set this option to **yes** and set the **/usedhcpports** option to **no**. |
| Use DCHP ports.<br><br>`wdsutil /set-server`<br>`/usedhcpports:yes \| no`<br>`C:\>wdsutil /set-server`<br>`/usedhcpports:yes` | Specifies whether the WDS server should use the DHCP port, port 67.<br><br>If DHCP and Windows Deployment Services are running on the same computer, you should set this option to **no** to enable the DHCP server to use the port, and set the **/DhcpOption60** parameter to **yes**.<br><br>Figure 33-5 shows these settings in the WDS server properties page. |
| Name prestaged computers with MAC.<br><br>`wdsutil /set-server`<br>`/prestageusingmac:yes \| no`<br>`C:\>wdsutil /set-server`<br>`/prestageusingmac:yes` | This setting specifies whether Windows Deployment Services should use the MAC address rather than the GUID/UUID when creating computer accounts in Active Directory Domain Services (AD DS). |
| Configure PXE settings.<br><br>`[/answerclients:{all \| known`<br>`\| none}]`<br>`wdsutil /set-server`<br>`/answerclients:all \| known \|`<br>`none`<br>`C:\>wdsutil /set-server`<br>`/answerclients:known` | Specifies which clients this server will answer. If you set this value to **known**, a computer must be prestaged in AD DS before it will be answered by the Windows Deployment Services server.<br><br>Figure 33-6 shows these settings in the WDS Server properties page. |

**TIP** This section covers some basics with **wdsutil** and the **/set-server** switch. To dig deeper, check out the **/set-server** page on TechNet: http://technet.microsoft.com/library/cc816898.aspx.

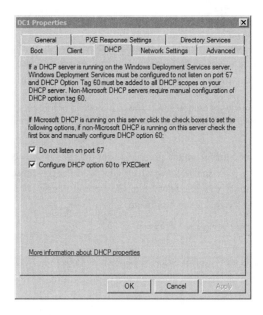

**Figure 33-5**   DHCP settings in WDS server Properties

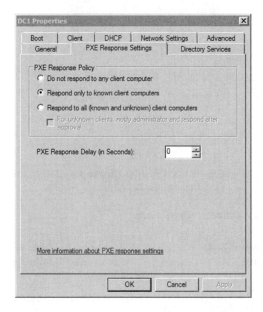

**Figure 33-6**   PXE Response Settings in WDS server Properties

## Running the sysprep GUI

The System Preparation (**sysprep**) tool removes unique information on computers prior to imaging them. It removes a wide variety of computer-specific and user-specific settings on Windows computers, including the system's security identifier (SID).

> **TIP**   The SID needs to be unique in a domain. If multiple computers have the same SID, you end up with significant problems that can be difficult to troubleshoot.

You can run **sysprep** either from the graphical user interface (GUI) or from the command prompt. Figure 33-7 shows the **sysprep** GUI with the typical settings selected. This file is located in the c:\windows\system32\sysprep folder by default. You can launch the GUI with the following command:

```
c:\windows\system32\sysprep\sysprep
```

> **NOTE**   The path to the **sysprep** GUI is not known by default, so you must include the full path.

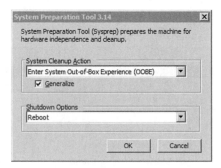

**Figure 33-7**   Running the sysprep GUI

Figure 33-7 shows two sections titled **System Cleanup Action** and **Shutdown Options**, and the **Generalize** checkbox. The following tables describe these settings.

| System Cleanup Action Selections | Comments |
| --- | --- |
| **Enter System Out-of-Box Experience (OOBE)** | Prepares the computer to be delivered to the user. It causes the system to enter the Windows Welcome phase when it reboots.<br><br>**NOTE**   Windows Welcome is also called Machine OOBE. |
| **Generalize** | The **Generalize** checkbox resets the user-specific and computer-specific settings, including the SID and the activation data. |

| System Cleanup Action Selections | Comments |
|---|---|
| Enter System Audit Mode | Audit mode bypasses the Windows Welcome phase and is used to add additional devices or applications to an installation. Audit mode is primarily used by original equipment manufacturers (OEM) and some large organizations to add additional customization settings.<br><br>**NOTE**  Because audit mode bypasses the Windows Welcome phase of the installation, it can't be used to deploy an operating system to an end user. You still must select **OOBE** after booting into audit mode. |

You have several choices of what **sysprep** will do after it runs. The most common choice is **Shutdown**. The following table shows these choices.

| Shutdown Options | Comments |
|---|---|
| Shutdown | The system shuts down. The image is now ready to be captured. When you're ready to capture the image, turn on the system and follow the procedures based on the image capture tool you're using. |
| Reboot | If you are ready to capture the image immediately, you can select **Reboot**. This setting is also commonly used with the Audit mode by OEMs. |
| Quit | This simply quits the **sysprep** application. You can shut it down later. |

**TIP**  If the system reboots before the image is captured, it enters the Windows Welcome phase and a new SID is created. You need to rerun **sysprep** again to prepare the system before imaging it.

# Running sysprep from the Command Line

You can also run **sysprep** from the command line. The most commonly used command is

```
c:\windows\system32\sysprep\sysprep /generalize /oobe
```

**TIP**  This command is the same as selecting the settings shown in Figure 33-7.

The following table shows the different switches available with **sysprep**.

| sysprep Switches | Comments |
|---|---|
| /?<br>C:\>c:\windows\system32\sysprep\<br>sysprep /? | Retrieves help on **sysprep**. |

| sysprep Switches | Comments |
|---|---|
| /generalize<br>C:\>c:\windows\system32\sysprep\<br>sysprep /generalize /oobe | Removes all unique system information from the Windows installation. It resets the SID, clears system restore points, and deletes event logs.<br><br>**NOTE** A new SID is created during the specialize configuration pass when the system is rebooted. Windows activation also resets (as long as activation hasn't already been reset three times). |
| /oobe<br>C:\>c:\windows\system32\sysprep\<br>sysprep /generalize /oobe | The out-of-box experience (**/oobe**) switch ensures the system enters the Windows Welcome mode when it restarts. Either an answer file can be used to answer the installation GUI's questions or users can answer the questions in the Windows Welcome mode. |
| /quiet<br>C:\>c:\windows\system32\sysprep\<br>sysprep /generalize /oobe /quiet | On-screen confirmation messages are suppressed. This option is useful if you are automating **sysprep**. |
| /audit<br>C:\>c:\windows\system32\sysprep\<br>sysprep /audit | Audit mode is used by OEMs but is rarely used by organizations. It enables you to boot into the system and add additional devices or applications. |
| /shutdown<br>C:\>c:\windows\system32\sysprep\<br>sysprep /generalize /oobe /shutdown | Shuts down the computer after **sysprep** completes. |
| /reboot<br>C:\>c:\windows\system32\sysprep\<br>sysprep /generalize /audit /reboot | Reboots the computer after running **sysprep**. Use this option to audit the computer and verify that the first-run experience operates correctly. |
| /quit<br>C:\>c:\windows\system32\sysprep\<br>sysprep /generalize /oobe /quit | Closes **sysprep** after running the specified commands but does not shut down the system. |
| /unattend:*filename*<br>C:\>c:\windows\system32\sysprep\<br>sysprep /generalize /oobe /shutdown<br>/unattend:answer.xml | Applies settings from the specified answer file to Windows during an unattended installation.<br><br>You can create answer files with the Windows System Image Manager (WSIM) included with the Windows Automated Installation Kit (WAIK). |

**NOTE**   You can view the full **sysprep** technical reference pages from http://technet.microsoft.com/library/dd744263.aspx.

# Manipulating IIS with appcmd

This chapter provides information and commands concerning the following topics:

- Managing sites with **appcmd**
- Adding a site with **appcmd**
- Adding an application to a site with **add app**
- Adding a virtual directory with **add vdir**
- Starting and stopping application pools with **appcmd** and **appcmd stop**

**TIP** You should be familiar with the **appcmd** command when preparing for the 70-643 exam.

## Managing Sites with appcmd

You can use the **appcmd** tool to manage IIS websites. This might be useful if you're running IIS on a Server Core installation.

**TIP** You can also manage Microsoft Management Consoles, including the Internet Information Services (IIS) Manager, remotely. Chapter 20, "Configuring Server Core for Remote Administration," shows how to configure a Server Core installation for remote management. Because many of the commands are not repeated, it's often easier to use the GUI instead of the **appcmd** tool.

The **appcmd** tool is located in the c:\windows\system32\inetsrv folder. Because this path isn't included in the path, you have to include it in commands. For example, to get help for the **appcmd**, you can use the following command:

```
C:\>c:\windows\system32\inetsrv\appcmd /?
```

The basic syntax of the **appcmd** is

```
appcmd command object
```

Most objects accept one of the following four commands: **list**, **add**, **set**, and **delete**. Some objects can also be stopped and started with the **stop** and **start** commands. The following table shows the different objects, and the basic syntax used with the **list** command.

**NOTE** You can get additional help on any of these topics by combining one of the four commands with one of the objects in the format of **appcmd** command object **/?**.

| Using the list Command for Each of the Objects | Comments |
|---|---|
| Sites<br><br>`C:\>c:\windows\system32\inetsrv\appcmd list site` | Administration of virtual sites |
| Applications<br><br>`C:\>c:\windows\system32\inetsrv\appcmd list app` | Administration of applications |
| Virtual directories<br><br>`C:\>c:\windows\system32\inetsrv\appcmd list vdir` | Administration of virtual directories |
| `apppool`<br>`C:\>c:\windows\system32\inetsrv\appcmd list apppool` | Administration of application pools |
| `config`<br>`C:\>c:\windows\system32\inetsrv\appcmd list config` | Administration of general configuration sections |
| `backup`<br>`C:\>c:\windows\system32\inetsrv\appcmd list backup` | Management of server configuration backups |
| `wp`<br>`C:\>c:\windows\system32\inetsrv\appcmd list wp` | Administration of worker processes |
| `request`<br>`C:\>c:\windows\system32\inetsrv\appcmd list request` | Display of active HTTP requests |
| `module`<br>`C:\>c:\windows\system32\inetsrv\appcmd list module` | Administration of server modules |
| `trace`<br>`C:\>c:\windows\system32\inetsrv\appcmd list trace` | Management of server trace logs |

# Adding a Site with appcmd

You can also add a site with the **appcmd** tool.

| Adding a Site with appcmd | Comments |
|---|---|
| Add a site.<br><br>`appcmd add site /name:`*`site-name`*<br>`/bindings:http/`*`port`*`:[`*`host-header`*`]`<br>`C:\>c:\windows\system32\inetsrv\`<br>`appcmd add site /name:"Success"`<br>`/bindings:http/8080`<br>`C:\>c:\windows\system32\inetsrv`<br>`\appcmd add site /name:"Success2"`<br>`/bindings:http/80:success2` | The **add site** command adds a website. You only need to identify the site name, the port, and a host header if one is used.<br><br>The first example creates a site named **Success** on port 8080. The second example adds a site named **Success2** on port 80 with a host header of **success2**. |

## Adding an Application to a Site with add app

| Adding an Application with add app | Comments |
|---|---|
| Add an application to a site.<br><br>`appcmd add app /site.name:`*`site-name`*<br>`/path:`*`app-name`*<br>`C:\>c:\windows\system32\inetsrv\appcmd`<br>`add app /site.name:"success" /path:/app` | You can add applications to existing websites with the **add app** command.<br><br>The example creates an application named **app** for the site named **success**. |

## Adding a Virtual Directory with add vdir

| Adding a Virtual Directory with add vdir | Comments |
|---|---|
| Add a virtual directory to a site.<br><br>`appcmd add vdir /app.name:"web-`<br>*`site/app-name`*`" /path:`*`/Web-site-virtual-`*<br>*`path`* `/physicalpath:`*`actual-path`*<br>`C:\>c:\windows\system32\inetsrv\appcmd`<br>`add vdir /app.name:"default web site`<br>`/app1" /path:/svdir /physicalpath:g:`<br>`/svdir` | You can add virtual directories to existing websites with the **add vdir** command.<br><br>The example adds a virtual directory named **svdir** to the **app1** application in a website named **default web site**. The actual path to the directory is identified in the **/physicalpath** switch as **g:/svdir**.<br><br>Figure 34-1 shows the result of this command. The virtual directory (named svdir) is added within the Default Web Site. The Advanced Settings of the virtual directory show the physical path is on g:\svdir (instead of in the same path as the Default Web Site). |

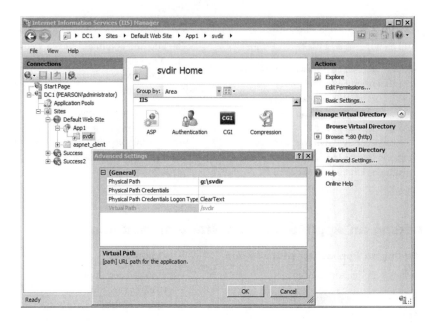

**Figure 34-1**    Viewing the virtual directory created from **appcmd**

## Starting and Stopping Application Pools with appcmd and appcmd stop

You can start and stop application pools with the **appcmd start** and **appcmd stop** commands. The basic syntax is

```
appcmd start apppool application-name
appcmd stop apppool application-name
```

For example, if the application pool is named **successpool**, you can stop and start it with the following commands:

```
appcmd start apppool successpool
appcmd stop apppool successpool
```

> **TIP**  This chapter provided the syntax for some basics with the **appcmd**. If you want to dig deeper, check out the TechNet website: http://technet.microsoft.com/library/cc772200.aspx.

# Creating Basic Visual Basic Scripts

This chapter provides information and commands concerning the following topics:

- Working with **filesystemobject**
- Accessing a network share with **filesystemobject**
- Calling scripts from a batch file
- Displaying a message box with a Visual Basic script
- Using **if** statements
- Checking for a value with a message box

**TIP** You should be familiar with the concept of Visual Basic scripting when preparing for the 70-640, 70-642, and 70-647 exams.

## Working with filesystemobject

Visual Basic (VB) script has access to many precompiled objects. These objects give you access to advanced capabilities through the scripting language without having to program the underlying code.

Objects have properties and methods that provide the means to interact with an instance of the object. For example, the **filesystemobject** provides access to the file system.

**NOTE** Some objects also have events that perform an action when a specific trigger occurs.

| Object Elements | Comments |
| --- | --- |
| Properties | Properties are values that you can set or retrieve on an object. For example, a file can have a name and a path. You can use the **filesystemobject** **getabsolutepathname** method to view the path of a file and the **getfilename** method to get the name of the file. |
| Methods | Methods are actions that you can invoke. For example, **filesystemobject** includes methods such as **createtextfile** to create a file, **writeline** to put text into the file, and **close** to close the file. |

The following code shows how to interact with the **filesysptemobject**, and the lines are explained in the following table.

```
set objfso = createobject("scripting.filesystemobject")
set txtfile = objfso.createtextfile("c:\scripts\log.txt",true)
```

```
txtfile.writeline("Logging an event")
txtfile.close
wscript.echo "getabsolutepathname = " & objfso.getabsolutepathname
("c:\scripts\log.txt")
wscript.echo "getfilename = " & objfso.getfilename("c:\scripts\log.txt")
if objfso.fileexists("c:\scripts\log.txt") then
 wscript.echo "File exists."
end if
```

| Code | Explanation |
|---|---|
| `set objfso = createobject ("scripting.filesystemobject")` | This line creates an instance of the **filesystemobject** and names it **objfso**.<br><br>**NOTE**  It's a common practice to prefix object names with the letters **obj**. Instead of naming it **objfso**, it can be named simply **fso**, or anything else such **x** or **y**. However, if you name it **x**, it's clear what the variable represents, but if you name it **objfso**, it's a reminder that it is an object representing the file's system object. |
| `set txtfile = objfso.createtextfile ("c:\scripts\log.txt",true)` | The **createtextfile** method creates a text file named c:\scripts\log.txt and creates an object named **txtfile** that refers to the created file.<br><br>**NOTE**   If the file exists, it will be overwritten because the value at the end of the line is **true**. If this value was omitted or set to false, the command would fail if the file exists. |
| `txtfile.writeline("Logging an event")` | The **writeline** method writes the message into the text file. |
| `txtfile.close` | The **close** method closes the file so that it no longer consumes resources and can be accessed by other processes. |
| `wscript.echo "getabsolutepathname = " & objfso.getabsolutepathname ("c:\scripts\log.txt")` | The **getabsolutepathname** method retrieves the full path and name of the file (c:\scripts\log.txt). The **wscript.echo** command displays it to the command prompt as shown in Figure 35-1. |
| `wscript.echo "getfilename = " & objfso.getfilename("c:\scripts\ log.txt")` | The **getfilename** method retrieves just the name of the file without the path and echoes it to the command prompt. |

| Code | Explanation |
|------|-------------|
| `if objfso.fileexists("c:\scripts\`<br>`log.txt") then`<br>`  wscript.echo "File exists."`<br>`end if` | The last line in the script checks whether the file exists and uses the **echo** method to show that it does exist.<br><br>**NOTE**  Syntax for **if** statements is shown later in this chapter in the "Using **if** Statements" section. |

In addition to showing the output of the preceding script, Figure 35-1 also includes the line **type c:\scripts\log.txt** to show the contents of the log file. After running the script, it has only one line, "Logging an event."

**Figure 35-1**   Viewing the results of the script

You can use the following steps to create this script.

| Step | Action |
|------|--------|
| 1. | Start a command prompt. |
| 2. | Type the following text and press **Enter**:<br><br>`notepad c:\scripts\fso.vbs` |
| 3. | When prompted to create the file, click **Yes**. |
| 4. | Add the following lines to the script:<br><br>`set objfso = createobject("scripting.filesystemobject")`<br>`set txtfile = objfso.createtextfile("c:\scripts\log.txt",true)`<br>`txtfile.writeline("Logging an event")`<br>`txtfile.close`<br>`wscript.echo "getabsolutepathname = " &`<br>`objfso.getabsolutepathname ("c:\scripts\log.txt")`<br>`wscript.echo "getfilename = " &`<br>`objfso.getfilename("c:\scripts\log.txt")`<br>`if objfso.fileexists("c:\scripts\log.txt") then`<br>`  wscript.echo "File exists."`<br>`end if` |
| 5. | Press Ctrl+S to save the script. |
| 6. | Return to the command prompt, type the following text, and press **Enter**:<br><br>`Cscript c:\scripts\fs0.vbs` |

> **TIP**   There is much more you can do with the **filesystemobject**. If you want to dig deeper into different **filesystemobject** methods, check out the MSDN website: http://msdn.microsoft.com/library/6tkce7xa.aspx.

## Accessing a Network Share with filesystemobject

You can use the **filesystemobject** to access a network share. The following code connects to the **apps** share on **DC1**:

```
set objfso = createobject("scripting.filesystemobject")
set objdrive = objfso.getfolder("\\dc1\apps")
```

> **TIP**   To connect to a different share, just substitute **\\dc1\apps** with the Universal Naming Convention (UNC) path of your share.

## Calling Scripts from a Batch File

There might be times when you want to run a script from a batch file. You precede the path and the name of the script with the **cscript** statement.

> **TIP**   **cscript** is the command-based script host. There are times when the script runs without the **cscript** command, but if you want to ensure the script runs without problems, you should use **cscript**.

For example, if you want a batch file to run a script named logon.vbs, you can use the following line:

```
cscript c:\scripts\logon.vbs
```

## Displaying a Message Box with a Visual Basic Script

There are many times when you want to create a pop-up message box to provide feedback to the user, or even to send a message to a user after logon. The basic syntax is

```
msgbox "message",[msg-box-style], "title"
```

| msgbox Commands | Comments |
|---|---|
| Display a basic message.<br><br>`msgbox "Only Pearson employ-`<br>`ees should use this computer.",`<br>`vbinformation, "Warning"` | Displays a simple message to the user. It includes an information icon and the title bar includes the text "Warning." |

| msgbox Commands | Comments |
|---|---|
| Add blank lines in a message.<br><br>msgbox "Only Pearson employees<br>should use this computer." &<br>vbcrlf & vbcrlf & "If you are<br>not an employee of Pearson, you<br>should terminate this session<br>immediately.", vbinformation,<br>"Warning" | If you have a long message, you can choose where line breaks are added with the **vbcrlf** constant.<br><br>Figure 35-2 shows how script is displayed when it is executed.<br><br>**NOTE**  The **msgbox** command is entered as a single line in Notepad without pressing Enter at all. |

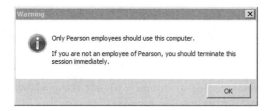

**Figure 35-2**   Dialog box with line feeds

The following table shows some of the message box styles you can use as the second parameter in a dialog box.

**NOTE**  These styles are actually constants (integers). For example, **vbinformation** is a constant for the number 64. You can enter the integers instead but the constants are easier to remember.

| Style | Comments |
|---|---|
| **vbinformation** | Shows a white "i" in a blue circle. |
| **vbexclamation** | Shows a black exclamation mark in a yellow triangle. |
| **vbcritical** | Shows a black "x" in a red circle. |
| **vbquestion** | Shows a white "?" in a blue circle. |
| **vbokonly** | Displays OK button only (default). The OK button has a return value of 1. |
| **vbokcancel** | Displays OK and Cancel buttons. The OK button has a return value of 1 and Cancel returns 2. |
| **vbabortretryignore** | Displays Abort, Retry, and Ignore buttons. The Abort button has a return value of 3, Retry returns 4, and Ignore returns 5. |
| **vbyesnocancel** | Displays Yes, No, and Cancel buttons. The Yes button has a return value of 6, No returns 7, and Cancel returns 2. |
| **vbyesno** | Displays Yes and No buttons. The Yes button has a return value of 6, and No returns 7. |

| Style | Comments |
|---|---|
| **vbretrycancel** | Displays Retry and Cancel buttons. The retry button has a return value of 4, and Cancel returns 2. |
| **msgboxsetforeground** | Sets the message box as the foreground window. |

You can combine the buttons using the plus character (**+**) to concatenate message box styles. For example, if you want to use the question mark icon with the **Yes** and **No** buttons, you can use the following code: **vbquestion + vbyesno**.

## Using if Statements

You can use **if** statements to add choices to your script. The **if** statement tests for a condition, and when the condition is true, it takes the specified action. The basic syntax is

```
if condition then action
```

You can also add **else** and **elseif** statements. If you add **else** and **elseif** statements, you must end with an **end if** statement. The extended syntax is

```
if condition then action
  elseif condition then
    action
  else condition then
    action
endif
```

> **TIP**  The spaces before the **elseif**, **else**, and action statements are not necessary; however, they do make the code easier to read.

The following section shows how to use the **if elseif** statement block to check which button a user pressed from a message box.

## Checking for a Value with a Message Box

You can identify which button a user presses by checking for a value after the message box is dismissed. The following code shows a basic check:

```
intbutton = msgbox ("Do you want to continue", vbquestion +
vbyesno,"Question")
If intbutton = 6 then
   msgbox "User pressed Yes",,"Answer"
 elseif intbutton = 7 then
   msgbox "User pressed No",,"Answer"
end if
```

| Code Lines | Explanation |
| --- | --- |
| `intbutton = msgbox ("Do`<br>`you want to continue",`<br>`vbquestion + vbyesno,`<br>`"Question")` | The first line assigns a value to the **intbutton** variable based on which button the user presses.<br><br>**TIP**  When using the **msgbox** in an assignment statement (assigning the result to a variable), you must enclose it in parentheses. However, if you use the **msgbox** statement by itself, you must omit the parentheses. |
| `If intbutton = 6 then`<br>`    msgbox "User pressed`<br>`Yes",vbokonly, "Answer"`<br>`  elseif intbutton = 7 then`<br>`    msgbox "User pressed`<br>`No",,"Answer"`<br>`end if` | The second line is an **if elseif** statement. It checks for the two possible values (**6** for **yes** and **7** for **no**).<br><br>Although this code simply displays another message box to indicate which button the user pressed, you can put in any other code here desired.<br><br>**NOTE**  The **msgbox** style (between the message and the title text) is omitted in the last example with two commas. The default is **vbokonly** to display an **OK** button. |

**TIP**  This section provided only some basic information on the VB Scripting language. If you want to dig deeper, check out this TechNet page: http://msdn.microsoft.com/library/d1wf56tt.aspx.

**TIP**  Any script you create can be scheduled to run through Group Policy or with the Task Scheduler. Chapter 15, "Group Policy Overview," shows the nodes where you can add scripts for computer startup, computer shutdown, user logon, and user log events. Chapter 29, "Using the Reliability and Performance Monitor," shows how you can use the Task Scheduler to schedule a batch file to run Data Collector Sets. You can substitute a .vbs file for the batch file and it works exactly the same.

# Manipulating Active Directory with Visual Basic Scripts

This chapter provides information and commands concerning the following topics:

- Connecting to Active Directory with a VB script
- Creating an OU with a VB script
- Creating a user account with a VB script
- Modifying the tombstone lifetime

**TIP** You should be familiar with the concept of VB scripting when preparing for the 70-640, 70-642, and 70-647 exams.

## Connecting to Active Directory with a VB Script

When working with Active Directory, the first step is to connect the instance of Active Directory. The basic syntax to connect with a Visual Basic (VB) script is

```
set objdom = getobject("LDAP://dn")
```

**NOTE** LDAP, which is an acronym for Lightweight Directory Access Protocol, must be in all capital letters.

For example, to connect to the pearson.pub domain, the *dn* is "**dc=pearson,dc=pub**", so the syntax is

```
set objdom = getobject("LDAP://dc=pearson,dc=pub")
```

## Creating an OU with a VB Script

The following script creates an OU named **Project Team**:

```
set objdom = getobject("LDAP://dc=pearson,dc=pub")
set objou = objdom.create("organizationalunit","ou=Project Team")
objou.setinfo
```

The following table explains each of these three lines.

| Creating an OU | Comments |
|---|---|
| `set objdom = getobject("LDAP:// dc=pearson,dc=pub")` | This line sets the context to the pearson.pub domain. It creates an object named **objdom** and uses the **getobject** method to connect to the pearson.pub domain.<br><br>**NOTE**   LDAP must be all uppercase. |
| `set objou = objdom.create ("organizationalunit", "ou=Project Team")` | This command uses the **create** method of the **objdom** object to create an OU named **Project Team**. However, the OU isn't created yet.<br><br>**NOTE**   The case of Project Team can be uppercase, lowercase, or any combination. However, it is displayed the way it's included in this line. |
| `objou.setinfo` | The **setinfo** method creates the previously defined OU. |

You can use the following steps to create this script.

| Step | Action |
|---|---|
| 1. | Start a command prompt. |
| 2. | Type the following text, and then press **Enter**:<br><br>`notepad c:\scripts\createou.vbs` |
| 3. | When prompted to create the file, click **Yes**. |
| 4. | Add the following three lines to the script:<br><br>`set objdom = getobject("LDAP://dc=pearson,dc=pub")`<br>`set objou = objdom.create("organizationalunit","ou=Project Team")`<br>`objou.setinfo` |
| 5. | Press Ctrl+S to save the script. |
| 6. | Return to the command prompt, type the following text, and then press **Enter**:<br><br>`Cscript c:\scripts\createou.vbs` |
| 7. | Launch **Active Directory Users and Computers** from the **Administrative Tools** menu and you'll see the Project Team OU created. |

**TIP**   You can use these steps to create and run any of the scripts in this chapter by just replacing the lines in step 4.

## Creating a User Account with a VB Script

The following script creates a user named **Jackie** in the **Project Team OU**:

```
set objOU = getobject("LDAP://ou=project team,dc=pearson,dc=pub")
set objuser = objou.create("user", "cn=Jackie")
objuser.put "samaccountname", "Jackie"
objuser.setinfo
```

The following table explains each of these lines.

| Creating an OU | Comments |
|---|---|
| `set objOU = getobject("LDAP:// ou=project team,dc=pearson,dc=pub")` | This line sets the context to the **pearson.pub** domain. It creates an object named **objdom** and uses the **getobject** method to connect to the **pearson.pub** domain. <br><br>**NOTE**  LDAP must be all uppercase. |
| `set objuser = objou. create("user", "cn=Jackie")` | This command uses the **create** method of the **objdom** object to create a user named **Jackie**. However, the user isn't created yet. <br><br>**NOTE**  The case of **Jackie** can be uppercase, lowercase, or any combination. However, it will be displayed the way it's included in this line. |
| `objuser.put "samaccount- name", "Jackie"` | You can assign values to any properties with the **put** method of the user object. This line sets the value of the **samaccountname** property to **Jackie**. |
| `objou.setinfo` | The **setinfo** method creates the previously defined user. |

## Modifying the Tombstone Lifetime

You can use the following script to set the tombstone lifetime. This script sets the tombstone lifetime to 365, but you can change the number 365 in the script to any number desired.

**NOTE**  The tombstone lifetime identifies the maximum age of a deleted object before it is permanently deleted. Tombstoned objects can be authoritatively restored. However, once the tombstone lifetime expires, they can no longer be restored.

```
set objdom = getobject("LDAP://rootdse")
set objds = getobject("LDAP://cn=directory service,cn=windows nt,"
 & "cn=Services," & objdom.get("configurationnamingcontext") )
objds.put "tombstonelifetime",365
objds.setinfo
```

**NOTE**  Notice that the second line spans two lines but should only be entered as a single line.

The following table explains each of these lines.

| Creating an OU | Comments |
|---|---|
| `set objdom = getobject("LDAP://` `rootdse")` | This line sets the context to the domain used by the computer using the **rootdse** shortcut. You can use this instead of naming the domain. The benefit is that the script is portable to any domain.<br><br>**NOTE**  LDAP must be all uppercase. |
| `set objds = getobject("LDAP://` `cn=directory service,cn=windows` `nt," & "cn=Services," &` `objdom.get` `("configurationnamingcontext") )` | This command uses the **getobject** method to connect to the directory services container. Figure 36-1 shows the directory services container in the **adsiedit** tool. |
| `objds.put "tombstonelifetime",365` | You can assign values to properties with the **put** method. This line sets the value of the **tombstone lifetime** property to **365**. Figure 36-1 shows the current value as 180. |
| `objou.setinfo` | The **setinfo** method makes the change. |

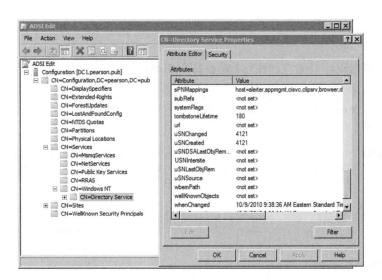

**Figure 36-1**  ADSI Edit tool

You can use the following steps to view the ADSI Edit tool on a domain controller.

| Step | Comments |
|---|---|
| 1. | Click **Start**, type **ADSI Edit**, and double-click **ADSI Edit** in the **Programs** list. |
| 2. | Right-click **ADSI Edit** and select **Connect to**. |

| Step | Comments |
|------|----------|
| 3. | In the **Connection Point** section, Ensure that **Select a Well Known Naming Context** is selected. Select **Configuration** from the drop down menu. Click **OK**. |
| 4. | Select **Configuration** and expand it by clicking the plus (+). |
| 5. | Select **CN=Configuration** and expand it. |
| 6. | Select **CN=Services** and expand it. |
| 7. | Select **CN=Windows NT** and expand it. |
| 8. | Select **CN=Directory Service**. Right-click **CN=Directory Service** and select **Properties**. |
| 9. | Scroll down to **Tombstone Lifetime** to view the value.<br><br>**NOTE**   You can double-click it to set the value from here. |

# Starting and Using PowerShell

This chapter provides information and commands concerning the following topics:

- Installing and Launching PowerShell
- Understanding PowerShell verbs and nouns
- Tabbing through PowerShell commands
- Understanding the different types of PowerShell commands
- Creating aliases
- Discovering Windows PowerShell commands
- Exploring **get-member**
- Redirecting output with Windows PowerShell
- Understanding PowerShell errors
- Understanding PowerShell variables
- Using comparison operators
- Understanding pipelining

**TIP** You should be familiar with PowerShell when preparing for the 70-640, 70-643, and 70-647 exams.

## Installing and Launching PowerShell

PowerShell is installed by default in Windows Server 2008 R2, but you have to add it in Windows Server 2008. You can use the steps in the following table to add it to Windows Server 2008.

**TIP** Windows does not support installing PowerShell on a Server Core installation of Windows Server 2008. However, the Server Core installation of Windows Server 2008 R2 does support PowerShell. This page (see http://support.microsoft.com/kb/976736) shows how to install it on Server Core 2008 R2.

| Steps | Action |
|-------|--------|
| 1. | Launch Server Manager from the **Administrative Tools** menu. |
| 2. | Select **Features**. Click **Add Features**. |
| 3. | Scroll down to **Windows PowerShell** and click the checkbox to add it. Click **Next.** |
| 4. | Click **Install**. When the installation completes, click **Close**. |

After it is installed, you can launch the PowerShell command prompt by clicking **Start**, typing **PowerShell** in the **Start Search** text box, and pressing **Enter**. You can also click the Windows PowerShell icon on the **Quick Launch** bar to the right of the **Start** menu.

> **TIP**   Many PowerShell commands require administrative permissions. You can launch Windows PowerShell with elevated permissions by right-clicking **Windows PowerShell** and selecting **Run As Administrator**.

Figure 37-1 shows the Windows PowerShell window. In the figure, the **$host** and **get-help** commands were executed after launching PowerShell.

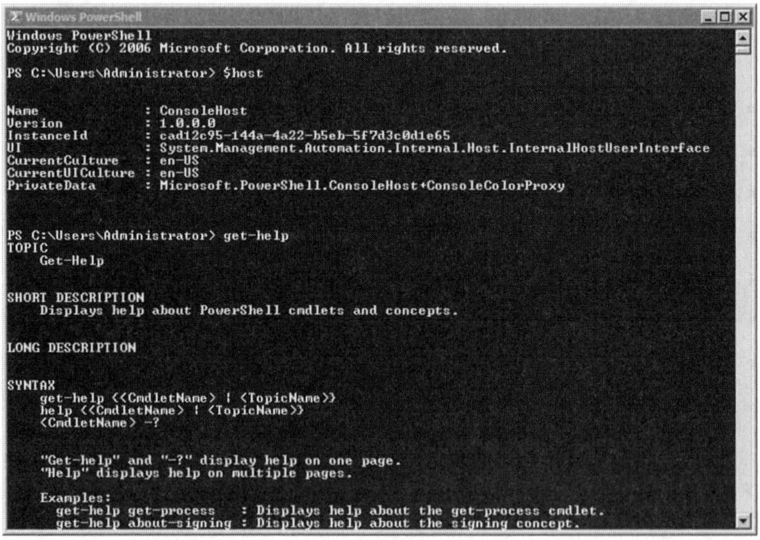

**Figure 37-1**   Windows PowerShell with the **get-help** command

> **TIP**   Windows 2008 R2 includes Windows PowerShell v2.0 and Windows Server 2008 includes Windows PowerShell v1.0. This chapter and Chapters 38, 39, and 40 cover version 2.0 commands.

You can check the PowerShell version by typing **$host** and pressing **Enter** in the PowerShell prompt.

> **TIP**   You can upgrade to Windows PowerShell v 2.0 by installing the Windows Management Framework (update KB 968930) available here: http://support.microsoft.com/kb/968930. You should also download and install the most recent version of the .NET Framework from here: http://go.microsoft.com/fwlink?linkid=124150.

## Understanding PowerShell Verbs and Nouns

Windows PowerShell commands use basic verbs and nouns. You can usually determine what the command does just by its name. For example, the **get-help** command combines the **get** verb with the **help** noun, and just as you'd expect, it gets help.

**NOTE**   PowerShell commands follow Pascal casing rules, which are also known as camel casing. Pascal casing joins words without spaces but uses uppercase to distinguish them. For example, camel case is written as CamelCase. However, PowerShell commands are mostly case insensitive and PowerShell commands are shown in all lowercase to match the style of this book. If uppercase is required, a note will be added.

Common verbs are as shown in the following table.

| Verbs with Examples | Comments |
|---|---|
| Get<br><br>`get-command`<br>`PS C:\> get-command` | Retrieves information.<br><br>For example, the **get-command** cmdlet retrieves a listing of all PowerShell commands. |
| Set<br><br>`set-executionpolicy policy`<br>`PS C:\> set-executionpolicy`<br>`remotesigned` | Configures a setting.<br><br>The example sets the PowerShell execution policy to remote signed, allowing local scripts to run. |
| Format<br><br>`format-table columns`<br>`PS C:\> get-service |`<br>`format-table Name, Status,`<br>`DependentServices -auto` | Formats the output.<br><br>The example gets a listing of all services but picks specific columns to include in the table.<br><br>**TIP**   The pipe command (\|) sends the output from the previous command to the next command. In other words, the output if **get-service** is sent to **format-table**.<br><br>**TIP**   The **-auto** switch helps the output fit on the screen. |
| Out<br><br>`Out-file filename`<br>`PS C:\> get-process |`<br>`out-file processes.txt`<br>`PS C:\> get-process >`<br>`processes.txt` | Sends data out to a file.<br><br>The example uses **get-process** to retrieve a listing of all running processes and sends it to a text file named **processes.txt**. You can achieve the same result using the redirect symbol (>), as shown in the second example. |
| Gridview<br><br>`Get-service | out-gridview`<br>`PS C:\> get-service |`<br>`where-object {$_.status -eq`<br>`"running"} | sort-object`<br>`-property displayname |`<br>`out-gridview` | Sends the output to a grid view window similar to Figure 37-2.<br><br>The example command uses the **where-object** cmdlet to list only running services, the **sort-object** cmdlet to sort on the **displayname**, and the **out-gridview** cmdlet to send the output to a gridview window.<br><br>**TIP**   The gridview window allows dynamic sorting by simply clicking on any column to reorder the data.<br><br>**NOTE**   The gridview requires the Microsoft .NET Framework 3.5 Service Pack 1 (available at http://go.microsoft.com/fwlink?linkid=124150). On Windows Server 2008 R2, it requires that the Windows Integrated Scripting feature be installed via Server Manager. |

| Verbs with Examples | Comments |
|---|---|
| Selected columns in **gridview**<br><br>`Get-process | select`<br>`columns | out-gridview`<br>`PS C:\> get-process |`<br>`select-object name,`<br>`description, handles, vm,`<br>`ws, pm, npm, cpu,`<br>`totalprocessortime |`<br>`out-gridview` | This example shows how to select specific columns in the gridview by using the **select-object** cmdlet. The output of this command is shown in Figure 37-3.<br><br>**TIP** You can view a list of all selectable columns (and their name in the header) by running **get-process | select-object * | out-gridview**. |
| Test<br><br>`test-path` *path*<br>`PS C:\> test-path c:\data\`<br>`processes.txt` | Tests various conditions like the existence of a file or the existence of a registry key.<br><br>The example tests to see whether the path and filename exist. If it exists, it returns a true. If it doesn't exist, it returns a false. |
| Write<br><br>`write-warning` *message*<br>`PS C:\> write-warning`<br>`"Success!"` | Writes data to various sources such as the screen or event logs.<br><br>The example writes the message to the screen in yellow text. |
| Start<br><br>`start-service` *servicename*<br>`PS C:\> start-service`<br>`msftpsvc` | You can use this to start jobs, processes, services, and more.<br><br>The example starts the FTP Publishing Service using the service's name.<br><br>**TIP** You can get a list of all services (including their service name) with the **get-service** command. The service name is displayed in the **Name** column. |
| Stop<br><br>`stop-service` *servicename*<br>`PS C:\> stop-service`<br>`msftpsvc` | You can use this to stop jobs, processes, services, and more.<br><br>The example stops the FTP Publishing Service using the service's name. |
| Measure<br><br>`measure-object`<br>`PS C:\> get-command |`<br>`measure-object` | Provides counts, averages, and other metrics for various objects.<br><br>The example command counts the number of Windows PowerShell commands and provides the total. There are more than 400 built-in commands. |

**NOTE** This is not a complete list of verbs available in Windows PowerShell. You can get a complete list of all commands by entering **get-command** at the PowerShell command prompt.

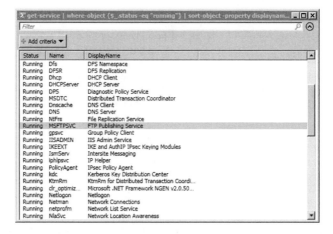

**Figure 37-2**   Windows PowerShell **gridview** output

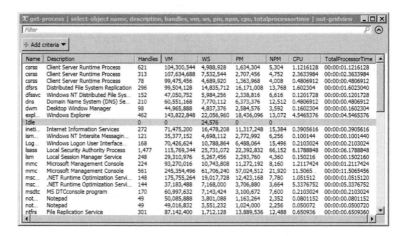

**Figure 37-3**   Selected columns in Windows PowerShell **gridview**

You can also use **get-command** to retrieve information on commands with specific verbs or with specific nouns.

| Get-commands | Comments |
|---|---|
| Getting verbs.<br><br>`get-command -verb` *verb*<br><br>`PS C:\> get-command -verb get`<br><br>`PS C:\> get-command -verb out`<br><br>`PS C:\> get-command -verb write` | Provides a listing of all commands associated with a specific verb.<br><br>The examples show all the commands using the **get** verb, the **out** verb, and the **write** verb. You can also use other verbs, such as **set, select, start**, and **stop**.<br><br>**TIP** You can get a list of all verbs, including the number of commands, using the verb with the following command:<br><br>**get-command \| group-object verb \| sort-object count -descending** |
| Getting nouns.<br><br>`get-command -noun` *noun*<br><br>`PS C:\> get-command -noun event` | Provides a listing of all commands associated with a specific noun.<br><br>The example shows all the commands using the noun **event**. You can also use other nouns such as **service, variable**, and **error**.<br><br>**TIP** You can get a list of all nouns, including the number of commands, using the noun with the following command:<br><br>**get-command \| group-object noun \| sort-object count -descending** |
| Looking for strings with wildcards.<br><br>`get-command *`*string*<br><br>`PS C:\> get-command *service`<br><br>`PS C:\> get-command *object*` | Provides a listing of all commands associated with the string.<br><br>In the first example, all commands that end in **service** are shown. The second example shows all commands with the word **object** anywhere in the command. |

# Tabbing Through PowerShell Commands

One of the benefits of knowing the verbs is that it enables you to easily discover the commands using the tab completion, or tab expansion feature. With more than 400 commands, you simply can't remember them all. However, you can remember common verbs such as **get, set, start**, and **stop**. You enter the name of the verb, and then simply press the Tab key to discover all the available commands. The following steps show this process.

| Step | Comments |
|---|---|
| 1. Launch PowerShell. | Click **Start**, type **PowerShell** in the **Search** text box, and double-click **Windows PowerShell**. |
| 2. Type **get-**. | **get** is a common noun. It retrieves information. |

| Step | Comments |
| --- | --- |
| 3. Press the Tab key. | The **get** command changes to **Get-Acl**. If you press Enter at this point, it executes the **get-acl** command.<br><br>**NOTE**   PowerShell is not case sensitive, but it does automatically change to Pascal casing, or camel case, for easier readability. Camel casing uses an uppercase letter for each new word. |
| 4. Continue to press the Tab key to discover all of the commands beginning with **get**-. | There are about 50 get commands that you can discover using this method.<br><br>**NOTE**   The command **get-command get\* \| measure-object** shows the exact number of commands. |
| 5. Press the **Esc** key to clear the PowerShell command. | Pressing **Esc** clears the command line the same way in PowerShell as it works from the command prompt. |
| 6. Type **set**-. | **set** is another common noun. It is used to configure settings. |
| 7. Press the Tab key. | The **set** command changes to **Set-Acl**. If you press Enter at this point, it tries to execute the **set-acl** command. However, because the **set-acl** command requires additional parameters, it won't complete.<br><br>**TIP**   You can get additional help on any command by entering the **get-help** command. For example, **get-help set-acl** retrieves information on this command. |
| 8. Continue to press the Tab key to discover all of the commands beginning with **set**-. | There are about 35 **set** commands that you can discover using this method.<br><br>**NOTE**   The command **get-command set\* \| measure-object** shows the actual count based on the version of PowerShell you're running. |
| 9. Try the same method with any of the other verbs, such as **out** or **write**. | This is one of the core self-discovery methods built into Windows PowerShell. |

**TIP**   Windows PowerShell has the equivalent of the command prompt's doskey. It keeps a history of previous commands, and you can use the up arrow, down arrow, F7, home, end, page up, and page down keys to navigate through the history. The **get-command \*history\*** command shows all the commands you can use with history. For example, you can execute **get-history** to show a listing of all commands you've entered during this session.

## Understanding the Different Types of PowerShell Commands

All PowerShell commands aren't the same. There are actually three distinct types of commands, as shown in the following table.

| Type | Comments |
|---|---|
| Cmdlet | Cmdlets are mini-programs. They are created as objects with properties and methods. Properties describe the object and methods perform actions. |
| Alias | Aliases are simpler names for common commands. For example, you can enter the command **get-alias** to list all aliases. The **get-alias** command actually has two aliases that you can execute instead of **get-alias**: **gal** and **alias**. All three commands (**get-alias**, **gal**, and **alias**) perform the same command. |
| Function | Functions perform a specific action. For example, the **E:** function changes the drive to E. The **clear-host** function clears the screen. |

**NOTE**   You can create your own cmdlets, aliases, and functions. Creating cmdlets can be complex, but creating aliases and functions is easy. The next section shows how to create aliases. Chapter 38, "Creating and Running a PowerShell Script," shows how to add functions to the profile in the "Creating and Modifying the Global PowerShell Profile" section.

## Creating Aliases

Windows PowerShell includes many built-in aliases, but you can also create your own. The following table shows you how to list the aliases and create your own.

| Command | Comments |
|---|---|
| `Alias`<br>`PS C:\> alias` | Provides a listing of all aliases. It includes built-in aliases and user-defined aliases. This returns the same data as **get-alias** and **get-command -commandtype alias**. |
| `set-alias` *alias command*<br>`PS C:\> set-alias gh get-help` | Creates or changes an alias.<br><br>The example creates an alias named **gh** that can be entered instead of the command **get-help**. |

## Discovering Windows PowerShell Commands

Few people will master all of the PowerShell commands; however, you can master a basic self-discovery method used to learn and master any specific command. This method includes three important commands, as described in the following table.

| PowerShell Discovery Commands | Comments |
|---|---|
| `get-command [switches]`<br>`PS C:\> get-command`<br>`PS C:\> get-command -commandtype cmdlet`<br>`PS C:\> get-command -commandtype alias`<br>`PS C:\> get-command -commandtype function` | The **get-command** cmdlet shows all of the possible commands.<br><br>You can list the cmdlets, aliases, or functions separately as shown by the three examples. |
| `get-help`<br>`get-help command [-full \|`<br>`-detailed \| -examples]`<br>`PS C:\> get-help`<br>`set-executionpolicy -full`<br>`PS C:\> get-help get-process`<br>`-detailed`<br>`PS C:\> get-help start-service`<br>`-examples` | The **get-help** command provides access to a rich set of built-in help.<br><br>You can follow **get-help** with the name of any command. By default, it provides basic help. However, you can also add the **-full, -detailed,** or **-examples** switches.<br><br>The **-detailed** switch expands the basic information with more details and includes examples.<br><br>The **-full** switch provides verbose help, including technical information. It includes all available help information including examples. It often includes online links for more information.<br><br>The **-examples** switch shows a brief synopsis with examples. |
| `get-member`<br>`command or object \| get-member`<br>`PS C:\> get-service \| get-member`<br><br>`$variable \| get-member`<br>`PS C:\> $profile \| get-member` | The **get-member** command provides information about properties and methods you can use with the command. Almost all of the commands are objects, meaning they have properties and methods.<br><br>Properties are descriptions that you can retrieve and sometimes configure. Methods are actions you can take with the item. |

There are also many help topics available on conceptual PowerShell topics. These are called "about" topics and they all start with **about_**.

| List all about topics.<br><br>`PS C:\> get-help about_*` | The * (asterisk) wildcard can be used to list all about topics (all topics that start with **about_**). |
|---|---|
| View any specific about topic.<br><br>`get-help about_topic`<br>`PS C:\> get-help about_execution_policies` | You can then use the **get-help** command to view the **about_ topic**. |

## Exploring get-member

The **get-member** cmdlet shows what properties and events are available for a command. The following listing shows a partial output of the **get-date | get-member** command:

```
PS C:\ > get-date | get-member


    TypeName: System.DateTime


Name                MemberType Definition
----                ---------- ----------
Add                 Method     System.DateTime Add(System.TimeSpan value)
AddDays             Method     System.DateTime AddDays(double value)
AddHours            Method     System.DateTime AddHours(double value)

       . . .

ToShortDateString Method       string ToShortDateString()
ToShortTimeString Method       string ToShortTimeString()

       . . .

Date                Property   System.DateTime Date {get;}
Day                 Property   System.Int32 Day {get;}
DayOfWeek           Property   System.DayOfWeek DayOfWeek {get;}
DayOfYear           Property   System.Int32 DayOfYear {get;}
Hour                Property   System.Int32 Hour {get;}
Kind                Property   System.DateTimeKind Kind {get;}
Millisecond         Property   System.Int32 Millisecond {get;}
Minute              Property   System.Int32 Minute {get;}
Month               Property   System.Int32 Month {get;}
Second              Property   System.Int32 Second {get;}
Ticks               Property   System.Int64 Ticks {get;}
TimeOfDay           Property   System.TimeSpan TimeOfDay {get;}
Year                Property   System.Int32 Year {get;}
```

The following table shows how you can use this information retrieved with the **get-member** cmdlet by accessing properties or executing methods.

> **NOTE** Most properties and methods can be accessed using the dot operator, but the command must be in parentheses. The format is *(command).property*. As you can see, the dot operator is a period after the command. The following table includes some dot operator examples.

| Exploring get-date | Comments |
|---|---|
| Get available members.<br><br>PS C:\> get-date \|<br>get-member<br><br>PS C:\> get-date \|<br>get-member -force | This shows all of the members of the **get-date** cmdlet. The **MemberType** column identifies the members as methods and properties.<br><br>The **Definition** column identifies how the member can be used, such as {**get**;} to indicate a property can be retrieved, {set;} to indicate a property can be configured, or both.<br><br>The **-force** shows all members including intrinsic members. |
| Format member output to view definitions.<br><br>PS C:\> get-date \|<br>get-member \| format-list | Displayed data often won't fit on the screen and instead ends with an ellipsis (...). which usually simply means "there's more." You can use the **format-list** command to view all the data in a list format instead of a table format. |
| Retrieve a property using the dot operator.<br><br>(command).property<br>PS C:\><br>(get-date).hour<br>19 | Most properties can be retrieved simply by enclosing the cmdlet in parentheses and using a dot and the property name.<br><br>The example shows the hour as 19 (or 7 PM) on a 24-hour clock.<br><br>TIP   This works when there is only one instance of a class. There is only one current date and time, so this works. It wouldn't work for **get-service** because there are multiple instances of services running. The next table shows how to handle objects with multiple instances. |
| Execute a method with the dot operator.<br><br>(command).method()<br>PS C:\> (get-date).<br>toshorttimestring()<br>9:13 AM | Methods are executed with parentheses () at the end. Some methods accept (and require) parameters that can be included in the parentheses, but an empty parameter list often works.<br><br>NOTE   The **get-member** output shows that the **toshorttimestring** method has an empty parameter list in the description.<br><br>The example shows the output of the **toshorttimestring** method. |
| Execute a method with a parameter.<br><br>command.<br>method(parameter)<br>PS C:\> (get-date).<br>addhours(5).<br>toshorttimestring()<br>2:13 PM | The **addhours**() method requires a parameter and adds the provided number to the current hours.<br><br>NOTE   The **get-member** output shows that the **addhours** method requires a parameter of type double. Double is a number.<br><br>Notice that you can sometimes use more than one method by separating them with dots. The example adds five hours to the current time of 9:13 AM and then converts it to a short time string (such as 2:13 PM). |

There is a difference in syntax when there's just a single instance of an object and when there are multiple instances of an object. For example, the **get-date** cmdlet returns today's date, and there is only one value of today's date. However, there are always multiple services identified when you execute the **get-service** cmdlet.

Different procedures are required when you have multiple instances. The following table shows some examples.

| Exploring get-service | Comments |
|---|---|
| Get available members.<br><br>`PS C:\> get-service │`<br>`get-member` | This shows all of the members of the **get-service** cmdlet. The **MemberType** column identifies the members as methods and properties.<br><br>The **Definition** column identifies how the member can be used, such as {**get;**} to indicate a property can be retrieved. |
| Retrieve a property.<br><br>(*command* -**name**<br>*name*).*property*<br>(**get-service** -**name**<br>*servicename* ).**status**<br>`PS C:\ > (get-service`<br>`-name msftpsvc).status`<br>`Running` | Properties of specific services can be retrieved using a unique identifier such as the name.<br><br>**NOTE** The (**get-service).status** command returns a null value because it doesn't know which service to query.<br><br>You can use the **get-service** command to identify the names of services to use with the **-name** switch.<br><br>The example checks the status of the FTP Publishing Service (**msftpsvc**). It returns running, stopped, or paused. |
| Execute a method.<br><br>(*command* -**name**<br>*name*).**method()**<br>`PS C:\> (get-service`<br>`-name msftpsvc).stop()`<br>`PS C:\> (get-service`<br>`-name`<br>`msftpsvc).start()` | Methods are executed with parentheses () at the end. Some methods accept parameters that can be included in the parentheses, but an empty parameter list often works.<br><br>**NOTE** The output of **get-service │ get-member st*** shows that the **stop** and **start** methods have empty parameter lists, as listed in the definition as **Start()** and **Stop()**.<br><br>These examples show how to stop and start the FTP Publishing Service. |

# Redirecting Output with Windows PowerShell

Often you'll want data sent to a file. Windows PowerShell includes several redirection operators.

| Operator and Example | Description |
|---|---|
| `>`<br>`Command > `*`filename`*<br>`PS C:\> get-help`<br>`about_execution_policies >`<br>`exec.txt` | Sends output to a file. The file is created if it doesn't exist and overwritten if it exists. |
| `>>`<br>`Command >> `*`filename`*<br>`PS C:\> get-help`<br>`about_execution_policies >>`<br>`about.txt` | Appends output to a file. Existing data is not overwritten. |
| `2>`<br>`Command 2> `*`filename`*<br>`PS C:\> get-help`<br>`about_execution_polic 2>`<br>`errors.txt` | Sends errors to a file. If there aren't any errors, the file is blank.<br><br>**NOTE**   The command fails and gives an error output because the last three letters (ies) in **about_execution_policies** are missing. |
| `2>>`<br>`Command > `*`filename`*<br>`PS C:\> get-help`<br>`about_execution_polic 2>>`<br>`errors.txt` | Appends errors to a file. Existing data is not overwritten.<br><br>**NOTE**   The command fails and gives an error output because the last three letters (ies) in **about_execution_policies** are missing. |

# Understanding PowerShell Errors

PowerShell provides excellent feedback when you make an error. However, unless you know what to look for, it can look just like a huge red blob.

**NOTE**   Errors are in red text on a black background and clearly indicate something is wrong with the previous command.

Figure 37-4 shows an example of what an error looks like, and the error is explained in the following table.

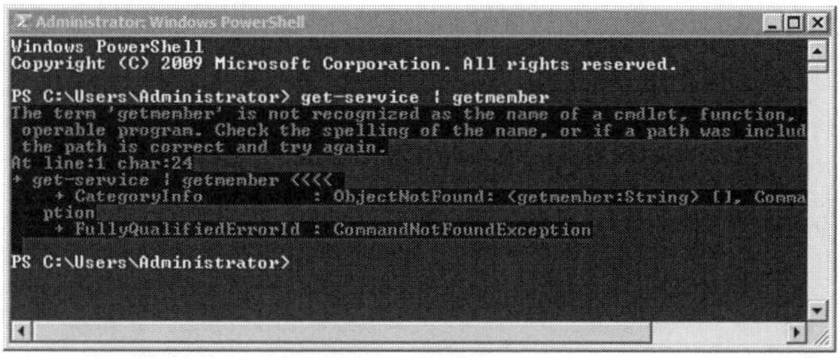

**Figure 37-4**   Windows PowerShell error

| Operator and Example | Description |
|---|---|
| Command with an error:<br><br>`PS C:\ > get-service \|`<br>`getmember` | This command is missing the dash (-) between **get** and **member**. It results in an error. |
| First part of error message:<br><br>`The term 'getmember' is`<br>`not recognized as the`<br>`name of a cmdlet, func-`<br>`tion, script file, or op-`<br>`erable program. Check the`<br>`spelling of the name, or`<br>`if a path was included,`<br>`verify that the path is`<br>`correct and try again.` | The first line indicates what isn't understood. In this case, **getmember** is not understood because it's missing the dash. It should be **get-member**. |
| Second part of error message showing location:<br><br>`At line:1 char:24` | This gives the specific line number and character number where the error was encountered. In this case, it gives the character number where the unknown command (**getmember**) ended.<br><br>**NOTE**  Most commands are on line 1, but if you're running a script, this tells you which line of the script is at fault. |
| Third part of error message pointing at error:<br><br>`+ get-service\| getmember`<br>`<<<<` | The `<<<<` characters are arrows or pointers to the offending command. In this case, the arrows point directly at **getmember**. |
| Additional information:<br><br>`    + CategoryInfo`<br>`: ObjectNotFound:`<br>`(getmember:String) [],`<br>`CommandNotFoundException` | The error closes with some technical information. If you're writing a script, this can be useful, but usually, the first lines give you the information you need to resolve the problem. |

# Understanding PowerShell Variables

Variables are units in memory that hold different values. Both built-in and user-defined variables are available in PowerShell.

**NOTE**  All PowerShell variables start with the dollar sign ($).

The following table shows some of the commonly used variables built-in to Windows PowerShell.

| Built-in Variables | Comments |
|---|---|
| `$pshome`<br>`PS C:\> cd $pshome`<br>`PS C:\Windows\System32\`<br>`WindowsPowerShell\v1.0>` | Location of PowerShell command and associated configuration files. A profile can be placed here.<br><br>The example changes the directory to the location of **$pshome**. |
| `$profile`<br>`PS C:\> $profile`<br>`C:\Users\Darril\Documents\`<br>`WindowsPowerShell\Microsoft.`<br>`PowerShell_profile.ps1`<br>`PS C:\> test-path $profile` | Shows the perceived location of the **profile.ps1** file. This path does not exist by default. The **test-path $profile** command returns false if it does not exist and true if the file does exist. |
| **$error** | An array of all the errors from the current session. The most recent error can be retrieved with **$error[0]** (the first item in the array). |
| **$_.**<br><br>`PS C:\> get-service | where`<br>`{$_.status -eq "`*stopped*`" }` | The $_. string is a special variable that indicates the current cmdlet being piped.<br><br>In the example, the **get-service** command retrieves all services and is then piped to the **where** clause. The $_. variable is used with dot notation to identify the status of each service and see if they are stopped.<br><br>**NOTE**  This effectively works like a **foreach** clause. It lists the information for each service that matches the status of **stopped**. |
| `$pwd` | Current working directory. |

**NOTE**  You can retrieve a full list of variables with the **get-variable** cmdlet or the variable alias. The output lists the variables and their current values.

You can also create your own variables. Variables are assigned with the equal sign (=) and prefixed with the dollar sign ($). You can then use the variable in the current session or within a script.

The following table shows the methods used to assign and manipulate variables.

| Assigning Variables | Comments |
|---|---|
| `PS C:\>  $d = get-date`<br>`PS C:\> $d` | Assigns the current date and time value to **$d**.<br><br>You can view the value of the variable by entering **$d** by itself. |
| `PS C:\> $counter = 0` | Assigns the value **0** to a variable. |

| Assigning Variables | Comments |
|---|---|
| PS C:\> $counter = $counter + 1<br>PS C:\> $counter++<br>PS C:\> $counter | Increments a variable by 1.<br><br>If the **$counter** started as 0, the first line would add 1 to it, and the second line would add 1 again. The third line would show the value is 2. |
| PS C:\> $counter = $counter - 1<br>PS C:\> $counter--<br>PS C:\> $counter | Decrements a variable by 1.<br><br>If the **$counter** started as 0, the first line would subtract 1 from it and the second line would subtract 1 again. The third line would show the value is -2. |
| PS C:\> $msg = "Success!"<br>PS C:\> $msg | Assigns a string of characters to a variable.<br><br>You can view the value of the variable by entering **$msb** by itself. |

When working with numeric variables, you can use different mathematical assignment values, as shown in the following table.

| Working with Numeric Variables | Comments (Including the Value $x if it Starts with 10) |
|---|---|
| =<br>PS C:\> $x = 10 | Assignment. The value of **$x** is **10** after this command. |
| +<br>PS C:\> $x = $x + 5 | Addition. If **$x** started at **10**, the value of **$x** would be **15** after this command. |
| -<br>PS C:\> $x = $x - 5 | Subtraction. If **$x** started at **10**, the value of **$x** would be **5** after this command. |
| *<br>PS C:\> $x = $x * 5 | Multiplication. If **$x** started at **10**, the value of **$x** is **50** after this command. |
| /<br>PS C:\> $x = $x / 5 | Division. If **$x** started at **10**, the value of **$x** is **2** after this command. |
| %<br>PS C:\> $x = $x % 3 | Module (remainder). If **$x** started at **10**, the value of **$x** is **1** after this command. |
| +=<br>PS C:\> $x += $x | Additive assignment. If **$x** started at **10**, the value of **$x** is **20**. |
| -+<br>PS C:\> $x -= $x | Subtractive assignment. If **$x** started at **10**, the value of **$x** is **0** after this command. |
| *=<br>PS C:\> $x *= 10 | Multiplicative assignment. If **$x** started at **10**, the value of **$x** is **100** after this command. |
| /=<br>PS C:\> $x /= 2 | Quotient assignment. If **$x** started at **10**, the value of **$x** is **1** after this command. |
| %=<br>PS C:\> $x /= 3 | Remainder assignment. If **$x** started at **10**, the value of **$x** is **1** after this command. |
| ++<br>PS C:\> $x ++ | Increment. If **$x** started at **10**, the value of **$x** is **11** after this command. |

| Working with Numeric Variables | Comments (Including the Value $x if it Starts with 10) |
|---|---|
| `--`<br>`PS C:\> $x --` | Decrement. If $x started at 10, the value of $x is 9 after this command. |

## Using Comparison Operators

When you're trying to compare two values, you have to use specific syntax. For example, you can't use the equal sign (=) as a comparison operator. The equal sign is used as an assignment operator to assign a value to a variable (such as $x = 10 to assign the value of 10 to the $x variable).

This command works to compare two strings:

```
PS C:\scripts> If ("abc" -eq "abc") {write-host "equal"}
equal
```

However, this command fails with an error, as shown in the following:

```
PS C:\scripts> If ("abc" = "abc") {write-host "equal"}
```

The following table lists the commonly used comparison operators.

| Comparison Operator | Comments |
|---|---|
| -eq | Equals |
| -ne | Not equal |
| -gt | Greater than |
| -lt | Less than |
| -le | Less than or equal |
| -ge | Greater than or equal |

## Understanding Pipelining

Pipelines enable you to combine multiple commands. The output of one command is used as the input for another command.

**NOTE** These are called pipes for two reasons. It represents a metaphor of data being sent through a pipe to another location. Also, the pipe character (|) looks similar to a pipe.

This chapter has already demonstrated many uses of the pipeline. This table shows some of the examples used and adds a few others.

| Pipeline Examples | Comments |
|---|---|
| Retrieve list of services.<br><br>`PS C:\>get-service | format-table Name,`<br>`Status, DependentServices -auto` | The output of the **get-service** cmdlet is used as the input for the **format-table** cmdlet. The **format-table** cmdlet gives you the ability to format the output. |
| Retrieve list of processes and send to file.<br><br>`PS C:\>get-process | out-file`<br>`processes.txt` | The output of **get-process** is piped to **out-file** to send the data to a file. |
| Count commands.<br><br>`PS C:\>get-command | measure-object`<br>`PS C:\>get-command -type cmdlet |`<br>`measure-object` | The **measure-object** cmdlet counts the number of commands retrieved by **get-command**. In the second example, the **get-command** cmdlet looks only for cmdlets with the **-type** switch. |
| Learn properties and methods for commands.<br><br>`PS C:\>get-service | get-member` | The **get-member** cmdlet is used to retrieve all the members of the **get-service** cmdlet. |
| Identify running services.<br><br>`PS C:\> get-service | where {$_.status`<br>`-eq "running" }` | The **$_** combination is a special pipeline variable that allows you to use dot notation with pipelines. The **$_.** refers to the cmdlet being piped (**get-service**).<br><br>This example retrieves a list of running services.<br><br>**NOTE** The **get-service** cmdlet by itself returns a list of all services whether they are running or not. |
| Count list of running services.<br><br>`PS C:\> get-service | where {$_.status`<br>`-eq "running" } | measure-object` | Pipes all the services to the **where** filter to restrict the result to only running services. It then pipes this result to the **measure-object** command to count the result. It returns an integer that indicates the number of services that are running. |
| Sort a list of running processes.<br><br>`PS C:\> get-process | sort-object`<br>`-property handles` | Retrieves a listing of running processes and sorts the output on the property "handles." |
| Retrieve verbose details on any running process.<br><br>`PS C:\> get-process | where-object {`<br>`$_.processname -eq "powershell" } |`<br>`format-list *` | Lists all data (the * wildcard in the **format-list** * indicates all the data) on any running process (**get-process**) identified by the process name (**$_.processname -eq "name"**). |

| Pipeline Examples | Comments |
|---|---|
| Retrieve top 10 list of memory consuming processes.<br><br>`PS C:\> get-process | sort-object workingset -descending | select-object -first 10` | Uses two pipelines. It starts by getting a listing of all processes. It then uses the **sort-object** cmdlet with descending sort order to list the processes using the most memory (**workingset**). It then limits the output to only the top 10 with the **select-object** cmdlet. |
| `PS C:\> get-process | where-object {$_.workingset -gt 30000000}` | This uses the **where-object** to list only the processes that use more than 30 MB of memory (**working set -gt 30000000**). |
| `PS C:\> get-eventlog system -newest 10 | Format-List *` | The **format-list** * cmdlet formats the last 10 system event log entries in a list format. The * ensures that all items are listed. |
| Get a listing of files and folders in a wide format.<br><br>`PS C:\> get-childitem | format-wide` | Retrieves a directory listing of the current folder and uses the **format-wide** cmdlet to format the output. |
| Get a listing of folders only.<br><br>`PS C:\> get-childitem | where-object { $_.psiscontainer }` | Gets a listing of folders in the current directory using the **psiscontainer** (PowerShell is container) value. |
| Get a listing of files only.<br><br>`PS C:\> get-childitem | where-object { !$_.psiscontainer }` | Gets a listing of files in the current directory. This uses the not operator (!) looking for all items that aren't folders using the **psiscontainer** (PowerShell is a container) value. |
| List drives including type, capacity, and freespace.<br><br>`PS C:\> get-wmiobject win32_volume | select name,drivetype, capacity, freespace | export-csv drivelist.csv` | Uses the Windows Management Instrumentation (WMI) cmdlet to retrieve a list of volumes with specific columns. The **export-csv** cmdlet formats the output as a comma-separated value file. |

**TIP**   You can get more detailed help on pipelines with the following command: **get-help about_pipelines**.

**TIP**   A great source for more information is the Windows PowerShell Tips section on Microsoft TechNet. You can get it here: http://technet.microsoft.com/library/ee692948.aspx.

This chapter provides information and commands concerning the following topics:

- Setting the security context
- Creating a PowerShell profile
- Creating and modifying the global PowerShell profile
- Running PowerShell scripts
- Logging processes with a **get-process** script
- Testing for the existence of a file
- Creating output as HTML
- Running a script against multiple computers
- Scheduling PowerShell scripts

**TIP** You should be familiar with PowerShell when preparing for the 70-640, 70-643, and 70-647 exams.

## Setting the Security Context

PowerShell has different levels of security set by an execution policy. If you don't modify the execution policy, you won't be able to run any scripts. These security contexts or security levels define what PowerShell scripts can run. The following table shows the available security contexts that you can configure.

**TIP** By default, PowerShell scripts cannot run until the execution policy is changed. It's common to change the policy to **remote-signed**. You can still run individual commands.

| Execution Policy | Comments |
|---|---|
| Restricted | No scripts can run. PowerShell does not load configuration files or run scripts.<br><br>**TIP** This is the default and must be changed to run any scripts. |
| Unrestricted | All configuration files are loaded and any scripts can run. If you run an unsigned script that was downloaded from the Internet, you are prompted for permission before it runs. |

| Execution Policy | Comments |
|---|---|
| Remote-signed | Local scripts can run without being signed. All scripts and configuration files downloaded from the Internet must be signed by a trusted publisher. |
| All-signed | All scripts and configuration files must be signed by a trusted publisher. This includes scripts running on the local computer. |
| Bypass | Nothing is blocked and there are no warnings or prompts. This works like unrestricted without the prompts. |
| Undefined | Removes the currently assigned execution policy from the current scope. It does not remove an execution policy that is set in a Group Policy scope. |

You can view and set the execution policy with the following commands.

| PowerShell Command | Comments |
|---|---|
| `PS C:\> get-executionpolicy` | Returns the currently assigned execution policy. |
| `PS C:\> get-executionpolicy -list` | Lists the state of the execution policy for all scopes including the machine policy, the user policy, the process, the current user, and the local machine. |
| `set-executionpolicy (restricted | remotesigned | allsigned | unrestricted | bypass )` `PS C:\> set-executionpolicy remotesigned` | Sets the execution policy. The example sets the policy to allow local scripts to run, but requires any scripts downloaded from the Internet to be signed. |

# Creating a PowerShell Profile

The PowerShell profile is a PowerShell script file (named **profile.ps1** or **Microsoft. PowerShell_profile.ps1**) that creates the PowerShell environment every time Windows PowerShell is started. It can include aliases, PowerShell functions, or any other type of PowerShell modifications you want.

> **TIP** The default location of the user's PowerShell profile is C:\Users\username\ Documents\WindowsPowerShell\Microsoft.PowerShell_profile.ps1. However, it doesn't exist by default.

You can view the location and name of the profile using the **$profile** variable executed at the PowerShell prompt as follows:

```
PS C:\> $profile
C:\Users\Darril\Documents\WindowsPowerShell\
Microsoft.PowerShellISE_profile.ps1
```

It's important to realize that even though the **$profile** points to this file and this location, it doesn't mean the file actually exists. The steps in the following table show how to test for and create a profile used for the current user.

> **NOTE**  You can also modify the profile with **Notepad** or the **Windows PowerShell Integrated Scripting Environment** (covered in Chapter 39, "Using the Integrated Scripting Environment"). These steps use Notepad.

| PowerShell Command | Comments |
|---|---|
| PS C:\> $profile<br>C:\Users\Darril\Documents\<br>WindowsPowerShell\Microsoft.<br>PowerShellISE_profile.ps1 | Displays the path and name of the profile. |
| PS C:\> test-path $profile | The **test-path** cmdlet identifies if the path exists. Returns true if it exists and false if not. |
| PS C:\> new-item -path $profile<br>-type file -force | The **new-item** cmdlet creates the path and the profile file identified in the **$profile** variable. If **test-path $profile** returned false before, it will return true now.<br><br>**NOTE**  The **-force** switch overwrites the profile file, if one exists. |
| PS C:\> notepad $profile | Opens the profile file with Notepad. If it was just created, it will be blank. At this point, you can modify the profile as desired. |

Both local and global PowerShell profiles can exist. The following table compares these two profiles.

| Global and Local Profiles | Comments |
|---|---|
| Global profile<br><br>C:\windows\system32\<br>WindowsPowerShell\v1.0\profile.ps1<br><br>Open with:<br><br>PS C:\> notepad c:\windows\system32\<br>WindowsPowerShell\v1.0\profile.ps1 | If a global profile exists, it is used for all users.<br><br>**NOTE**  Even though the path includes "v1.0," this profile does apply to Windows PowerShell v2, which is installed on Windows 2008 R2. |

| Global and Local Profiles | Comments |
|---|---|
| Local profile<br><br>`c:\users\username\documents\`<br>`windowspowershell\`<br>`microsoft.powershell_profile.ps1`<br><br>Open with:<br><br>`PS C:\> notepad $profile` | Applies to currently logged-on user and takes precedence over global profile. The **$profile** variable holds the path for the local profile.<br><br>**TIP** If PowerShell profiles exist in both locations, the local profile takes precedence over the global profile if there are any conflicts. For example, if the global profile sets the location to c:\data, but the local profile sets the location to c:\scripts, the location would be set to c:\scripts. |

## Creating and Modifying the Global PowerShell Profile

The steps in the following table show how to create and modify the global profile.

**TIP** You can use most of these steps to modify the local profile too.

| Steps | Comments |
|---|---|
| 1. Launch PowerShell with administrative permissions. | Some of the steps will not work correctly if PowerShell is not started using **Run As Administrator**. |
| 2. Create the global profile:<br><br>`PS C:\> notepad c:\windows\system32\`<br>`windowspowershell\v1.0\profile.ps1` | If the file doesn't exist, Notepad prompts you to create the file. Click **Yes**. |
| 3. Change the PowerShell starting folder:<br><br>`set-location c:\scripts` | Because **cd** is an alias, you can also enter **cd c:\scripts**.<br><br>**NOTE** The path must exist for this to work. In other words, if **c:\scripts** isn't a valid folder, PowerShell gives an error when it launches. |
| 4. Add an alias to the profile in Notepad:<br><br>`set-alias gh get-help` | Creates an alias called **gh** that executes **get-help**. After this alias is created, you can use the following line to get help on the **set-alias** command:<br><br>PS C:\> **gh get-alias** |

| Steps | Comments |
|---|---|
| 5. Add a function to the profile:<br><br>```<br>function get-topprocesses<br>{<br>get-process | sort-object<br>-property ws -descending |<br>select-object -first 10 |<br>out-gridview<br>}<br>``` | After this is added to the profile, you can enter the following line at the PowerShell prompt:<br><br>PS C:\> **get-topprocesses** to run the function.<br><br>**TIP**  You can name the function anything you like. For example, you can name it something shorter such as **gtp**, which is short for get top processes. Additionally, you can have multiple lines of code in the function. |
| 6. Press Ctrl+S to save the file. | Saves the profile. |
| 7. Close and restart PowerShell. | You see the default path is changed to **c:\scripts**. |
| 8. Run the alias from the profile:<br><br>PS C:\> **gh** | Runs the **get-help** command. |
| 9. Run the function from the profile:<br><br>PS C:\> **get-topprocesses** | Runs the **get-topprocesses function** command.<br><br>Your display looks similar to Figure 38-1. |
| 10. Run other scripts from the profile:<br><br>. *path-script*.**ps1**<br>. **c:\scripts\setenvironment.ps1** | You can run other scripts from within the PowerShell profile by typing a dot, a space, and the path to the script.<br><br>**TIP**  If there is not a space after the dot, the command fails and you see an error message when PowerShell is launched. |

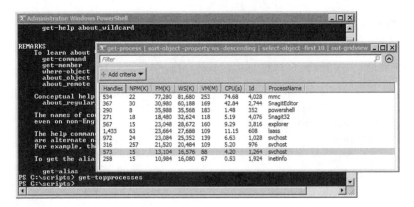

**Figure 38-1**  Top running processes shown in grid view

> **NOTE**  The profile is loaded only when Windows PowerShell is first launched. In other words, if you modify the profile, the modifications won't take effect until you close and restart PowerShell.

## Running PowerShell Scripts

Unlike normal command prompt commands, PowerShell doesn't look in the current path to run commands. In other, words, you have to include a prefix when running a PowerShell script. The following table shows the different prefixes.

| Running PowerShell Script Named test.ps1 in c:\scripts Folder | Comments |
|---|---|
| Include the full path.<br><br>PS C:\> **c:\scripts\ test.ps1** | You can run the script by including the full path. |
| Use the dot backslash ( .\) prefix.<br><br>.\*scriptname*.**ps1**<br>PS C:\scripts><br>.\**test.ps1** | If the file is in the current path, you can use the .\ prefix and PowerShell script name.<br><br>**NOTE**  There are no spaces between the dot, the back slash, or the script name. |
| Use the dot (.) prefix and the path.<br><br>. *path*\*scriptname*.**ps1**<br>PS C:\scripts><br>. **c:\scripts\test.ps1** | **NOTE**  When including the path, you must include a space after the dot. |

| Running PowerShell Script Named test.ps1 in c:\scripts Folder | Comments |
|---|---|
| Run from the command prompt.<br><br>`C:\>powershell c:\`<br>`scripts\test.ps1` | You can run PowerShell scripts from the command prompt.<br><br>**TIP**   You can also access PowerShell interactively from the command prompt by just typing **PowerShell** and pressing **Enter**. You then have the PowerShell prompt and can enter any PowerShell commands from here. |
| Run from the **Start** text box.<br><br>`powershell c:\scripts\`<br>`test.ps1`<br>`powershell -noexit c:\`<br>`scripts\test.ps1` | The **-noexit** switch leaves the PowerShell command prompt open so that you can see the results of the script, but it is not required. |

## Logging Processes with a get-process Script

You can create a PowerShell script from any PowerShell command or group of commands. Just as a batch file is one or more command-line commands, a PowerShell script is one or more PowerShell lines.

You can use the script shown in step 3 of the following table to capture all of the running processes at any given time. For example, if you suspect a rogue process is running at random times causing problems, you can schedule this script to run once an hour for a week to log running processes. At the end of the week, you can analyze the file.

| Steps | Action |
|---|---|
| 1. | Launch PowerShell. |
| 2. | At the PowerShell Prompt, type **notepad getproc.ps1** and press **Enter**. When prompted to create the file, click **Yes**. |
| 3. | Add the following four lines into the Notepad window:<br><br>`$dt = "Current date and time is: "`<br>`$dt = $dt + (get-date).tostring('MMM-dd-yyyy hh:mm')`<br>`$dt | out-file c:\data\runningprocesses.txt -append`<br>`get-process | out-file c:\data\runningprocesses.txt -append`<br><br>**NOTE**   If the c:\data folder doesn't exist, either create it or change the path in lines 3 and 4 to a folder that does exist. |
| 4. | Press Ctrl+S to save the file and close Notepad. |
| 5. | At the PowerShell prompt, type **.\getproc.ps1** and press **Enter**. This runs the script.<br><br>**TIP**   Ensure there is no space between the dot and the backslash. |
| 6. | In Notepad, type **c:\data\runningprocesses.txt** and press **Enter**. |

**TIP**   You can also use this script to identify a process with a memory leak. The script records the amount of memory the process uses, and if a memory leak exists, the memory usage steadily increases.

The following table explains the lines in this script.

| Script Lines | Comments |
|---|---|
| `$dt = "Current date and time is: "` | The script starts by creating a variable (**$dt**) that is used to record the current date and time in the file. |
| `$dt = $dt + (get-date).tostring ('MMM-dd-yyyy hh:mm')` | The **get-date** cmdlet is used with dot notation to get the actual day and time and convert it to a string. The plus (+) character concatenates (or appends) the data.<br><br>**NOTE**   The **MMM** for Month must be in uppercase, and the **mm** for minutes must be in lowercase.<br><br>You could also use a single line as<br><br>`$dt = "Current date and time is: " + (get-date).tostring('MMM-dd-yyyy hh:mm')` |
| `$dt | out-file c:\data\ runningprocesses.txt -append` | This line writes the current date and time to the file using the **out-file** cmdlet and the variable created in the previous step. The value of the string is something like<br><br>`Current date and time is: Oct-17-2010_09:02`<br>The **-append** switch ensures the data is added to the file and it doesn't overwrite the file. |
| `get-process | out-file c:\data\ runningprocesses.txt -append` | Get a list of all current running processes and output them to the same file using the **append** switch.<br><br>Of course, you can get fancier with the **get-process** command. For example, if you wanted to record only the top 10 processes based on memory usage, you could use this command:**get-process | sort-object -property ws -descending | select-object -first 10 | out-file c:\data\ runningprocesses.txt -append** |

**TIP**   You can use the same script to record the activity of a specific process. For example, if you wanted to see the activity of the lsass process only, you can modify the last line so that it looks like this: **Get-Process | Where-Object { $_.processname -eq "lsass" } | out-file c:\data\runningprocesses.txt -append.**

## Testing for the Existence of a File

You can use the following script snippets to test for the existence of a file and either delete or rename the file depending on which code snippet you choose. This has multiple uses. For example, if you want to create a listing of computers in the domain, but you don't want the new listing appended to the current file, you can either delete or rename the existing file. Similarly, if you have a script that writes data to a file for logging, you can use one of these scripts to handle existing files.

| Script Lines | Comments |
|---|---|
| Delete a file if it exists.<br><br>```\nIf (test-path c:\data\\ncomputerlist.txt)\n{\n   remove-item c:\data\\ncomputerlist.txt\n}\n``` | The **test-path** cmdlet checks for the existence of the file. If it exists, it returns true and the lines within the curly brackets execute.<br><br>The example checks for **C:\data\computerlist.txt** and deletes if it exists with the **remove-item** cmdlet. |
| Rename a file if it exists.<br><br>```\nIf (test-path c:\data\\ncomputerlist.txt)\n{\n   $dt = (get-date).\ntostring('MMM_dd_yyyy_hh_mm')\n   $newname = "computerlist_" +\n$dt + ".txt"\n   rename-item -path c:\data\\ncomputerlist.txt -newname\n$newname\n}\n``` | Alternatively, you can archive the item by renaming it with the **rename-item** cmdlet.<br><br>**NOTE**  Use this code *instead* of the **remove-item** code in the preview row if you want to archive the item.<br><br>This code renames the file by appending the date and time to the file name. |
| Copy a file if it doesn't exist.<br><br>```\nIf (test-path c:\gpo_adm\\ngrouppolicy-server.admx)\n{\n#do nothing\n}\nelse\n{\n   $objnet = $(new-object -com\nwscript.network)\n   $objnet.mapnetworkdrive\n("x:", "\\dc1\admx")\n   copy-item\nx:\grouppolicy-server.admx\n-destination\nc:\gpo_adm\n   $objnet.\nremovenetworkdrive("x:")\n}\n``` | This code checks for the existence of a file and copies it from a share if it doesn't exist.<br><br>If the file exists, the comment **#do nothing** is ignored. If the file doesn't exist, it's copied from a network share.<br><br>Because the **copy-item** cmdlet can't copy from a share directly, the share must first be created using the **new-object** cmdlet from the **wscript.network** object and the **mapnetworkdrive** method. The network object is stored in the **$objnet** variable.<br><br>**NOTE**  You cannot have any spaces between the **mapnetworkdrive** method and the first parentheses.<br><br>With the drive mapped, the **copy-item** can copy the file from the mapped drive to the local destination.<br><br>Last, the **removenetworkdrive** method is used to remove the x: mapped network drive.<br><br>**NOTE**  You cannot have any spaces between the **removenetworkdrive** method and the first parentheses. |

# Creating Output as HTML

You can use the following script to capture data and send the output to an HTML file. Although this script captures the output of a **get-service** command, you can use it for other commands as well.

```
$computer = get-content env:computername
get-service  |
sort-object -property status -descending |
convertto-html -title "Running Services" -body "<h1>Running
Services on $computer</h1> " -property DisplayName, Name, Status |
  foreach   {
      if($_ -like "*<td>Running</td>*")
          {$_ -replace "<tr>", "<tr bgcolor=ffffcc >"}
      elseif($_ -like "*<td>Stopped</td>*")
          {$_ -replace "<tr>", "<tr bgcolor=ffccff >"}
      else{$_}
  }   >  c:\scripts\get-service.html
c:\scripts\get-service.html
```

The following table explains the lines in this script.

| Script Lines to Send Output to HTML | Comments |
|---|---|
| `$computer = get-content env:computername` | This retrieves the name of the computer and stores it in the **$computer** variable. |
| `get-service  |` | The rest of the script (except the last line) is a single line with several pipes. The first cmdlet is the **get-service** cmdlet ending with the pipe symbol (\|). |
| `Sort-object -property status -descending  |` | Next, the output is sorted based on the status (running or stopped) in descending order so that running services are listed first. It finishes with a pipe. |
| `convertto-html -title "Running Services" -body "<h1>Running Services on $computer</h1> " -property DisplayName, Name, Status  |` | The **convertto-html** cmdlet converts the output to HTML with some HTML codes. The title is in the title bar of the web browser. The **<h1>** code provides a heading at the top of the page with the **$computer** variable displaying the name. Last, the **-property** switch identifies the three columns to include and lists them as column headings. **NOTE** The column headings are not case sensitive but are displayed in the same case you enter them. If you use this script for something other than the **get-service** applet, you need to modify the columns in the **-property** list. |

| Script Lines to Send Output to HTML | Comments |
|---|---|
| ```foreach   {     if($_ -like "*<td>Running</td>*")         {$_ -replace "<tr>", "<tr bgcolor=ffffcc >"}       elseif($_ -like "*<td>Stopped</td>*")         {$_ -replace "<tr>", "<tr bgcolor=ffccff >"}       else{$_}  } > c:\scripts\get-service.html``` | The **foreach** command loops through the page to change the background colors of the rows. If the service is running, the row is changed to a light yellow color. If the service is not running, the row is changed to a reddish color.<br><br>The redirector (>) then sends the output to the **c:\scripts\get-service.html** file. |
| ```c:\democode\ get-service.html``` | Last, the file is opened. It looks similar to Figure 38-2. Because it is an HTML file, it automatically launches the default web browser. |

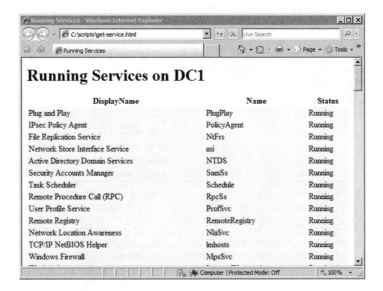

**Figure 38-2**   Display running services in an HTML file

# Running a Script Against Multiple Computers

Occasionally, you need to run a single script against multiple computers. One way of doing so is to read a list of the computers from a text file.

This script shows how to read the computer list from a text file and then run the script against each computer in the list. Although this script records the BIOS information for each computer in the list, you can use it to do any other task by modifying the content of the **foreach** loop.

The full script is presented here, with some comments on the lines in the following table.

```
$computers = get-content "c:\data\computerlist.txt"
"BIOS Information as of " + (get-date).tostring('MMM-dd-yyyy')
| out-file c:\data\computerbios.txt
foreach ($computer in $computers){
"Computer name: " + $computer -computername $computer
| out-file c:\data\computerbios.txt -append
get-wmiobject win32_bios | out-file c:\data\computerbios.txt -append
}
```

For this example, the computerlist.txt file has the following two lines:

```
DC1
DC2
```

> **TIP**   This script reads from a file named computerlist.txt file. You can create the script manually or automatically. Chapter 40, "Using PowerShell to Manage Active Directory," includes a script you can use to create a list of computers in a domain.

| Script Lines to Run Command Against Multiple Computers | Comments |
|---|---|
| `$computers = get-content "c:\data\` `computerlist.txt"` | This command reads the list of computer names from a file named computerlist.txt and places them in an array named **$computers**. You can view the array contents by entering **$computers**. <br><br>**NOTE**   If the file doesn't exist, the script fails. |
| `"BIOS Information as of " +` `(get-date).tostring('MMM-dd-yyyy')` `| out-file c:\data\computerbios.txt` | Next, a file header line is added, indicating what the file contains. The **get-date** cmdlet is used to add the month and year to the header, identifying when it was created. <br><br>**NOTE**   The **-append** switch is not used, so any existing data in the file is deleted. |

| Script Lines to Run Command Against Multiple Computers | Comments |
|---|---|
| ```foreach ($computer in $computers){ "Computer name: " + $computer   | out-file c:\data\computerbios.txt -append get-wmiobject win32_bios -computername $computer   | out-file c:\data\computerbios.txt -append }``` | The **foreach** command loops through the **$computers** array. For each computer name in the array, it outputs data.<br><br>First, it outputs the name of the computer. Next, it uses the **get-wmiobject** cmdlet to retrieve information on the BIOS for the computer identified as **$computer**. It does this for each computer name retrieved from the **computerlist.txt** file and stored in the **$computers** variable. |
| You can view the file with this command:<br><br>`PS C:\> notepad c:\data\ computerbios.txt` | Figure 38-3 shows a screen shot of the opened file. |

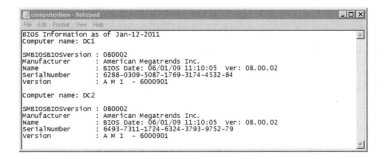

**Figure 38-3**  File created by script

**TIP**  This scripted used **get-wmiobject**, and there are thousands of commands you can execute using **get-wmiobject**. You can't know them all. However, Marc van Orsouw (AKA The PowerShell Guy) wrote a great script known as the PowerShell WMI Explorer. You can read about it and download it from http://thepowershellguy.com/blogs/posh/archive/2007/03/22/powershell-wmi-explorer-part-1.aspx. Figure 38-4 shows a screenshot of the WMI Explorer in action.

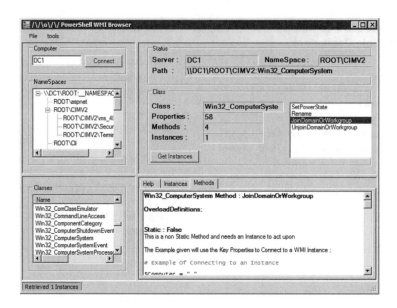

**Figure 38-4**  PowerShell WMI Explorer

## Scheduling PowerShell Scripts

You can schedule PowerShell scripts through the Task Scheduler, but it is a little trickier than simple batch files. If you try to schedule the .ps1 file, Notepad opens the file instead of the script running.

As an example, imagine that you created the following script and named it c:\scripts\ feedback.ps1:

```
$obj = new-object -comobject wscript.shell
$intButton = $obj.Popup("Your message",0,"Title", 0)
```

**TIP**  This script displays a popup dialog box similar to Figure 38-5, though you can change the title and message to anything desired. You can test your script from the command prompt (not the PowerShell prompt) by entering the following: **powershell c:\scripts\feedback.ps1**.

**Figure 38-5**  Dialog box created with PowerShell

You can use the following steps to schedule it with Task Scheduler.

| Steps | Comments |
|---|---|
| 1. Launch the Task Scheduler with administrative permissions. | Click **Start**, type **Schedule** in the **Start Search** text box, right-click **Task Scheduler,** and then select **Run As Administrator**. |
| 2. Select **Task Scheduler Library**. Click **Create Basic Task**. | The **Create Basic Task** button is in the right pane. |
| 3. Name the task **Testing** and click **Next**. | This is just for testing but you could create a schedule for a live script and change the name to anything desired. |
| 4. Select **Daily** and click **Next**. | You can also choose to run it weekly, monthly, or any other available timeframe. |
| 5. Accept the default daily schedule and click **Next**. | You can modify this time. |
| 6. Ensure **Start a Program** is selected and click **Next**. | This allows you to locate an executable file, including a script. |
| 7. Enter **powershell** in the **Program/Script** text box. Enter **c:\scripts\feedback.ps1** in the **Add Arguments** text box. Click **Next**. | This has the net effect of typing the following command from the command prompt: **powershell c:\scripts\feedback.ps1**. Your display should look similar to Figure 38-6. |
| 8. Click **Finish** to create the task. | This creates the script. |
| 9. Select **Task Scheduler Library**. Locate the **Testing** task in **Task Scheduler**. Right-click it and select **Run**. | The script runs and the message box displays. However, it doesn't appear as the top window so you might have to look for it. Although this isn't elegant for a message box, it does show how to make a PowerShell script run. |
| 10. Close all the open windows. | If desired, delete the test task you created. |

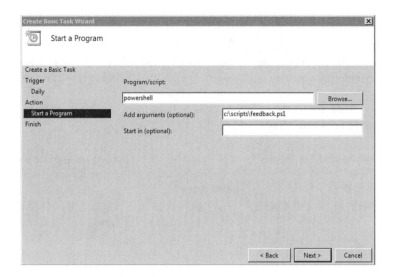

**Figure 38-6**   Scheduling a PowerShell script with Task Scheduler

The previous procedure creates a noninteractive command-line prompt in the background while the script runs. You can also run the PowerShell script by creating a batch file to run the script. The batch file would use the following line:

```
powershell -noexit c:\scripts\feedback.ps1
```

The **-noexit** switch keeps the PowerShell window open after the script runs, but you can omit it to ensure that PowerShell closes after the script runs.

> **TIP**   Although it is not a native feature, you can download a free copy of the specops tool that enables you to schedule scripts similar to how you can with the Task Scheduler but with a few more features. You can check it out here: http://technet. microsoft.com/en-us/library/ff730969.aspx.

# Using the Integrated Scripting Environment

This chapter provides information and commands concerning the following topics:

- Launching the ISE
- Exploring the ISE
- Executing commands in the ISE
- Creating and saving a script with the ISE

## Launching the ISE

The Windows PowerShell Integrated Scripting Environment (ISE) is a handy tool you can use to create, test, and debug PowerShell scripts. You can launch the ISE by clicking **Start**, **All Programs**, **Accessories**, **Windows PowerShell**, **Windows PowerShell ISE**.

Figure 39-1 shows the ISE in action with the different areas labeled, and the following table explains these sections.

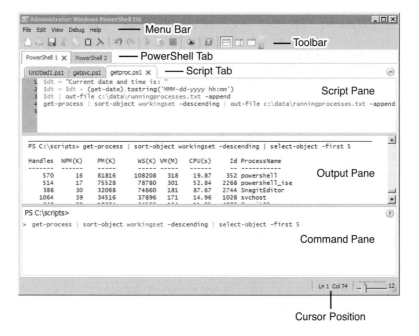

**Figure 39-1** Windows PowerShell ISE

| PowerShell ISE | Comments |
|---|---|
| Menu bar | Windows dropdown menus. |
| Toolbar | Buttons for key tools. |
| PowerShell tab | Different PowerShell tabs can have separate scripts and variables. It's common to create a different PowerShell tab when connecting to a remote computer.<br><br>**NOTE**   You can have as many as eight PowerShell tabs open at a time. |
| Script tab | Shows the name of script you're currently working on. Multiple scripts can be open at a time.<br><br>**TIP**   Hover over the tab and the full path to the script displays in a tooltip. |
| Script pane | Shows the script you're currently working on. The line numbers automatically display in the script pane but are not in the script. |
| Output pane | The script output goes here when scripts or PowerShell commands are executed. |
| Command pane | A regular PowerShell command prompt. Any PowerShell commands can be executed here. |
| Cursor position | Shows the current position of the cursor.<br><br>**NOTE**   PowerShell error outputs show the cursor position. You can use this hint to get right to the source of the problem when troubleshooting a script. |

## Exploring the ISE

The following table shows the default buttons on the toolbar in order from left to right.

| PowerShell ISE Toolbar Buttons | Use |
|---|---|
| New | Creates a new script tab. |
| Open | Opens an existing script or file. |
| Save | Saves the script or file in the current tab. |
| Cut | Cuts selected text and copies it to the Clipboard. |
| Copy | Copies selected text to the Clipboard. |
| Paste | Pastes contents of the Clipboard to the cursor location. |
| Clear Output Pane | Clears all content in the Output Pane. |
| Undo | Reverses the action that was just performed. |
| Redo | Performs the action that was just undone. |
| Run Script (Green arrow) | Runs a script. F5 also runs the script. |

| PowerShell ISE Toolbar Buttons | Use |
|---|---|
| Run Selection | Runs a selected portion of a script.<br><br>**TIP**   You can highlight any portion of a script and run it by itself by clicking this button or by pressing the **F8** key. |
| Stop Execution | Stops a script that is running. The Ctrl+Break and Ctrl+C combinations also stop the script. |
| New Remote PowerShell Tab | Creates a new PowerShell Tab that establishes a session on a remote computer. A dialog box displays and prompts you to enter details required to establish the remote connection. |
| Start PowerShell. exe | Opens a PowerShell Console. |
| Show Script Pane Top | Moves the Script Pane to the top in the display. This is the default display. |
| Show Script Pane Right | Moves the Script Pane to the right in the display. The output pane moves to the top with the command pane at the bottom. |
| Show Script Pane Maximized | Maximizes the Script Pane. |

You can use several keyboard shortcuts with the ISE. The following tables show many of these.

| PowerShell Shortcuts Keys | Comments |
|---|---|
| F1 | Launches Help. |
| F3 | Launches the Find dialog box to search the script. |
| F5 | Runs the script. |
| F8 | Runs a selected portion of a script. |
| Ctrl+T | Creates a new PowerShell tab. |
| Ctrl+Shift+P | Starts PowerShell. |
| Ctrl+N | Creates a new script tab. |

Breakpoints allow you to pause a script when it reaches the breakpoint. You can set breakpoints on any line in the script. The following keyboard shortcuts are used with breakpoints.

| Breakpoint shortcut keys | Comments |
|---|---|
| F9 | Toggles breakpoint. Position the cursor where you want the breakpoint and press **F9** to create it. The script pauses at the breakpoint. |
| Ctrl+Shift+F9 | Removes all breakpoints. |
| Ctrl+Shift+L | Lists all breakpoints. |
| F10 | Steps over. |

| Breakpoint shortcut keys | Comments |
|---|---|
| F11 | Steps into. |
| Shift+F11 | Steps out. |
| F5 | Runs/Continues. |
| Shift+F5 | Stops Debugger. |
| Ctrl+Shift+D | Displays the call stack. |

## Executing Commands in the ISE

You can execute any commands in the ISE that you can execute from the normal PowerShell prompt. Simply enter the command in the command pane and press **Enter**. Also, the command pane keeps a running history of your commands just as the normal PowerShell prompt does.

For example, Figure 39-2 shows the result of entering the **[System.DirectoryServices. ActiveDirectory.Domain]::GetCurrentDomain**() command.

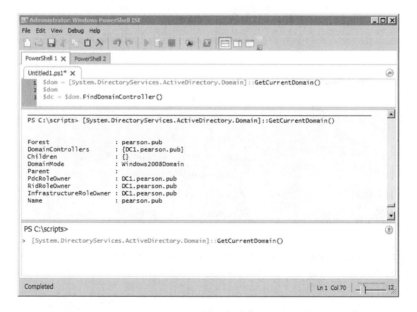

**Figure 39-2**   Executing commands in the Windows PowerShell ISE

**TIP**   Although the figure indicates the command on the command line in the bottom pane, it actually disappears after the command is entered. For the figure, the up arrow was pressed before the screenshot was captured to show the command.

## Creating and Saving a Script in the ISE

You can build scripts and test the progress from within the ISE. The steps in the following table show how to build a script from within the ISE that will

- Read a text file of computer names
- Store the computer names in an array
- Start writing output to a text file beginning with the date
- Loop through the list of computer names retrieving a list of hot fixes and writing them to the text file

| Steps | Comments |
|---|---|
| 1. Use Notepad to create a text file named computerlist.txt in the c:\data folder. | This text file includes a list of computer names in your network. To start, you can use a text file with just two computer names, such as DC1 and DC2. |
| 2. Launch the **Windows PowerShell ISE** with administrative permissions. | Click **Start**, type **PowerShell** in the **Search Programs and Files** text box, right-click **Windows PowerShell ISE,** and then click **Run As Administrator**. |
| 3. Type the following line in the script pane:<br><br>`$list = get-content`<br>`"c:\data\computerlist.txt"` | Reads the text file and stores the list in the variable named **$list**. Because there is more than one name in the list, the variable is created as an array. |
| 4. Press **F5** to run the script. | This should run successfully.<br><br>**NOTE**  You can view the contents of the array by entering **$list** and pressing **Enter** in the command pane. |
| 5. Type the following three lines in the script pane:<br><br>`$outputline = "Hotfix list as of: "`<br>`+ (get-date).tostring`<br>`('MMM-dd-yyyy hh:mm')`<br>`$outputline | out-file c:\data\`<br>`hotfixlist.txt -append`<br>`$outputline = "-------------------"`<br>`| out-file c:\data\`<br>`hotfixlist.txt -append` | The first line creates a variable and populates it with some text and the current date. It then appends it to a text file.<br><br>**TIP**  The **MMM** in the date format field must be entered as all caps to ensure the month is displayed.<br><br>The second line opens the hotfixlist.txt file and sends the Hotfix line to the file.<br><br>The third line sends a line of dashes to the text file. All of this is combined to create a header in the output file. |

| Steps | Comments |
|---|---|
| 6. Highlight the three lines you just typed and press the **F8** key to execute just these lines. | This should run successfully.<br><br>**NOTE**  You can view the output of this by entering **notepad c:\data\ hotfixlist.txt** and pressing **Enter** in the command pane. |
| 7. Type the following line in the command pane and press **Enter**:<br><br>```get-wmiobject<br>win32_quickfixengineering<br>-computername localhost```<br> | Retrieves a list of hot fixes installed on the local computer.<br><br>**TIP**  The term **localhost** runs this on the local computer. However, you can substitute the name of any computer in place of **localhost**.<br><br>The purpose of this line is to ensure that the **get-wmiobject** command is formatted correctly prior to placing it in the **foreach** loop in the next step. |
| 8. Type the following lines in the script pane:<br><br>```foreach ($i in $list)<br>    {<br>    $outputline = "Computername: "<br>+ $i ;<br>    $outputline | out-file c:\data\<br>hotfixlist.txt -append;<br>    $outputline = gwmi<br>win32_quickfixengineering<br>-computername $i<br>    $outputline = gwmi<br>win32_quickfixengineering<br>-computername $i | sort-object<br>-descending installedon<br>    $outputline | out-file c:\data\<br>hotfixlist.txt -append;<br>    }```<br> | The **foreach** command loops through the script lines within the curly brackets (**{ }**). The **$list** variable is an array of all the computers read from the text file. The **$i** holds the value of the first computer name in the list the first time it loops, then the second name on the next loop, and continues until the computer list is exhausted.<br><br>The loop starts by writing the name of the computer in the file with the first two **$outputline** lines.<br><br>It then populates the **$outputline** with the hotfix information for the computer after sorting the output in descending order on the **installedon** column. This lists the most recent hotfixes first.<br><br>**NOTE**  If your computerlist.txt file doesn't include names of valid computers or these computers can't be reached, the **gwmi (get-wmiobject)** command fails.<br><br>The last line writes the hotfix information to the file.<br><br>**TIP**  **gwmi** is an alias for **get-wmiobject**. |

| Steps | Comments |
|---|---|
| 9. Press F5 to run the script. | At this point, your display looks similar to Figure 39-3.<br><br>**TIP**  It's common to have typos. A simple space added in the wrong place causes problems. Use the error output and the cursor position information to identify the line and the position of the error. |
| 10. Save your script by clicking the **Save** button. Browse to a location on your computer and save the script as **hotfix.ps1.** | **NOTE**  You might not be able to run the script if the execution policy hasn't been modified. Chapter 38, "Creating and Running a PowerShell Script," in the "Setting the Security Context" section covers how to set the execution policy if necessary.<br><br>If the execution policy has been modified, you can execute the script from the command prompt with the following command:<br><br>**c:\data\hotfix.ps1**<br><br>If the script is in the same path as your current path, you can run it with this command:<br><br>**.\hotfix.ps1** |

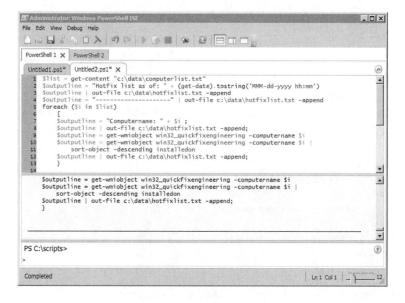

**Figure 39-3**  Building a script in the Windows PowerShell ISE

If you look at the file created by the hotfix.ps1 script, it looks something like this:

```
Hotfix list as of: Jan-07-2011 06:19
---------------------
Computername: DC1


Source Description HotFixID    InstalledBy          InstalledOn
------ ----------- --------    -----------          -----------
DC1    Update      KB948610    S-1-5-21-23182879... 1/7/2011 12:04:40 PM
DC1    Update      KB948609    S-1-5-21-23182879... 1/7/2011 12:04:40 PM
DC1    Update      KB968930    S-1-5-21-23182879... 1/7/2011 11:25:37 AM



Computername: DC2
Source Description HotFixID    InstalledBy          InstalledOn
------ ----------- --------    -----------          -----------
DC2    Update      KB948610    S-1-5-21-23182879... 1/7/2011 12:24:40 PM
```

After you start writing scripts, you'll probably realize that there is always an improvement you can add. Getting it to work is the first objective. You can then tweak it to make it better. For example, once you see the output of the hotfix.ps1 script, you might want to adjust it. The following table shows how you can tweak it.

| Breakpoint Shortcut Keys | Comments |
|---|---|
| Test this line from the command pane:<br><br>`gwmi Win32_QuickFixEngineering \|`<br>`format-table -property hotfixid,`<br>`description, installedon,`<br>`installedby` | Changes the output using the **format-table** cmdlet to pick specific columns.<br><br>When you're happy with the output, you can then put the line into the script.<br><br>TIP You can use \| **format-table \*** to view all the possible columns that you can add to the **format-table -property** list. |
| Modify the tenth line in the script so that it looks like this:<br><br>`$outputline = gwmi`<br>`    Win32_QuickFixEngineering`<br>`-computername $i`<br>`        \| sort-object -descending`<br>`installedon`<br>`        \| format-table -property`<br>`hotfixid,`<br>`            description, installedby,`<br>`installedon` | You can now run the script with the modified line by pressing the **F5** key. |

At this point, the modified script looks like the following text.

**TIP**  The lines are numbered for readability only. Do not add the numbers. However, they do show the only places where you should press the **Enter** key. In other words, line 2 extends two lines in the book but you should not press **Enter** until you get to the end of the line before line 3 starts.

```
1  $list = get-content "c:\data\computerlist.txt"
2  $outputline = "Hotfix list as of: " +
(get-date).tostring('MMM-dd-yyyy hh:mm')
3  $outputline | out-file c:\data\hotfixlist.txt -append
4  $outputline = "---------------------" | out-file 5 c:\data\hotfix-
list.txt -append
5  foreach ($i in $list)
6  {
7    $outputline = "Computername: " + $i ;
8    $outputline | out-file c:\data\hotfixlist.txt -append;
9    $outputline = gwmi win32_quickfixengineering -computername $i
10   $outputline = gwmi Win32_QuickFixEngineering -computername $i
| sort-object -descending installedon | format-table -property
hotfixid, description, installedby, installedon
11   $outputline | out-file c:\data\hotfixlist.txt -append;
12  }
```

# Using PowerShell to Manage Active Directory

This chapter provides information and commands concerning the following topics:

- Using the Active Directory Module in Windows Server 2008 R2
- Creating and manipulating objects in Windows Server 2008
- Working with the domain object
- Working with the system.directoryservices namespace
- Creating a list of domain computers

**NOTE** PowerShell commands in this chapter are run on a domain controller named DC1 in the pearson.pub domain.

**TIP** You should be familiar with PowerShell when preparing for the 70-640, 70-643, and 70-647 exams.

## Using the Active Directory Module in Windows Server 2008 R2

The Active Directory Module for Windows Server 2008 R2 includes more than 70 commands you can use to easily create and manipulate Active Directory objects.

**TIP** The Active Directory Module is not available for Windows Server 2008 at this writing. It is available only on Windows Server 2008 R2.

You can use this as a feature after you have promoted a Windows Server 2008 R2 server to a domain controller and imported the module with the following two commands:

```
PS C:\> import-module servermanager
PS C:\> add-windowsfeature rsat-ad-powershell


Success Restart Needed Exit Code Feature Result
------- -------------- --------- --------------
True    No             NoChan... {}

PS C:\>
```

After it's added, you need to launch **Active Directory Module for Windows PowerShell** via the **Administrative Tools** menu with administrative permissions.

**NOTE**   You do not have access to the extended commands in a normal PowerShell window.

The following table shows some of the usages of these objects. As long as you can create a distinguished name (DN), these commands are quite simple to use. See Chapter 7, "Using Basic ds Commands," if you need a review on DNs.

**TIP**   You have access to the same help with all of these commands. For example, you can enter **get-help** command, **get-help** command **-full**, and **get-help** command **-examples**. You can also tab through the commands by typing **get-ad**, or **set-ad**, or **new-ad**, and then pressing **Tab** to tab through the available commands.

| PowerShell Commands to Create AD Objects | Comments |
|---|---|
| Create an OU.<br><br>`new-adorganizationalunit -name`<br>`ou-name -path dn`<br>`PS C:\> new-adorganizationalunit`<br>`-name ITAdmins -path`<br>`"dc=pearson,dc=pub"` | The **new-adorganizationalunit** cmdlet creates new OUs. It requires a name and a path.<br><br>The example creates an OU named **ITAdmins** in the pearson.pub domain. |
| Create a user.<br><br>`new-aduser -samaccountname`<br>`username -name username -path`<br>`"dn"`<br>`PS C:\> new-aduser`<br>`-samaccountname Dawn`<br>`-name Dawn -path`<br>`ou=itadmins,dc=pearson,dc=pub` | You can create a new user with the **new-aduser** cmdlet.<br><br>The example creates a user named **Dawn** in the **itadmins** OU.<br><br>**NOTE**   If any of the properties have spaces, they must be enclosed in quotes. |
| Move a user.<br><br>`get-aduser username \|`<br>`move-adobject -targetpath dn`<br>`PS C:\> get-aduser Dawn \|`<br>`move-adobject -targetpath`<br>`ou=sales, dc=pearson,dc=pub` | You can move a user with the **move-adobject** cmdlet.<br><br>The example first gets the user named **Dawn** with the **get-aduser** cmdlet, and then it pipes the result to the **move-adobject** cmdlet.<br><br>The **move-adobject** specifies the target OU using the DN and moves the user to the Sales OU. |

**TIP**   There are many more capabilities and uses with the Active Directory Module. If you're running Active Directory on Windows Server 2008 R2 and want to dig deeper, check out the TechNet website: http://technet.microsoft.com/library/dd378937.aspx.

# Creating and Manipulating Objects in Windows Server 2008

If you're not running Windows Server 2008 R2, you can still create and manipulate objects with Windows PowerShell, but there is a little more coding. The following examples show how to create an OU, create a user, and move the user.

## Creating an OU with PowerShell

You can use the following script to create an OU.

```
$objdom = [adsi]""
$objou = $objdom.create("organizationalunit", "ou = IT Admins")
$objou.setinfo()
```

The lines in the script are explained in the following table.

| PowerShell Commands to Create AD Objects | Comments |
|---|---|
| `$objdom = [adsi]""` | Creates an object named **$objdom** and populates it with the value of the current domain. |
| `$objou = $objdom.create("organizationalunit", "ou = IT Admins")` | Creates an object named **$objou** and populates it using the **$objdom.create** method. This method needs two parameters: the type of object (**organizationalunit** in this case) and the name of the object after **ou=**.<br><br>NOTE   Both parameters in the create method must be enclosed in quotes. |
| `$objou.setinfo()` | The **setinfo** method actually creates the object. |

## Creating a User with PowerShell

The following code shows how you can create a user in a domain, and the table explains this code:

```
$objou = [adsi]("LDAP://ou=it admins, dc=pearson, dc=pub")
$objuser = $objou.create("user", "cn=Sally Pearson")
$objuser.put( "samaccountname", "Sally" )
$objuser.setinfo()
```

| Code | Explanation |
|---|---|
| `$objou = [adsi]("LDAP://ou=it admins, dc=pearson, dc=pub")` | The first line creates an object pointing to the target OU using the ADSI helper.<br><br>NOTE   LDAP must be entered in all capital letters. |

| Code | Explanation |
|------|-------------|
| `$objuser = $objou.create("user", "cn=Sally Pearson")` | The **$objou.create** method identifies the object as a user object and then gives the common name (**cn**). This results in a distinguished name for the user of<br><br>`"cn = Sally Johnson" ou=it admins, dc=pearson, dc=pub"` |
| `$objuser.put ( "samaccountname", "Sally" )` | You can add any properties for the user that are desired with the **put** method. This line adds the **samaccountname** for the user. |
| `$objuser.setinfo()` | The **setinfo** method creates the object using the properties and settings identified in the previous lines.<br><br>Figure 40-1 shows the user created in the OU as a result of the previous script used to create the OU, and the script used to create the user. |

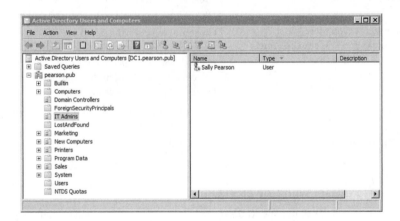

**Figure 40-1**    User created in the IT Admins OU using Windows PowerShell

## Moving Objects with PowerShell

You can use the following three lines to move an object in Active Directory, and the following table explains this code:

```
$obj = [adsi]("LDAP://cn=sally pearson,ou=it admins,dc=pearson,dc=pub")
$target = [adsi]("LDAP://ou=sales,dc=pearson,dc=pub")
$obj.MoveTo($target)
```

| Code | Explanation |
|------|-------------|
| `$obj = [adsi]("LDAP://`<br>`cn=sally pearson,ou=it`<br>`admins,dc=pearson,dc=pub")` | The first line identifies the object that you want to move and places it into the object named **$objuser**.<br><br>**NOTE   LDAP** must be all uppercase.<br><br>**TIP**   Although the example uses the DN of a user object, you can use the DN of any object that you want to move. |
| `$target = [adsi]("LDAP://`<br>`ou=sales,dc=pearson,dc=pub")` | The next line identifies the DN of the new location and places it in the object **$target**. |
| `$obj.MoveTo($target)` | You can then use the **moveto** method of the **$objuser** object. The **$target** parameter identifies where it will be moved. |

## Working with the Domain Object

PowerShell includes an Active Directory Service Interface (ADSI) that you can use to interact with Active Directory. The basic command to invoke it is

```
$objdom = [adsi]""
```

This creates an object named **$objdom** and populates it with the value of the current domain. You can see this value with the **$objdom** command, as shown in the following listing:

```
PS C:\> $objdom


distinguishedName : {DC=pearson,DC=pub}
Path              :
```

The following table shows you how to invoke and interact with the ADSI helper.

| ADSI Commands | Comments |
|---------------|----------|
| Get all members of the object.<br><br>`PS C:\> $objdom | get-member` | Shows all members of the object and gives you an idea of what you can do with it. |
| List all OUs and containers.<br><br>`PS C:\> $objdom.children` | Lists children of the domain (the top-level OUs and containers, such as the Users and Computers containers). |
| List the DN.<br><br>`PS C:\> $objdom.distinguishedname` | In the pearson.pub domain, the output is<br><br>**DC=pearson,DC=pub** |

**TIP**   You can also type **$objdom.** (with the period) and then tab through all the commands that are available.

# Working with the system.directoryservices Namespace

You can also use the **system.directoryservices** namespace to retrieve basic information about the domain. You first populate an object with the domain information and then query the object. The syntax to do each is shown in the following code:

```
PS C:\> $objdom =
[system.directoryservices.activedirectory.domain]::getcurrentdomain()
PS C:\> $objdom
```

```
Forest                     : pearson.pub
DomainControllers          : {DC1.pearson.pub}
Children                   : {}
DomainMode                 : Windows2008Domain
Parent                     :
PdcRoleOwner               : DC1.pearson.pub
RidRoleOwner               : DC1.pearson.pub
InfrastructureRoleOwner    : DC1.pearson.pub
Name                       : pearson.pub
```

> **TIP**  This is a long line to remember, but of course, you can place it in your profile so that you always have the **$objdom** object available to you. You don't even have to remember the command because you can type in **$objdom.** (with the period) and tab through the available commands.

Some other commands you can use are listed in the following table.

| ADSI Commands | Comments |
|---|---|
| `PS C:\> $objdom.forest` | Provides the following information on the forest: Name, Sites, Domains, GlobalCatalogs, ApplicationPartitions, ForestMode, RootDomain, Schema, SchemaRoleOwner, and NamingRoleOwner. |
| `PS C:\> $objdom.domaincontrollers` | Provides the following information on domain controllers in the domain: CurrentTime, HighestCommittedUsn, OSVersion, Roles, Domain, IPAddress, SiteName, SyncFromAllServersCallback, InboundConnections, OutboundConnections, Name, and Partitions |
| `PS C:\> $objdom.`<br>`FindAllDiscoverableDomainControllers()` | Lists the domain controllers that can be reached. |

Similarly, you can also use the **system.directoryservices** namespace to retrieve basic information about the forest. You first populate an object with the forest information, and then query the object. The syntax to do so is shown in the following code:

```
PS C:\> $objfor =
[system.directoryservices.activedirectory.forest]::getcurrentforest()
PS C:\> $objfor

Name                   : pearson.pub
Sites                  : {Default-First-Site-Name}
Domains                : {pearson.pub}
GlobalCatalogs         : {DC1.pearson.pub}
ApplicationPartitions  : {DC=pcgpartition,DC=pearson,DC=pub,
DC=DomainDnsZones,DC=pearson,
                         DC=pub, DC=ForestDnsZones,DC=pearson,DC=pub}
ForestMode             : Windows2003Forest
RootDomain             : pearson.pub
Schema                 : CN=Schema,CN=Configuration,DC=pearson,DC=pub
SchemaRoleOwner        : DC1.pearson.pub
NamingRoleOwner        : DC1.pearson.pub
```

Some other commands you can use on the forest are shown in the following table.

| ADSI Commands | Comments |
|---|---|
| PS C:\> $objfor.FindAllDiscoverableGlobalCatalogs() | Lists global catalog servers that can be reached. |
| PS C:\> $objfor.ApplicationPartitions | Lists application partitions. |

## Creating a List of Domain Computers

You can use the following script to create a list of computers with computer accounts in a domain:

> **TIP**  You must run this on a computer that is joined to a domain, with an account that has permissions to query the domain.

```
$strfilter = "computer"
$dom = [adsi]""

$searcher = new-object system.directoryservices.directorysearcher
$searcher.searchroot = $dom
$Searcher.searchscope = "Subtree"
$searcher.filter = "(objectCategory=$strfilter)"
$results = $searcher.findall()
foreach ($entry in $results)
    {
```

```
        $computer = $entry.getdirectoryentry().name
        $computer | out-file c:\data\computerlist.txt -append
}
```

The following table provides brief explanations of this code, including how you can slightly modify it for other uses.

| List Domain Computers Script | Comments |
|---|---|
| `$strfilter = "computer"` | If you want to get a list of all users in the domain, change this to **$strFilter = "user"**. |
| `$dom = [adsi]""` | This line uses the ADSI accelerator to get the current domain. |
| `$searcher = new-object`<br>`system.directoryservices.`<br>`directorysearcher`<br>`$searcher.searchroot = $dom`<br>`$Searcher.searchscope = "Subtree"` | These lines set up the Active Directory searcher object to search the entire domain. |
| `$searcher.filter =`<br>`"(objectCategory=$strfilter)"`<br>`$results = $searcher.findall()` | The filter specifies computer objects from the first line in the script (**$strfilter = "computer"**). The **$results** variable is an array that contains all computer objects in the domain. |
| `foreach ($entry in $results)`<br>`{`<br>`        $computer = $entry.`<br>`getdirectoryentry().name`<br>`        $computer | out-file`<br>`c:\data\computerlist.txt -append`<br>`}` | The **foreach** loop then loops through the array (**$results**) that holds all the computer objects. Each computer object is named **$i** on each pass through the loop.<br><br>The name of the computer is retrieved using the **$entry.getdirectoryentry(). name** line.<br><br>You can get the distinguished name using this line:<br><br>**$ocomputer = $i.getdirectoryentry(). distinguishedname**<br><br>You can get the LDAP path using this line:<br><br>**$ocomputer = $i.getdirectoryentry(). path** |

# Create Your Own Journal Here

Use this appendix to make notes about your day-to-day tasks and information specific to your job to make this journal truly your own.

_____

_____

_____

_____

_____

_____

_____

_____

_____

_____

_____

_____

_____

_____

_____

_____

_____

_____

_____

_____

_____

_____

_____

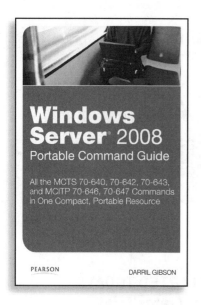

**FREE Online Edition**

Your purchase of **Windows Server 2008 Portable Command Guide** includes access to a free online edition for 45 days through the Safari Books Online subscription service. Nearly every Pearson IT Certification book is available online through Safari Books Online, along with more than 5,000 other technical books and videos from publishers such as Addison-Wesley Professional, Cisco Press, Exam Cram, IBM Press, O'Reilly, Prentice Hall, and Sams.

**SAFARI BOOKS ONLINE** allows you to search for a specific answer, cut and paste code, download chapters, and stay current with emerging technologies.

## Activate your FREE Online Edition at
## www.informit.com/safarifree

> **STEP 1:** Enter the coupon code: NVTFQGA.

> **STEP 2:** New Safari users, complete the brief registration form.
> Safari subscribers, just log in.

If you have difficulty registering on Safari or accessing the online edition, please e-mail customer-service@safaribooksonline.com

Addison Wesley • AdobePress • ALPHA • Cisco Press • BT Press • IBM Press • lynda.com • Microsoft Press • New Riders

O'REILLY • Peachpit Press • PRENTICE HALL • QUE • Redbooks • SAMS • SAS Publishing • Sun Microsystems • WILEY